REBALANCE YOUR RELATIONSHIP WITH FOOD

Reassuring recipes and nutritional support for positive, confident eating

EMMA BACON

SINGING
DRAGON

LONDON AND PHILADELPHIA

The 'Wellness Self-assessment' on page 274 is adapted from the 'Checklist for Full Recovery' in Noordenbos, G. (2013) *Recovery from Eating Disorders: A Guide for Clinicians and Their Patients* and printed with kind permission from John Wiley and Sons.

Disclaimer: While every effort has been made to ensure that the information in this book is correct, it should not be substituted for medical advice. The recipes in this book should be used in combination with a healthy lifestyle. If you are concerned about any aspect of your health, speak to your doctor. Neither the author nor the publisher takes any responsibility for any decisions made as a result of the information included in this book.

Notes:
- Both British (metric) and American (imperial plus US cups) are included in these recipes for your convenience, however it is important to work with one set of measurements and not alternate between the two within a recipe.
- If using a fan assisted oven, adjust temperatures according to the manufacturer's instructions.

First published in 2017
by Singing Dragon
an imprint of Jessica Kingsley Publishers
73 Collier Street
London N1 9BE, UK
and
400 Market Street, Suite 400
Philadelphia, PA 19106, USA

www.singingdragon.com

Library of Congress Cataloging in Publication Data
Names: Bacon, Emma, 1978- author.
Title: Rebalance your relationship with food : reassuring recipes and
   nutritional support for positive, confident eating / Emma Bacon.
Description: London ; Philadelphia : Singing Dragon, 2017. | Includes index.
Identifiers: LCCN 2016014464 | ISBN 9781785921193 (alk. paper)
Subjects: LCSH: Eating disorders--Popular works. | Nutrition--Psychological
   aspects--Popular works. | Food habits--Psychological aspects--Recipes. |
   Natural foods--Recipes. | Self-care, Health--Popular works.
Classification: LCC RC552.E18 B26 2017 | DDC 641.5/63--dc23 LC record available at https://urldefense.
proofpoint.com/v2/url?u=https-3A__lccn.loc.gov_2016014464&d=BQIFAg&c=euGZstcaTDllvimEN8b7jXrwqOf-v5A_
CdpgnVfiiMM&r=jDhEGaIRBceh95Jy34lINgmWR9tnCifzbrA2NWHfaH8&m=4ojNadCQ9TC3s25BeEpOTmHXl5Q2Oo15dEXA1v_
P26E&s=grRVY9Q6NU-ADRFIVHqpR4m8baXze3_r_ow7yK2TX-E&e=

British Library Cataloguing in Publication Data
A CIP catalogue record for this book is available from the British Library

ISBN 978 1 78592 119 3
eISBN 978 0 85701 278 4

Printed and bound in China

Every
ACCOMPLISHMENT
BEGINS
WITH THE
DECISION
to
TRY

Endorsements

'The importance of optimal nutrition for a healthy lifestyle cannot be overstated. Emma's inspirational book is a comprehensive guide with easy-to-follow sections, providing a wide variety of tasty and nutritionally balanced recipes and meal ideas. It is accompanied by detailed nutritional information, for every taste and culinary skill level. However, the true power of *Rebalance Your Relationship with Food* is that it is not just another cookbook. The Self-Help Tools section provides holistic information that enables the reader to understand and address their relationship with food. Emma's passion to help affected people understand and overcome their conditions shines through, and I will certainly be recommending *Rebalance Your Relationship with Food* for clients in my nutritional therapy clinic.'

Dr Elisabeth Philipps PhD, Nutritional Therapist

'One of the most useful and practical books for people recovering from food and body issues that I have read for a long time. It is a must for people who journey through recovery. The meal planner and the food diary…combine well with the motivational messages and self-care ideas to remind the person that recovering is about the balance of food and self. I would recommend this book to my patients with great pleasure.'

Deborah Meddes-Carpenter, Specialist Therapist, Nightingale Hospital, London

'This is such a helpful book. The way in which the recipes are written, inclusive of equipment and time required will enable people with eating disorders to implement the skills that are learnt in treatment… I can see it could be helpful for parents to use with a young person in order to do some joint preparation. I know I will be using it when doing skills training with my patients.'

Kathryn Weaver, Nurse Practitioner, NHS Adult Eating Disorder Team, Milton Keynes

'For families familiar with the roller coaster ride of supporting a loved one with an eating disorder, this book is a true gift… Often misguided understandings about different food types are addressed with clear, sound advice. This is a book for families to use together and rebuild trust on the journey to recovery.'

Jacqui Wheeler, parent of child with an eating disorder

'Emma's book is a brilliant tool for those that are nervous about food to use as a means to help build confidence and knowledge in a very unintimidating, user friendly way… This book is great for taking those first steps towards managing a healthy, nutritious diet with some very simple options and on to something more challenging when you are ready.'

Laura Bowley, Personal Trainer and Owner of Happy Bodies Gym

'Rebalance Your Relationship with Food is a brilliant mix of self-help, nutrition and life advice. It is a guide I wish I'd had when I was escaping my own diet prison and longing to live a life that was more than counting calories, stepping on scales and valuing myself based on the size of my jeans.'

Anne-Sophie Reinhardt, Eating Psychology Coach and founder of Escape Diet Prison

'Emma has written *Rebalance Your Relationship with Food* with considerable empathy and understanding.

The book is thoughtfully and beautifully presented with nutritional facts and a variety of recipes which are clearly explained. These range from basic recipes to more ambitious meals, yet all are simple to prepare. Carbohydrates, proteins, fats, sugars, vitamins and minerals are explained with clarity and brevity. It is particularly impressive in the way that the photos of the meals have captions to show the health benefits of the various ingredients.

It is wonderful to see how the reader is supported in their struggle by so many positive messages to live a healthy and balanced life. The book includes a helpful tool kit section as a motivator and a check of progress. Our daughter has been recovering from anorexia for many years and we can honestly say that this is the first ever recipe book we have seen to approach eating disorders in such a practical and supportive way. It will be invaluable to both the person challenged by disordered eating and their supporters.

We are deeply grateful to Emma for the extraordinary effort in undertaking this inspirational book.'

Supportive parent

'I think this is a beautiful book, with lovely illustrations, that will be very useful to all kinds of people who have worries about feeding themselves properly. The simplicity of the recipes and the clarity of the instructions will be very reassuring to those who are nervous of trying to make food. The nutritional information will be tremendously helpful to those who feel that food might poison them or who can see no reason to eat. I liked the comments on each recipe from someone who has used it and found it helpful. The quantities are small – two servings at most; that should enable both over- and under-eaters to feel confident that the food is safe and will not trigger too much anxiety. This is a big book with lots of recipes, so for the person who works their way through it, it will last a long time. For the person who wants to sample it, there is lots of choice. The tone of the book is calm and authoritative; I am sure that many people will feel that they can trust it and use it as a guide to establishing a better relationship with food and better day-to-day nutrition.'

**Julia Buckroyd, BACP Eating Disorder Therapist, Author,
Broadcaster and Emeritus Professor of Counselling**

'Wow...what an amazing book! Over the 20 years of fighting an eating disorder I have been given many nutritional booklets, handouts and diet plans from eating disorder specialists trying their hardest to help me in my recovery. Sadly, despite my determination and desire that these would help, many of them didn't and instead I was left feeling hopeless and alone, whereas I can honestly say that Emma's book has helped me and continues to do so. Emma has managed to achieve the incredibly hard and delicate task of producing a book that provides both practical and emotional support.

Most people are aware that someone with an eating disorder finds eating difficult. However, before the actual 'eating' bit, there are many stages that one needs to get through, such as deciding what to eat, then the shopping, preparation and cooking. I often found that I got overwhelmed at one of these stages and subsequently abandoned everything before getting to the eating stage! Eating disorders can over-complicate even the simplest of tasks! This is where Emma's book has really helped as it breaks everything down into calm, simple steps.

Throughout the book there is a strong sense of realism and empathy which is balanced beautifully with hope and encouragement that life can improve. For example, every recipe has an empathetic quote which has been written by someone challenged by their relationship with food. I find these quotes both motivating and reassuring, all of which help me to feel less alone in the battle against my eating disorder. In addition to these quotes each recipe has nutritional facts about the key ingredients. These have provided me with great ammunition against the negative thoughts. I am now able to use this knowledge to reassure myself that what I am eating is natural, real, nutritious food.

At the back of the book is the doodle page; I love this page! When my head is spinning with negative thoughts I often need something quick and simple to stop this cycle. The positive affirmations on the doodle page do just this! I have at times been eating my meal and reading one of the affirmations over and over! It is nice that there is space for people to write their own personal affirmations. This simple exercise demonstrates Emma's sensitivity and refreshing awareness that although people share common concerns, everyone is different and their individuality must be respected.

In many ways I find that this book takes on the role of a positive mentor that is available whenever needed and at the times most needed, such as when cooking or eating. It gently nudges me in the right direction, enabling me to challenge myself kindly, responsibly and sensibly. I cannot recommend this book highly enough! I am confident that it will be an invaluable resource for anyone wanting to improve their relationship with food and body image. Thank you Emma for creating it!'

Eating disorder sufferer

Thank You

Firstly, I'd like to say a heartfelt thank you to everyone who has ever helped me to appreciate what is meant by 'balanced eating'. Over the years, I have had the privilege to meet many people affected by disordered eating, body-image issues and low self-esteem – you have enriched my understanding and inspired me to represent a good example. I thank you from the bottom of my heart and hope this book will provide you with some helpful support.

In particular, I'd like to say an important thank you to Sally, for motivating me to create this book – you are a wonderful person who deserves to feel proud of your achievements and the positive impact you have on this world.

Also, Julia Buckroyd – thank you for your continued support, guidance and wisdom. Your professional insight has been invaluable.

I'd like to thank Laura for helping me to photograph the beauty of natural food in a way the reader would find non-threatening and yet inspiring.

And Lezlee – I am so grateful for your kindness, enthusiasm and generosity. This book wouldn't be the same without your involvement. You are simply wonderful!

I thank Singing Dragon for enabling my vision to become a reality. I very much appreciate the experience and professional support provided by everyone in the team.

I thank my family and friends for their encouragement and unconditional love. Your words of support and listening ears have meant a lot to me.

And lastly, but perhaps most importantly, I'd like to thank my wonderful husband, Andy, and our two children, Joshua and Savannah. You are my world. Thank you for entertaining our Wednesday 'Try Night'. Thank you for believing in me. And thank you for the rest of our lives still to come.

Contents

Journey to Self-acceptance..............................3
About This Book...4
Key Ingredients for a Balanced Life................7
General Nutritional Advice.........................8
Considering Carbohydrates........................10
Simplifying Sugars 11
Positive Proteins 12
Facts About Fats......................................13
Vitamin Chart..14
Mineral Chart 16

SIMPLE BEGINNINGS
Berry and Almond Smoothie.......................20
Toast with Almond Butter..........................22
Porridge (Oatmeal) with Milk....................24
Simple Eggy Bread 26
Cheese and Tomato on Toast 28
Yoghurt with Fruit, Nuts and Seeds 30
Poached Eggs on Toast 32
Crumpets with Marmite.............................34
Beans on Toast..36
Simple Cereals...38
Bagel with Cream Cheese 40
Tuna Salad 42
Pasta in Herby Tomato Sauce 44
Pasta with Peas and Parmesan 46
Baked Potato with Beans 48
Simple Popcorn 50
Fresh Fruit 52
Dried Fruit and Nut Mix 54

BREAKFAST
Homemade Granola 58
Pancakes with Fruit Compote.....................60
Porridge (Oatmeal), Apple and Walnuts 62
Blueberry Nut Muffins and Yoghurt...............64
Banana and Pecan Smoothie......................66
Cinnamon Eggy Bread with Berries 68
Darissa – Yoghurt Granola Fruit Pot 70
Mug Muffin with Yoghurt 72

BREAKFAST OR LUNCH
Scrambled Egg and Smoked Salmon............76
Homemade Baked Bean Burrito...................78
Ham, Spinach and Parmesan Eggs.............80
Poached Egg and Avocado on Toast 82
Cheese and Mushrooms on Toast 84
Kipper (Smoked Herring) and Spinach...........86
Egg, Bacon, Lettuce and Tomato.................88

LUNCH
Tuna Pasta Salad 92
Mackerel Pâté 94
Ham and Pea Frittata 96
Turkey Sandwich 98
Mango and Feta Salad 100
Salmon and Spinach Frittata.....................102
Cranberry and Almond Couscous 104
Chicken and Sweetcorn Wrap....................106
Sweet Potato and Red Pepper Soup 108
Red Lentil Pâté 110
Mixed Bean Salad 112
Pea Soup 114
Rainbow Salad with Hummus 116
Egg Mayo and Red Pepper Sandwich 118
Quinoa Greek Salad 120
Butternut Squash and Feta Pitta.................122
Tomato, Avocado and Quinoa Salad 124
Falafel and Hummus Salad Wrap 126
Leek and Potato Soup 128
Bagel, Cream Cheese and Salmon 130
Sweet Potato with Cottage Cheese 132
Tuna Salad Pitta 134

DINNER
Chilli Con Carne and Rice 138
Lentil Cottage Pie 140
Pesto Pasta with Chicken 142
Chickpea and Sweet Potato Stew 144
Chicken and Roast Veg Tray Bake 146
Simple Spaghetti Carbonara.....................148

Cosy Beef Stew..150
Asian Style Salmon with Veg Rice 152
Tuna, Sweetcorn and Broccoli Bake............154
Lemon, Basil and Pea Spaghetti 156
Veg Stir-Fried Noodles with Prawns..............158
Sweetcorn Salsa with Chicken....................160
Pitta Pizza 162
Avocado, Egg, Salmon and Lentils 164
Veg Couscous with Spiced Chicken.............166
Beef Burrito...168
Sweet Potato, Chicken and Spinach 170
Sea Bass, New Potatoes and Kale 172
Spaghetti and Meatballs.............................174
Lentil Stuffed Peppers 176
Grilled Lamb Burger with Salad 178
Roasted Veg with Garlic Chicken 180
Salmon, New Potatoes and Broccoli............182
Quinoa, Sundried Tomato and Feta 184
Fish Pie and Peas......................................186

SAVOURY SNACKS
Beetroot and Walnut Dip 190
Homemade Hummus with Crudités..............192
Green Smoothie...194
Artichoke and Cumin Dip...........................196
Ratatouille 198
Pistachio Dukka..200
Smoked Salmon Stuffed Celery 202
Seeded Crackers.......................................204
Guacamole 206
Rainbow Coleslaw.....................................208
Boiled Egg and Tomato..............................210
Root Vegetable Crisps 212
Lime and Pepper Cashew Nuts 214
Homemade Popcorn...................................216

NATURALLY SWEET
Bliss Balls..220
Oatie Biscuits..222
Banana, Almond Butter and Chia Seeds.......224

Five-Minute Raw Brownies 226
Pecan Bis-Cakes..228
Choc and Nut Raw Tart...............................230
Melon, Yoghurt and Seeds 232
No-Bake Date Cakes..................................234
Soft-Serve Banana Ice Cream......................236
Rejuvenating Chocolate Cake 238
Fruity Flapjacks..240

BREADS
No-Knead Seeded Spelt Loaf.......................244
Old-Fashioned Corn Bread..........................246
Wholemeal (Wholewheat) Soda Bread 248
Banana Bread...250
Simple Quick Bread....................................252

HEALTHY SPREADS AND SAUCES
Homemade Mayonnaise 256
Pizza/Pasta Sauce.....................................258
Cashew Butter...260
Pesto Sauce 262
Healthy Chocolate Spread 264
Fresh Berry and Lime Compote 266
Salad Dressings...268

SELF-HELP TOOLS
Self-reflection..272
Personal Bliss List......................................273
Wellness Self-assessment............................274
Doodle Page...280

INDEX
Example Food Plan.....................................284
My Food Plan..285
Measurement Index 286
Photographic Index of Ingredients 288
Photographic Index of Recipes 290
Contributors Information 295

Journey to Self-acceptance

My name is Emma and I have written this book to help people affected by disordered eating, poor body image and low self-confidence. I know how it feels to struggle with constant concerns about nutrition, exercise, a lack of self-esteem, anxiety, fear and general confusion. Over the last 20 years, I have been affected by tendencies towards a negative body image, bulimia, anorexia, obsessive compulsive disorder (OCD), depression, self-harm and orthorexia. I have travelled the road to recovery, back and forth, but am now in a healthy place, where I feel happy with my life balance. I am finally able to accept myself and appreciate how wonderful life can be!

I run a community-based eating disorder service in my local area and am also a personal trainer, nutrition advisor and martial arts instructor. I am privileged to share my life with my loving husband and two wonderful children. I hope this book, driven by my personal and professional experiences and education, can help you challenge negative thoughts and embrace a life full of positive energy.

Rebalance Your Relationship with Food is not a typical cookbook, nor is it simply a self-help book... It is a practical guide, offering a wide range of balanced recipes that can be trusted. Alongside each recipe is nutritional information that will help you develop a better relationship with food, and empathetic quotes from various people affected by eating disorders, body-image issues and low self-esteem.

Everybody is different, I understand that, but I also know that people share many common concerns. You may feel confused about what 'healthy eating' really means, obsess about eating only certain things at particular times, restrict calories, cut out entire food groups or over-exercise. Perhaps you struggle with trusting yourself, eat for comfort, succumb to negative internal voices, binge and purge, need emotional permission to care for yourself, or simply find life overwhelming and frightening. Whatever your specific challenges, this book has been created to help you develop a positive relationship with the food required to fuel a healthy mind and body.

Every recipe in this book provides a balance of nutrients. I encourage the use of natural foods and the inclusion of all food groups. 'Everything in moderation, including moderation itself' – as my husband has always told me!

After everything I've been through, I can honestly say I feel comfortable making and eating any of the recipes in this book, even when life is stressful and I have to work harder to avoid negative thoughts. I hope that you're able to trust my experience and empower yourself to explore the recipes with a new found confidence and self-belief.

Believe-Trust-Support...Yourself
Be inspired. Be brave. Be pro-active. Be empowered.
Stop living in a nightmare and start making your dreams come true.

About This Book

Rebalance Your Relationship with Food is a self-help book/cookbook written to support anyone affected by a negative relationship with food and body. It offers a variety of healthy meals and snacks alongside empathetic quotes and positive inspiration.

Chapter explanations

The recipes have been separated into sections, helping you to establish a regular eating pattern that includes breakfast, lunch, dinner and snacks. An example food plan has been provided on page 284, although this should be personalised according to your individual needs and preferences.

The first recipe section of the book, titled 'Simple Beginnings', is designed for people who struggle with more than a few basic ingredients on a plate, with hope that they can progress through the book over time. The chapters that follow give examples of meals and snacks relevant to anyone wanting to eat a well-balanced diet that supports emotional and physical health and wellbeing.

Natural nutrition

This book encourages the use of wholesome, natural ingredients from every food group. Nutritional information about key ingredients is provided to help you improve your knowledge and relationship with food. Understanding how food can fuel a healthy mind and body can help you to justify eating a variety of foods and retrain negative thinking patterns.

Choice of recipes

The selection of recipes has been developed with careful consideration of the following:

- common thoughts associated with body image issues, eating disorders and a lack of confidence
- simplicity of preparation and cooking methods
- practicality of including the recipe in everyday life, whether single or part of a family unit
- nutritional balance and benefits of each meal (with each photograph representing one portion).

Helpful advice

Each recipe page offers hints and tips that either help to simplify preparation or maximise the benefits of a meal. A list of required equipment has also been provided, helping you to gather the necessary items before beginning to cook.

Shared thoughts

Personal quotes from a variety of people affected by disordered eating or body-image issues offer an empathetic viewpoint on each recipe. These comments were provided by real people, all of whom are striving towards a more positive mindset about themselves (most of the names have been changed to protect confidentiality).

Self-help

Additional worksheets at the back of the book encourage personal reflection and an improved ability to self-soothe. Furthermore, a detailed questionnaire enables you to evaluate your current thoughts and behaviours in relation to physical and emotional health. This assessment tool can be revisited periodically to help you recognise positive change and aspects of your life that need further consideration.

Doodle page

This section offers positive affirmations that have helped other people overcome challenging thoughts about food and body issues. Space has been provided for you to add statements personal to you. Writing these statements down and regularly repeating them in your mind will encourage more positive thinking.

Compassion and planning

Challenge yourself responsibly. Be kind and considerate to yourself, avoiding self-sabotage whenever possible. Start by trying a recipe you feel comfortable with, make and eat it a number of times, and then expand your repertoire. If you find change overwhelming, consider introducing a specific day of the week to try something new. Try to see each recipe as an experimental adventure. Do this with the support of others, whether that is a partner, family member, friend or health professional.

Take note of the 'Key Ingredients for a Balanced Life' page in this section and the 'Self-help Tools' section later in the book to aid and evaluate your wellness. Combining this with support from trusted relationships will further benefit your journey to a fulfilled life.

> Positive thoughts generate positive feelings and attract positive life experiences.

Quick guide

To help you decide which meals to cook, a selection of icons can be found below each recipe photograph – see below:

| max cooking time | no measuring required | no cooking required | good to freeze | good to batch cook and store | suitable for vegetarians | promotes good health |

I may not
be
perfect,
but
I am
perfectly *me*

Key Ingredients for a Balanced Life

Everybody is different, with their own personal circumstances and challenges with food or body image. The journey to self-acceptance is equally individual, although there are common themes that seem to encourage emotional and physical wellbeing. The list below suggests important aspects of a balanced life, according to a variety of people who have overcome personal challenges. Allow yourself to be inspired by their experiences and add to the list as appropriate.

- Purpose and meaning

- A varied support network

- A positive appreciation for nutrition

- A healthy amount of exercise

- A positive attitude towards change

- Time spent outdoors

- Self-reflection, understanding and a desire for self-acceptance

- The ability to be honest with yourself and others

- A long-term view – on-going personal development

- Healthy hobbies and interests

- Open communication – don't be ashamed, be proud to be you

- Meaningful relationships

- Hope for the future

Add your own items here...

-

-

-

-

General Nutritional Advice

Eat regularly
Most people would benefit from having three main meals a day with snacks in between, spread two–four hours apart. Each meal should be substantial enough to satisfy hunger between meals and stimulate the metabolism (the process responsible for the breakdown of food into energy). The recipe pages in this book provide a photographic example of sensible portion sizes as a guide.

Enjoy variety
Eating a variety of foods ensures consumption of every food group and all essential vitamins and minerals.

Choose natural
Eat natural foods full of wholesome ingredients. Focus on enjoying foods that either 'grow, run, swim or fly', rather than ones that are processed, modified or man-made.

Never skip breakfast
Have a high-protein breakfast, preferably in conjunction with complex carbohydrate and natural fat – yes I said 'fat'. I know this might be a scary word, but it really is good for you and is NOT your enemy. Eating a good breakfast helps boost your metabolism and steady your blood sugar levels at the start of the day.

Eat fruit in moderation
Include fresh fruit in your diet to benefit from its antioxidant and health-boosting properties. However, it's best to eat just one to three portions a day so as to avoid excessive sugar in your diet.

Enjoy healthy fats
Fat is an essential part of your diet and body, relevant to insulation, protection of your vital organs, fertility and the absorption of certain vitamins and minerals. Include healthy natural fats from oily fish, nuts and seeds, vegetable oils, avocado, yoghurt and cheese, and so on.

Include protein
Protein is essential for the growth and repair of cells, healthy brain function, metabolism and the immune system. Try to eat some protein with every meal, for example chicken, fish, eggs, pulses, yoghurt, nuts, milk and so on.

Limit processed foods
As much as possible, avoid processed foods, especially items high in trans fats, refined sugar or salt, as they contain limited nutritional value and may leave your body craving more of these foods.

Replenish water
Drink plenty of water throughout the day, especially when participating in exercise or when the weather is hot. Water is a necessary ingredient of every single chemical reaction in your body!

Limit caffeine and alcohol
In order to encourage a stable mind and energy levels avoid overconsumption of caffeine and alcohol.

Enjoy cooking at home
Eat home-cooked foods whenever possible – this way you can guarantee the freshness of foods and avoid unnecessary additives. Regularly experimenting with recipes will help reduce anxiety about food in general. You may also find it helpful to cook with a supportive parent or friend.

Avoid excessive salt
Limit salt intake (often hidden in processed food), adding only small amounts to recipes. Having said this, people who are very sporty lose salt in their sweat. Deficient salt levels can cause muscular cramps, so it's important to be aware of replenishing significant salt loss in these circumstances.

Shop smart
Avoid unnecessary anxiety or compulsive purchases by avoiding food shopping when you're hungry or just before a meal. Stock your cupboards to ensure you have healthy options readily available to you (and limit unhealthy temptations from your list/cupboard).

Recognise hunger and satisfaction
It takes 15 minutes for your brain to register that you feel full. Eat steadily, allowing time to appreciate what you are eating and how you are feeling.

Appreciate food as fuel
Educate yourself on the nutritional benefits of different foods, encouraging positive affirmations about healthy choices to enhance your overall satisfaction. But don't become too obsessive. Note the doodle page at the back of the book, adding further comments that you find helpful.

Try new things
Be adventurous and embrace variety. Try to enjoy buying, making and eating your food. See each recipe as an experimental adventure focusing on the creativity of a dish rather than any anxiety associated with eating it. Challenge yourself to cook and eat new recipes on a regular basis, with others whenever you feel able.

> **Everything in moderation, including moderation itself**
> In other words, be sensible, but also allow yourself a treat every now and then without feeling guilty. A balanced diet encourages a balanced life.

Considering Carbohydrates

What are carbohydrates?

There are different types of carbohydrates: simple and complex.

Simple carbohydrates include naturally occurring sugars found in fruit and vegetables, white and brown sugar, honey and maple syrup, and processed foods, such as sweets and sauces. These are easily digested by the body, increasing blood sugar levels quickly, so should be eaten in moderation. Ideally, consume in conjunction with foods that provide a slow release of energy, from protein or complex carbohydrates.

Complex carbohydrates include bread, pasta, rice and flour, with wholemeal (wholewheat) varieties containing more fibre, vitamins and minerals. Other examples include oats (oatmeal), root vegetables, some fruits, chickpeas, lentils and nuts. Complex carbohydrates provide a slow release of energy, encouraging a steady feeling of satiety.

Why do carbohydrates have a bad reputation?

Processed foods tend to contain high levels of simple sugar carbohydrates, combined with saturated fat and salt, for example mass-produced biscuits and cakes. Overconsumption of such convenience foods results in an unhealthy body, whereas eating a sensible amount of complex carbohydrates (and a small amount of simple carbohydrates in conjunction with foods that produce slow-release energy) encourages a feeling of satiety that will help to maintain a healthy body.

Why do we need carbohydrates?

Carbohydrate provides the body with energy necessary to fuel everyday activities and bodily functions. Without carbohydrate, the body would have to break down fat and protein for energy, which should be available for growth and repair of the body instead. In turn, this may result in poor health, muscle wastage and a slower metabolism. Carbohydrate should form part of a healthy balanced diet.

How much should we eat?

The amount of carbohydrate someone should consume is variable according to their physical activity, but on average, one-third of your plate should be represented by complex carbohydrates.

What about fibre?

Ther are two types of fibre: insoluble and soluble.

Insoluble fibre is often found in wholemeal (wholewheat) foods. This can't be absorbed by the body, so plays an important role in digestion by aiding the passage of food through the gut.

Soluble fibre is found in oats, pulses, vegetables and fruit. This is digested by the good bacteria in the gut, promoting digestive health and helping to lower cholesterol.

Simplifying Sugars

What is sugar?

Sugar is a generic term for a sweet-tasting soluble crystalline substance found in various foods and drinks. Sugar provides quick-release energy that, when overconsumed, can upset blood sugar and insulin levels, causing potential health issues.

How can I avoid consuming hidden sugars?

There are many different words used for sugar, which can make it hard to avoid unnecessary consumption. Being aware of the terminology can help you to make an informed decision about your food, favouring natural sweeteners with additional health benefits over and above simple sugars. Here is a list of some words used to describe sugar:

brown rice syrup, corn sweetener, dextrin, dextrose, fructose, fruit juice concentrate, glucose, inverted sugar, lactose, malt syrup, maltose, palm sugar, rice syrup, sucrose and xylose.

Artificial sweeteners and natural sugar alternatives, such as honey, Xylitol and date syrup, are processed as sugar in the body. These shouldn't be avoided in the diet, but they should be limited, and eaten in conjunction with foods that provide slow-release energy whenever possible, for example foods containing protein.

Is sugar addictive?

Sugar causes a quick rise in blood sugar levels, which provides a feeling of satisfaction and energy, for a short period of time. Soon after consumption of sugar, blood sugar levels drop, leaving a feeling of wanting more. This can create a pattern of addictive behaviour that can cause emotional and physical issues.

Should I include sugar in my diet?

Avoiding any particular food group completely can lead to anxieties and disordered thoughts and behaviours. Eating natural sugars in moderation is the most sensible course of action.

Healthy foods, such as fruit, vegetables, dairy products and honey, contain natural sugars, alongside fibre and various other vitamins and minerals that support a healthy mind and body. So eat natural.

Everything in moderation, including moderation itself.

Positive Proteins

What is protein?

Protein is made up of 20 different amino acids, some of which can be made by the body and others, known as essential amino acids, which are sourced from food.

Complete proteins contain all essential amino acids, for example meat, fish, milk, eggs, cheese and quinoa.

Incomplete proteins contain only a selection of amino acids, for example nuts, seeds, beans, lentils, oats, cereals, peas, tofu and corn.

Consuming a mixture of proteins on a regular basis ensures that the body receives all the amino acids needed for a healthy body.

What does protein do?

Protein provides the building blocks of the body. It is essential for the growth and repair of muscles and other cells, as well as the creation of hormones that regulate body functions and brain activities. It is also a key component of enzymes that break down and absorb food and chemicals in the body, and antibodies that enable the immune system to fight disease.

How much protein do we need?

On average, approximately one-sixth of a balanced plate should be made up of protein. To achieve optimum health, try to eat at least two portions of oily fish a week (such as salmon or mackerel). The rest of the week should include meat-free protein sources such as quinoa, lentils and beans, some poultry and just a little red meat.

It's important to note that excessive consumption of protein, especially in conjunction with a low carbohydrate intake, can be bad for your health.

What about vegetarians and vegans?

Vegetarians and vegans should consume a variety of different protein sources to ensure receipt of a complete range of amino acids, including beans, pulses, legumes, lentils, quinoa, tofu, nuts and seeds.

It may be difficult for vegetarians and vegans to digest sufficient levels of vitamin B12, found mainly in meat. In such cases, it might be worth considering supplements to support an otherwise healthy life choice.

Facts About Fats

Are there different types of fat?

There are three types of fat:

Unsaturated fats, for example olive oil, nuts, seeds, avocado, omega-3-rich oily fish. These are mostly monounsaturated or polyunsaturated fatty acids, associated with health benefits (such as lowered cholesterol level) when consumed in moderation. Unsaturated fatty acids should be included in a healthy diet.

Saturated fats, for example lard, suet, butter, animal fats. Saturated fats are often combined with monounsaturated fats. Some research suggests that overconsumption of saturated fats is linked to an increased risk of health issues, whereas other studies have reported otherwise, so eating a small amount from natural sources would be advisable.

Trans fats, for example processed fat often found in ready-made convenience foods, processed cakes and pre-brought biscuits. These are linked to an increased risk of negative health issues so should be limited.

What does fat do and why do I need it?

Fat is an essential part of our diet and bodies, providing insulation and protection, boosting fertility, and enabling the absorption of fat-soluble vitamins and essential fatty acids (such as vitamin A, omega-3 and omega-6).

How much should we eat?

All fats should be eaten in moderation, favouring natural unsaturated fats most of the time.

Examples of healthy unsaturated oils

Olive oil and extra virgin olive oil, made from olives. This oil is rich in omega-9. The taste can vary according to its source and age. Use cheaper, lighter olive oil to cook at low temperatures and extra virgin olive oil for raw dressings.

Rapeseed oil, made from the yellow flowering plants that are seen in many English fields (called rape). This oil is a great source of omega-3, omega-6 and vitamin E. A neutral flavour makes this oil a good choice for cooking and condiments, such as mayonnaise. Affordable and healthy.

Virgin coconut oil, made from untreated coconut. This oil contains medium-chain triglycerides – healthy fats – that help to lower the risk of heart disease and boost metabolism. Suitable for use at low or high temperatures.

Sunflower oil, made from sunflower seeds. This oil is an affordable choice, rich in omega-6 and vitamin E. Suitable raw or cooking at low temperatures.

Vitamin Chart

Vitamins are essential nutrients that your body needs in small amounts to work properly. Fat-soluble vitamins, such as vitamin A, D, E and K, can be stored in the body. Water-soluble vitamins, such as vitamin C, B vitamins and folic acid, cannot be stored in the body, so they need to be consumed on a regular basis. A healthy balanced diet should provide you with all the minerals needed for good health, but if you are concerned about the amount you are consuming, speak to a health professional for advice (because having too little or too much of a vitamin or mineral can be harmful to health).

NUTRIENT	FUNCTIONS	RICH FOOD SOURCES	NOTES
Vitamin A and carotenoids	Vitamin A: Antioxidant; helps the immune system fight infection, aids vision in dim light, and is relevant to skin health. Carotenoids: Precursors to vitamin A; antioxidant; relevant to a healthy heart and circulation.	Vitamin A: Cheese, eggs, oily fish, milk and yoghurt. Carotenoids: Yellow, red and green (leafy) vegetables, such as spinach, carrots, sweet potatoes and red peppers. Also yellow fruit such as mango and apricots.	You should be able to get all the vitamin A you need by eating a varied and balanced diet.
Vitamin B1 (thiamin)	Relevant to the release of energy from carbohydrates, growth, appetite regulation, and a healthy digestion and nervous system.	Peas, fresh and dried fruit, wholemeal (wholewheat) flour, rye flour, sunflower seeds, brown rice, pecan nuts, Brazil nuts, beans, hazelnuts, cashew nuts, eggs, yeast extract.	Thiamin cannot be stored in the body so you need it in your diet every day. You should be able to get all the thiamine you need from a healthy balanced diet.
Vitamin B2 (riboflavin)	Combines with protein to regulate respiration, also relevant to growth, healthy skin and eyes.	Milk, egg yolks, rice, almonds, cashew nuts, wild rice, mushrooms, oily fish, kale, sunflower seeds/oil and yeast extract.	UV light can destroy riboflavin, so ideally these foods should be kept out of direct sunlight. Riboflavin cannot be stored in the body so you need it in your diet every day. You should be able to get all the riboflavin you need from a healthy balanced diet.
Vitamin B3 (niacin)	Required for energy release and synthesis of fatty acids, healthy digestion, skin and nervous system.	Brown rice, wild rice, wholemeal (wholewheat) flour, peanuts, turkey, mackerel, chicken, sesame seeds, sunflower seeds, lean red meat, almonds, milk and yeast extract.	Niacin cannot be stored in the body so you need it in your diet every day. You should be able to get all the niacin you need from a healthy balanced diet.
Vitamin B5 (pantothenic acid)	Regulates carbohydrate and fat metabolism, relevant to resistance to stress, a healthy immune system and digestive system.	Chicken, beef, peanuts, mushrooms, peas, brown rice, eggs, sunflower seeds, lentils, rye flour, cashew nuts, oily fish, turkey, broccoli, avocado, potatoes, porridge (oatmeal), tomatoes and yeast extract.	Pantothenic acid cannot be stored in the body so you need it in your diet every day. You should be able to get all the pantothenic acid you need from a healthy balanced diet.
Vitamin B6 (pyridoxine)	Relevant to the metabolism of carbohydrate and protein, the formation of haemoglobin, the synthesis of hormones and fatty acids, a healthy nervous system, hormone balance, growth and skin.	Sunflower seeds, yeast extract, soybeans, walnuts, peanuts, oily fish, lentils, beans, brown rice, hazelnuts, bananas, pork, chicken, avocado, wholewheat flour, egg yolk, kale, rye flour, potatoes and milk.	You should be able to get all the pyridoxine you need from a healthy balanced diet.

NUTRIENT	FUNCTIONS	RICH FOOD SOURCES	NOTES
Vitamin B12 (cobalamin)	Relevant to DNA synthesis, the production of new red blood cells, a healthy nervous system, the processing of folic acid, gut health and the skin.	Lamb, beef, shellfish, oily fish such as salmon, egg yolk, cod, milk and cheese.	If you eat meat, fish or dairy products you should be able to get enough cobalamin from a healthy balanced diet. Vitamin B12 is not found in plants, so vegans should consider a supplement.
Vitamin C (ascorbic acid)	Antioxidant; relevant to a healthy immune system, teeth, gums, bones, cartilage, capillaries, connective tissue, synthesis of hormones and the regulation of cholesterol.	Sweet peppers, kale, leafy vegetables, broccoli, watercress, strawberries, oranges, red and green peppers, potatoes, cabbage, lemon juice, mangoes, raspberries, asparagus, radishes and parsley.	Vitamin C cannot be stored in the body, so you need it in your diet every day. You should be able to get all the vitamin C you need from a healthy balanced diet.
Vitamin D (calciferol)	Controls calcium absorption, relevant to healthy bones and teeth, necessary for a healthy immune system and nervous system, and relevant to hormone balance.	Oily fish such as salmon, sardines and mackerel, but also tuna, shrimps, butter, sunflower seeds, eggs, fortified milk, mushrooms and cheese.	Vitamin D is also synthesised by the action of sunlight on the skin. People often struggle to get enough vitamin D from their diet and sunlight, so supplements should be considered.
Vitamin E (tocopherol, etc.)	Antioxidant; relevant to a healthy immune system, heart, circulation, as a sex hormone regulator, and fertility.	Sunflower seeds, sunflower oil, almonds, sesame oil, peanut oil, olive oil, butter, spinach, salmon, brown rice, rye flour, wholewheat bread, carrots and nuts.	You should be able to get all the vitamin E you need from a healthy balanced diet.
Vitamin K (phylloquinone, menaquinone)	Relevant to blood clotting, calcium metabolism, blood sugar balance, heart and circulation, metabolism, bones, skin and gut health.	Green leafy vegetables such as broccoli, lettuce, cabbage, spinach and watercress, but also asparagus, cheese, butter, oats, peas and vegetable oils.	You should be able to get all the Vitamin K you need from a healthy balanced diet.
Bioflavonoids (hesperidin, rutin, quercetin)	Antioxidant; anti-inflammatory, relevant to a healthy immune system and healthy blood.	Black and red berries, apples, blackcurrants, citrus fruit, apricots and onions.	You should be able to get all the bioflavonoids you need from a healthy balanced diet.
Folic acid	Relevant to DNA synthesis, new blood cells, protein synthesis, growth, a healthy digestive system and nervous system. Important during pregnancy because folic acid helps to reduce the risk of central nervous system defects, such as spina bifida, in unborn babies.	Eggs, green beans, kidney beans, black-eyed beans, soya beans, asparagus, lentils, chickpeas, walnuts, spinach, kale, peanuts, broccoli, pork, wholewheat cereal, almonds, oatmeal, cabbage, figs and avocado.	Folic acid cannot be stored in the body so you need it in your diet every day. Most people should be able to get all the folic acid they need from a healthy balanced diet, but pregnant women should seek advice about taking a supplement.

Mineral Chart

Minerals are necessary for three main reasons: building strong bones and teeth; controlling body fluids inside and outside cells; and turning food into energy. A healthy balanced diet should provide you with all the minerals needed for good health, but if you are concerned about the amount you are consuming, speak to a health professional for advice (because having too little or too much of a vitamin or mineral can be harmful to health).

NUTRIENT	FUNCTIONS	RICH FOOD SOURCES	NOTES
Boron	A trace element that activates vitamin D and is relevant to the synthesis of other minerals, bone and joint health.	Drinking water, almonds, apples, dates, nuts, beans, peanuts, prunes and soya.	Boron is naturally available from most plant sources. You should be able to get all the boron you need from a healthy balanced diet.
Calcium	Relevant to bone and teeth formation, hormones and blood pressure, blood clotting, nerve and muscle function, including the heartbeat.	Milk, cheese and other diary products, molasses, nuts, parsley, corn, watercress, yeast, goat's milk, tofu, sunflower seeds, yoghurt, green leafy vegetables, sesame seeds, olives and broccoli.	You should be able to get all the calcium you need from a healthy balanced diet.
Chromium	A trace element relevant to growth, insulin and cholesterol regulation, and metabolism.	Meat, wholewheat bread, porridge (oatmeal), rye flour, chilli, broccoli and potatoes.	Refining flour causes up to 50% losses so choose wholegrain varieties whenever possible. You should be able to get all the chromium you need from a healthy balanced diet.
Copper	A trace element relevant to red and white blood cell formation, synthesis of enzymes relevant to iron absorption, skin, bone and nerve formation.	Shellfish, almonds, hazelnuts, Brazil nuts, walnuts, pecan nuts, peanuts, legumes and lamb.	You should be able to get all the copper you need from a healthy balanced diet.
Iodine	Relevant to the synthesis of thyroid hormone.	Seaweed, prawns (shrimps), haddock, shellfish, salmon, sardines, liver, pineapple, eggs, peanuts, wholemeal (wholewheat) bread, cheese, pork and spinach.	Often added to table salt but not sea salt. You should be able to get all the iodine you need from a healthy balanced diet.
Iron	Relevant to red blood cell function, energy release, growth, healthy respiration, bones, skin and nails.	Red meat, beans, pumpkin seeds, sunflower seeds, parsley, almonds, cashew nuts, raisins, yeast, dates, eggs, most green leafy vegetables such as watercress and curly kale, lentils, brown rice, dried apricots and raw chocolate.	Vitamin C enhances iron absorption. You should be able to get enough iron from a healthy balanced diet.
Magnesium	Relevant to the synthesis of proteins, carbohydrates and fats, DNA repair, energy release, moderation of muscle activity, heart and circulation health.	Green leafy vegetables such as spinach, wheat bran, nuts, rye flour, tofu, coconut, soya, brown rice, figs, apricots, dates, fish, meat, sweetcorn, avocado and diary products.	Milling/refining of grains and cereals causes up to 90% loss, so choose whole grains whenever possible. You should be able to get all the magnesium you need from a healthy balanced diet.

NUTRIENT	FUNCTIONS	RICH FOOD SOURCES	NOTES
Manganese	Antioxidant; a trace element that activates enzymes, relevant to bone and ligament formation.	Pecans, Brazil nuts, almonds, rye flour, buckwheat flour, spinach, oats, raisins, Brussels sprouts, avocado and beans.	Milling/refining of cereals causes up to 90% losses. You should be able to get all the manganese you need from a healthy balanced diet.
Molybdenum	Relevant to the regulation of iron, copper and fat metabolism, also linked to dental health.	Lentils, cauliflower, spinach, brown rice, garlic, porridge (oatmeal), eggs, rye flour, corn, fish, chicken, beef, potatoes, peas, broccoli, onions and coconut.	Refining flour causes up to 80% losses. You should be able to get all the molybdenum you need from a healthy balanced diet.
Phosphorus	Relevant to healthy bones, calcium regulation, DNA synthesis, energy metabolism, and a vitamin B activator.	Red meat, pumpkin seeds, Brazil nuts, sesame seeds, almonds, cheese, bread, peanuts, cashews, chicken, brown rice, eggs, garlic, mushrooms and milk.	You should be able to get all the phosphorus you need from a healthy balanced diet.
Potassium	Relevant to heart function, blood pressure regulation, water balance, hormone balance, muscle and nerve health.	Sunflower seeds, almonds, raisins, nuts, dates, figs, garlic, spinach, mushrooms, broccoli, parsnips, banana, red meat, squash, chicken, turkey, carrots and potato.	Diuretics, sickness and certain medicines cause your body to lose potassium. You should be able to get all the potassium you need from a healthy balanced diet.
Selenium	Antioxidant; a trace element relevant to the detoxification of chemicals, reproductive health, fertility, thyroid health and DNA repair.	Butter, herring, Brazil nuts, prawns (shrimps), oats, shellfish, milk, fish, red meat, molasses, garlic, eggs and mushrooms.	Milling/refining of cereals causes up to 50% losses. If you eat meat, fish or nuts, you should be able to get all the selenium you need from a healthy balanced diet.
Zinc	Antioxidant; a trace element relevant to the immune system, DNA synthesis, an enzyme activator, wound healing, linked to skin, hair, muscle and respiratory health, the reproductive system, growth and insulin synthesis.	Red meat, nuts, milk, cheese, egg yolk, porridge (oatmeal), peanuts, chicken, sardines, oily fish, prawns (shrimps), white fish and wholewheat bread.	Milling/refining of cereals and flour can cause up to 80% losses. Freezing of vegetables causes up to 50% losses. You should be able to get all the zinc you need from a healthy balanced diet.

SIMPLE BEGINNINGS

Berry and Almond Smoothie 20
Toast with Almond Butter 22
Porridge (Oatmeal) with Milk 24
Simple Eggy Bread 26
Cheese and Tomato on Toast 28
Yoghurt with Fruit, Nuts and Seeds 30
Poached Egg on Toast 32
Crumpets with Marmite 34
Beans on Toast 36
Simple Cereals 38
Bagel with Cream Cheese 40
Tuna Salad 42
Pasta in Herby Tomato Sauce 44
Pasta with Peas and Parmesan 46
Baked Potato with Beans 48
Simple Popcorn 50
Fresh Fruit 52
Dried Fruit and Nut Mix 54

Berry and Almond Smoothie

A nutritious drink that provides the body with protein, vitamins and minerals. Contains 100% natural ingredients that help strengthen the heart, bones, muscles and immune system. Combines all ingredients in one glass, making this meal feel less overwhelming.

Total time: 00:05   Preparation time: 00:05   Cooking time: 00:00   Serves: 1

Ingredients

- ½ glass of milk of your choice, for example cow's milk, goat's milk, rice milk, coconut milk or almond milk
- 3 tablespoons natural yoghurt
- 1 handful of ground or flaked almonds
- 1 handful of berries, for example blueberries, raspberries or strawberries
- Drizzle of organic honey

Equipment

- Food processor
- Glass, for serving
- Tablespoon

Instructions

1. Place all ingredients in the food processor and blend until smooth.
2. Serve in a glass.

Hints and tips

- Use whichever nuts and berries you prefer.
- Natural Greek yoghurt contains probiotics that aid digestion.
- This smoothie makes a great high-protein breakfast, but is also suitable as a snack between meals.

> " I had to gradually build up my confidence to have this smoothie for breakfast by first having a simple glass of milk. I then added the other ingredients over time, once I was convinced of the benefits they provided. Experimenting with different types of nuts and berries enabled me to consider my personal preferences…a skill I need to develop in other aspects of life too. "
>
> Isabelle – recovering from anorexia

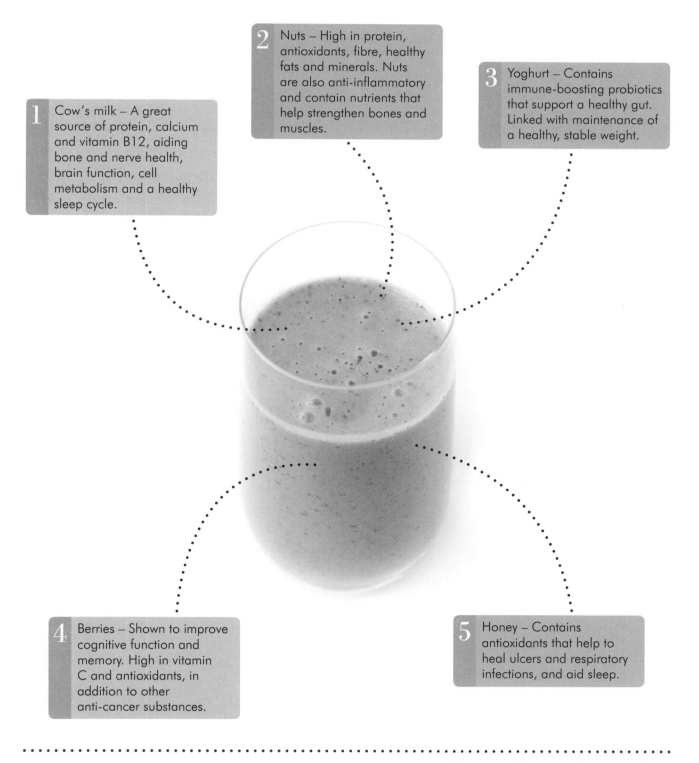

1 Cow's milk – A great source of protein, calcium and vitamin B12, aiding bone and nerve health, brain function, cell metabolism and a healthy sleep cycle.

2 Nuts – High in protein, antioxidants, fibre, healthy fats and minerals. Nuts are also anti-inflammatory and contain nutrients that help strengthen bones and muscles.

3 Yoghurt – Contains immune-boosting probiotics that support a healthy gut. Linked with maintenance of a healthy, stable weight.

4 Berries – Shown to improve cognitive function and memory. High in vitamin C and antioxidants, in addition to other anti-cancer substances.

5 Honey – Contains antioxidants that help to heal ulcers and respiratory infections, and aid sleep.

Toast with Almond Butter

A simple high-protein breakfast, containing antioxidants, fibre, omega-3 and omega-6. Quick and easy to prepare, with no fuss. This combination of complex carbohydrates and protein will provide a steady release of energy throughout the morning.

Total time: 00:05   Preparation time: 00:03   Cooking time: 00:02   Serves: 1

Ingredients

- 2 slices of wholemeal bread
- 1 tablespoon of almond butter

Optional: drizzle of organic honey

Instructions

1. Toast the wholemeal bread in a toaster or under the grill (turning when necessary).
2. Spread the almond butter evenly.
3. Add the honey, if desired.

Equipment

- Toaster or grill (broiler)
- Tablespoon
- Knife

Hints and tips

- Choose wholemeal or seeded bread over white varieties to benefit from additional nutrients and fibre.
- Choose no added salt/sugar almond butter.
- See page 261 for nutritional information about a variety of nuts.
- Choose local honey whenever possible, as this will have the most nutritional value and have the highest antibacterial/viral action.

> " This is a great 'emergency meal' for when I have finished late from work and haven't got the time or energy to cook. I always have a jar of almond butter in my cupboard, so there is never an excuse that I haven't got anything at home for dinner! PS: The fat in nut butter is good fat! "
>
> Jenni – recovering from anorexia

1 Wholemeal (wholewheat) bread – A great source of complex carbohydrate, offering slow-release energy. High in fibre, aiding digestive health. Often fortified with folate and B vitamins.

2 Almond butter – High in protein and a variety of minerals that support brain, cardiovascular and respiratory health.

3 Honey – Choose local or Manuka honey for maximum benefit. Can be a source of antioxidants that help to heal ulcers and respiratory infections, and aid sleep.

Porridge (Oatmeal) with Milk

Comforting porridge (oatmeal), served with calcium-rich milk, satisfying hunger and aiding a healthy heart. See page 62 for additional flavours and textures to enhance the taste and nutritional benefits of this recipe.

Total time: 00:05   Preparation time: 00:02   Cooking time: 00:03   Serves: 1

Ingredients

- 4–6 heaped tablespoons of porridge (oatmeal)
- Milk of your choice (for example cow's milk, goat's milk, rice milk, coconut milk or almond milk)

Optional: drizzle of organic honey and/or a handful of flaked almonds

Instructions

1. Place the porridge in a non-stick saucepan.
2. Completely cover with milk.
3. Cook on a medium heat until fully warmed through (approximately 2–3 minutes), stirring occasionally.
4. Add additional milk during cooking, if a looser consistency is preferred.
5. Add a drizzle of honey or a handful of almonds, if using.
6. If using a microwave, cover the porridge with milk and heat for 1½–2 minutes, stirring halfway.

Equipment

- Oven hob (stovetop)
- Non-stick saucepan (or microwave)
- Wooden spoon
- Tablespoon

Hints and tips

- Toast the almonds in a dry frying pan for 1–2 minutes to increase their flavour.
- Eating almonds with the skin on will more than double the nuts' antioxidant powers.
- Use 100% natural porridge (without added sugar).
- Digesting uncooked oats will encourage bloating so always heat or bake oats before eating them.

> Porridge is one of the foods that I find non-threatening, perhaps because the neutral colour and physical warmth of it makes me feel calmer. I used to make my porridge with just water, but now I appreciate the benefits of making it with milk instead.
>
> Sarah – recovering from bulimia

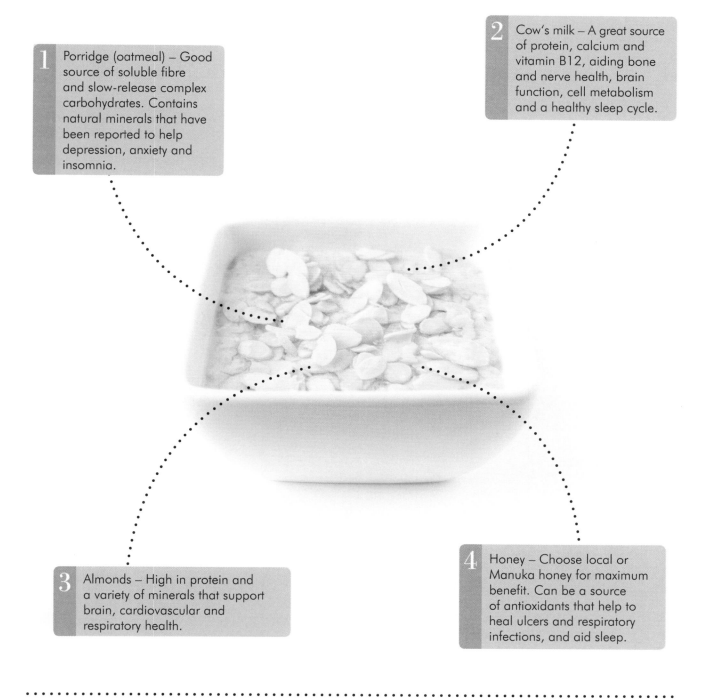

1 Porridge (oatmeal) – Good source of soluble fibre and slow-release complex carbohydrates. Contains natural minerals that have been reported to help depression, anxiety and insomnia.

2 Cow's milk – A great source of protein, calcium and vitamin B12, aiding bone and nerve health, brain function, cell metabolism and a healthy sleep cycle.

3 Almonds – High in protein and a variety of minerals that support brain, cardiovascular and respiratory health.

4 Honey – Choose local or Manuka honey for maximum benefit. Can be a source of antioxidants that help to heal ulcers and respiratory infections, and aid sleep.

Simple Eggy Bread

A simple breakfast of protein and complex carbohydrate, which boosts metabolism and energises the body. Contains natural ingredients providing an impressive variety of vitamins and minerals in one meal.

Total time: 00:10   Preparation time: 00:05   Cooking time: 00:05   Serves: 1

Ingredients

- 2 free-range eggs
- Pinch of salt and pepper
- 1–2 slices of wholemeal (wholewheat) bread

Instructions

1. Carefully break the eggs into a shallow bowl.
2. Add salt and pepper to the eggs and whisk with a fork.
3. Place the wholemeal bread into the egg mixture, coating both sides completely.
4. Heat the frying pan to a medium heat.
5. Place the eggy bread in the frying pan (one at a time if necessary), cooking for approximately 2 minutes each side, turning with a spatula when the eggy bread starts to brown.
6. Simply serve warm from the pan.

Equipment

- Oven hob (stovetop)
- Non-stick frying pan
- Mixing bowl
- Spatula

Hints and tips

- Research suggests that a high-protein breakfast served with some complex carbohydrate (such as wholemeal bread) is the healthiest way to start your day.
- To add a piece of fruit to your breakfast, replace one egg with a mashed banana.
- Delicious served with fresh tomatoes or baked beans.

"
I find it hard to eat lots of different ingredients on one plate so this recipe suits my needs. I can eat bread and eggs without it looking too overwhelming.
"

Isabelle – recovering from anorexia

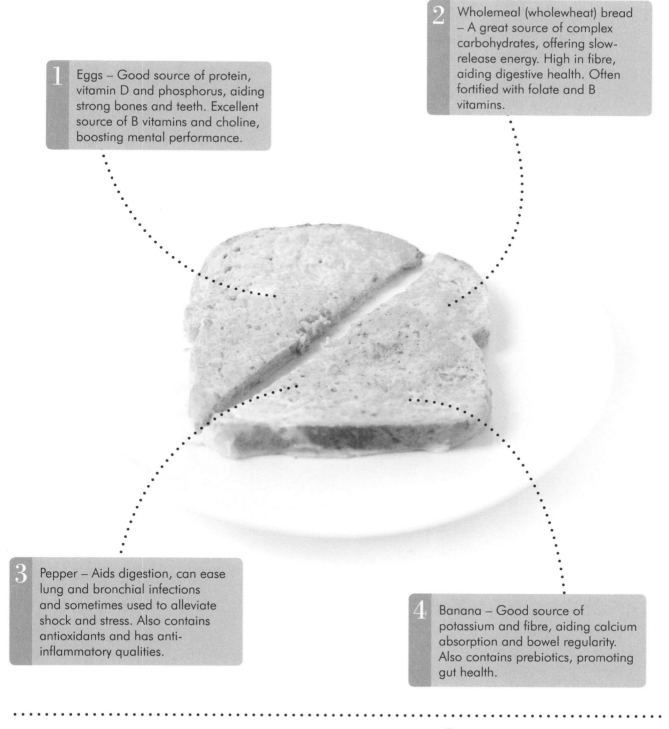

1 Eggs – Good source of protein, vitamin D and phosphorus, aiding strong bones and teeth. Excellent source of B vitamins and choline, boosting mental performance.

2 Wholemeal (wholewheat) bread – A great source of complex carbohydrates, offering slow-release energy. High in fibre, aiding digestive health. Often fortified with folate and B vitamins.

3 Pepper – Aids digestion, can ease lung and bronchial infections and sometimes used to alleviate shock and stress. Also contains antioxidants and has anti-inflammatory qualities.

4 Banana – Good source of potassium and fibre, aiding calcium absorption and bowel regularity. Also contains prebiotics, promoting gut health.

Cheese and Tomato on Toast

A well-balanced recipe combining complex carbohydrates, protein, healthy fats and vitamin-rich fruit. This meal encourages a feeling of physical satisfaction, reducing the likelihood of cravings later in the day.

Total time: 00:05   Preparation time: 00:02   Cooking time: 00:03   Serves: 1

Ingredients

- Approx. 30g (1oz) cheese
- 2–3 cherry tomatoes
- 1 slice of wholemeal (wholewheat) bread

Equipment

- Grill (broiler)
- Chopping board
- Sharp knife

Hints and tips

- Choose wholemeal bread over white varieties for additional nutrients.
- Be sure to cover the bread with cheese because the bread will burn faster than the cheese will melt.
- A small portion of cheese adds protein and natural fat, which will encourage a feeling of physical satisfaction, subsequently reducing the likelihood of unwanted cravings.

Instructions

1. Preheat the grill to a medium heat.
2. Thinly slice the cheese and tomatoes.
3. Toast one side of the bread under the grill.
4. Remove from the grill and turn the bread over.
5. Place the cheese and tomatoes evenly over the bread.
6. Return to the grill until the cheese begins to cook but the bread is not burnt.
7. Serve immediately.

"
Cheese on toast is a favourite of mine. Since using this book, I've changed to wholemeal bread and add tomatoes as well. Sometimes I even put tuna, tomato and then cheese on top. I need my food to be simple and quick, but want it to be nutritious and satisfying too.
"

Alex – recovering from over-eating

1 Cheese – Good source of calcium, aiding strong bones and teeth. Contains nutrients that promote healthy muscle and nerve function.

2 Wholemeal (wholewheat) bread – A great source of complex carbohydrate, offering slow-release energy. High in fibre, aiding digestive health. Often fortified with folate and B vitamins.

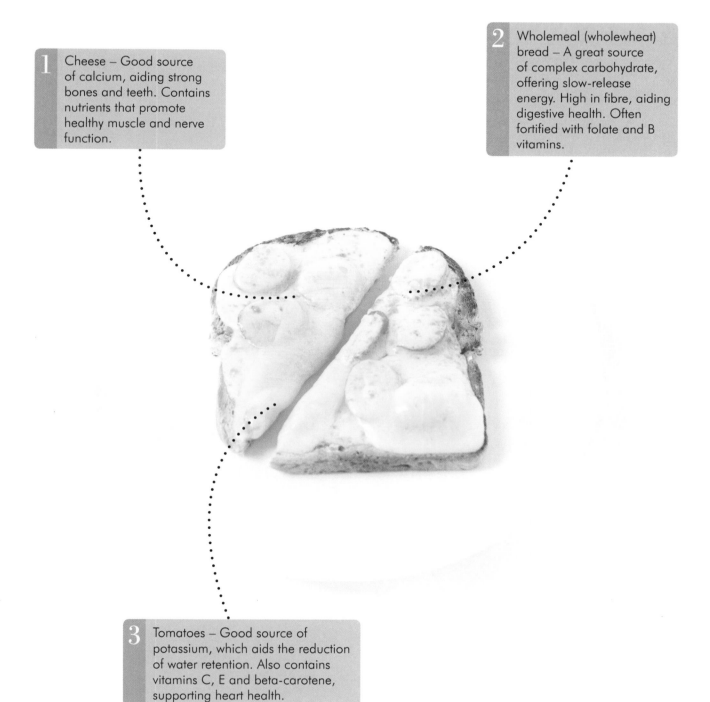

3 Tomatoes – Good source of potassium, which aids the reduction of water retention. Also contains vitamins C, E and beta-carotene, supporting heart health.

Yoghurt with Fruit, Nuts and Seeds

An amazing high-protein breakfast, offering slow-release energy and a variety of vitamins and minerals. Also suitable as a snack or dessert. Experiment with a variety of nuts and seeds to benefit from their individual properties.

Total time: 00:05   Preparation time: 00:05   Cooking time: 00:00   Serves: 1

Ingredients

- 1 small pot of natural yoghurt
- 2–3 tablespoons of dried fruit, nuts and seeds (for example dates, apricots, almonds, pecans, sunflower seeds, pumpkin seeds)

Instructions

1. Combine the natural yoghurt with the dried fruit, nuts and seeds, as preferred (see page 54 for dried fruit and nut mix).

Equipment

- Tablespoon

Hints and tips

- Enjoy full-fat, natural and plain probiotic yoghurts to maximise the benefits and avoid sweeteners.
- Make a batch of nuts, seeds and fruit that you can add to yoghurt and cereals without any fuss.
- Buy unsulphured apricots (darker in colour), as the orange apricots have been treated with a chemical that can irritate digestion.

> " Sometimes I have this for breakfast, along with a piece of toast. Other days I have this as my afternoon snack. I feel comfortable knowing that all of the ingredients are 100% natural. "
>
> Becky – overcoming body-image issues

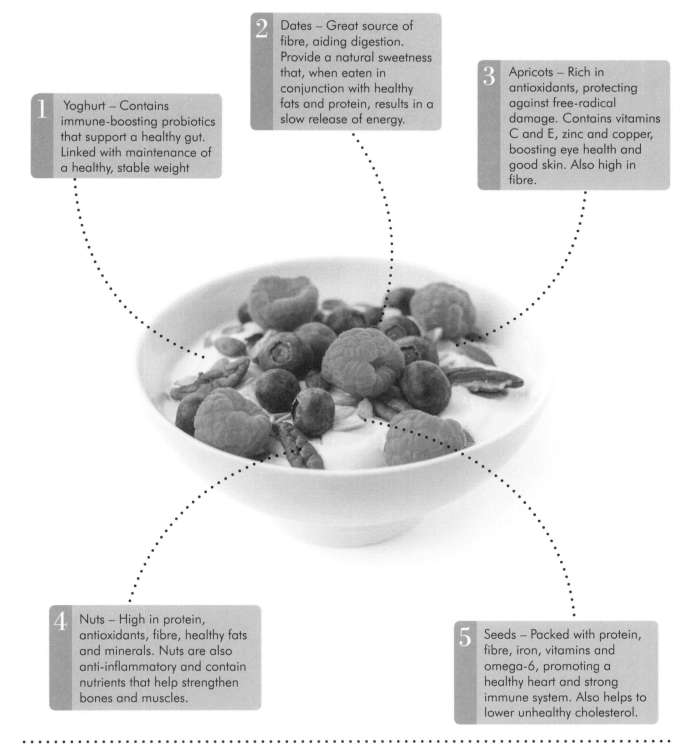

1 Yoghurt – Contains immune-boosting probiotics that support a healthy gut. Linked with maintenance of a healthy, stable weight

2 Dates – Great source of fibre, aiding digestion. Provide a natural sweetness that, when eaten in conjunction with healthy fats and protein, results in a slow release of energy.

3 Apricots – Rich in antioxidants, protecting against free-radical damage. Contains vitamins C and E, zinc and copper, boosting eye health and good skin. Also high in fibre.

4 Nuts – High in protein, antioxidants, fibre, healthy fats and minerals. Nuts are also anti-inflammatory and contain nutrients that help strengthen bones and muscles.

5 Seeds – Packed with protein, fibre, iron, vitamins and omega-6, promoting a healthy heart and strong immune system. Also helps to lower unhealthy cholesterol.

<15

Poached Eggs on Toast

Protein rich eggs containing essential vitamins and minerals alongside complex carbohydrates, helping to stabilise blood sugar levels and sustain energy levels for hours. Choose free-range eggs whenever possible.

Total time: 00:10   Preparation time: 00:05   Cooking time: 00:05   Serves: 1

Ingredients

- 1–2 slices of wholemeal (wholewheat) bread
- 2 free-range eggs
- Approx. 1 teaspoon of butter
- Pinch of salt and pepper

Equipment

- Oven hob (stovetop)
- Non-stick saucepan
- Toaster or grill (broiler)
- Tablespoon
- Knife

Instructions

1. Half fill a saucepan with water and bring to the boil.
2. Put the bread in a toaster or under the grill (turning when necessary).
3. Whilst the bread is toasting, carefully crack the eggs into the boiling water.
4. Butter the toast when ready.
5. Using a large spoon, remove the eggs from the hot water after 2–3 minutes, or once cooked to your preference. Place the eggs onto a piece of kitchen paper after cooking as this will soak up any excess water before serving.
6. Place the eggs on top of the toast and serve with salt and pepper to taste.

Hints and tips

- Research recommends a high-protein breakfast, served with some complex carbohydrate (such as wholemeal bread).
- You can buy various kitchen gadgets that help to produce the perfect poached eggs.
- Pink Himalayan salt contains good levels of iodine and other minerals compared to table salt.

" This is such a useful meal as you can usually find eggs in every shop. This is particularly useful when you go to the shop to find that what you had planned for dinner has sold out! Eggs are always my back-up plan! "

Charlie – recovering from anorexia

1 Eggs – Good source of protein, vitamin D and phosphorus, aiding strong bones and teeth. Excellent source of B vitamins and choline, boosting mental performance.

2 Wholemeal (wholewheat) bread – A great source of complex carbohydrates, offering slow-release energy. High in fibre, aiding digestive health. Often fortified with folate and B vitamins.

3 Butter – Contains healthy medium- and short-chain fatty acids that aid the absorption of fat-soluble nutrients.

4 Pepper – Aids digestion, can ease lung and bronchial infections and sometimes used to alleviate shock and stress. Also contains antioxidants and has anti-inflammatory qualities.

Crumpets with Marmite

A super-quick breakfast, rich in complex carbohydrate and B vitamins. Add a little grated cheese to further increase the recipe's content. The light and airy texture of crumpets can be reassuring for those who struggle with the thought of bread.

Total time: 00:05   Preparation time: 00:03   Cooking time: 00:02   Serves: 1

Ingredients

- 2 crumpets (or English muffins)
- Approx. 1 teaspoon of butter
- Approx. 1–2 teaspoons of Marmite or Vegemite

Equipment

- Toaster or grill (broiler)
- Tablespoon
- Knife

Instructions

1. Toast the crumpets (or English muffins) in a toaster or under the grill (turning when necessary).
2. Spread the butter evenly, followed by the Marmite or Vegemite.

Hints and tips

- Favour organic butter because it contains a higher percentage of healthy mono-saturated fats, which aid the digestion of fat-soluble nutrients.
- Alternatively, use almond or cashew butter on the crumpets.
- Choose wholemeal (wholewheat) muffins over white varieties for additional nutrients and fibre.

> " Crumpets are my 'safe' comfort food. I like to eat them with a nutritious spread to get a hit of vitamins and minerals at the same time. "
>
> M – recovering from over-eating

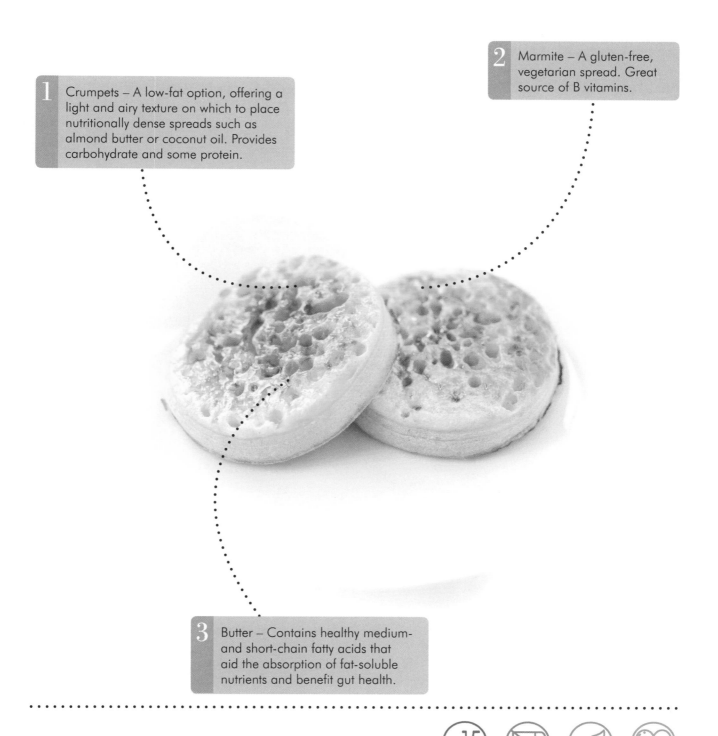

1 Crumpets – A low-fat option, offering a light and airy texture on which to place nutritionally dense spreads such as almond butter or coconut oil. Provides carbohydrate and some protein.

2 Marmite – A gluten-free, vegetarian spread. Great source of B vitamins.

3 Butter – Contains healthy medium- and short-chain fatty acids that aid the absorption of fat-soluble nutrients and benefit gut health.

Beans on Toast

A healthy, balanced meal providing the body with carbohydrate, protein, fibre, calcium, potassium and iron. A comforting combination at any time of day! Add a dash of Worcestershire sauce for a burst of flavour.

Total time: 00:05   Preparation time: 00:01   Cooking time: 00:04   Serves: 1

Ingredients

- ½ can of baked beans (approx. 200g/ 1 cup)
- 2 slices of wholemeal (wholewheat) bread
- Approx. 1 teaspoon of butter

Instructions

1. Put ½ a can of baked beans into a non-stick saucepan.
2. Cook on a medium heat, stirring occasionally, for approximately 4 minutes.
3. Toast the wholemeal bread in a toaster or under the grill (turning when necessary).
4. Spread the butter evenly over the toast.
5. Pour the baked beans over the top.

Equipment

- Oven hob (stovetop)
- Toaster or grill (broiler)
- Non-stick saucepan
- Can opener
- Wooden spoon
- Knife

Hints and tips

- Choose wholemeal or seeded bread over white varieties to benefit from additional nutrients and fibre.
- Try mixed baked beans to further increase the variety of nutrients in the recipe, or make your own – see recipe on page 78.
- Add a poached egg on top to further increase the protein content of this meal.
- Suitable for breakfast or lunch.

> " I like the fact that I could have this meal for breakfast, lunch or dinner. It's quick and easy to prepare, which is what I need, especially when my head is spinning with confusing thoughts. "
>
> Rosie – overcoming low self-esteem

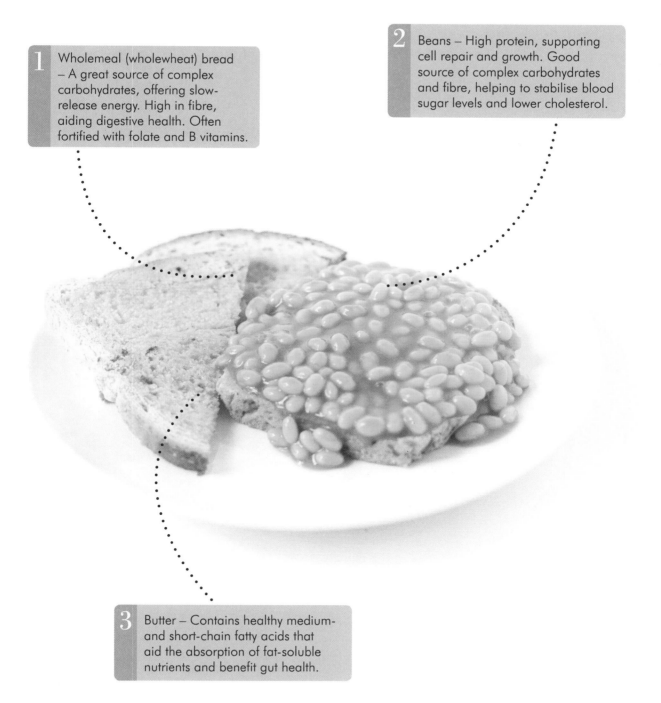

1 Wholemeal (wholewheat) bread – A great source of complex carbohydrates, offering slow-release energy. High in fibre, aiding digestive health. Often fortified with folate and B vitamins.

2 Beans – High protein, supporting cell repair and growth. Good source of complex carbohydrates and fibre, helping to stabilise blood sugar levels and lower cholesterol.

3 Butter – Contains healthy medium- and short-chain fatty acids that aid the absorption of fat-soluble nutrients and benefit gut health.

Simple Cereals

A quick wholegrain breakfast, offering slow-release energy when served with nuts and seeds. Adding a banana will provide extra fibre and a serving of potassium, aiding heart health. Alternatively, consider topping with fresh berries or flaked almonds.

Total time: 00:05   Preparation time: 00:05   Cooking time: 00:00   Serves: 1

Ingredients

- 4–6 heaped tablespoons of pre-bought cereal (for example Weetabix, Shredded Wheat or Bran Flakes)
- Milk of your choice (for example cow's milk, goat's milk, rice milk, coconut milk or almond milk)

Optional: sliced banana and/or 1 tablespoon of nuts and seeds

Instructions

1. Place the cereal in a bowl.
2. Pour on the milk.
3. Add a sliced banana and/or nuts and seeds on top, if desired.

Equipment

- Tablespoon

Hints and tips

- Choose wholegrain cereals to benefit from additional nutrients and fibre.
- Cereal goes well with milk or yoghurt – Enjoy full-fat, natural and plain probiotic yoghurts to maximise the benefits and avoid sweeteners.
- Adding nuts and seeds to wholegrain cereals will further increase the nutritional benefits of this recipe.

"
Sometimes, I just don't feel able to spend time cooking or preparing food. I need 'safe' options that don't involve much thought or time. So it's good to see such simple ideas included in this book.

Isabelle – recovering from anorexia
"

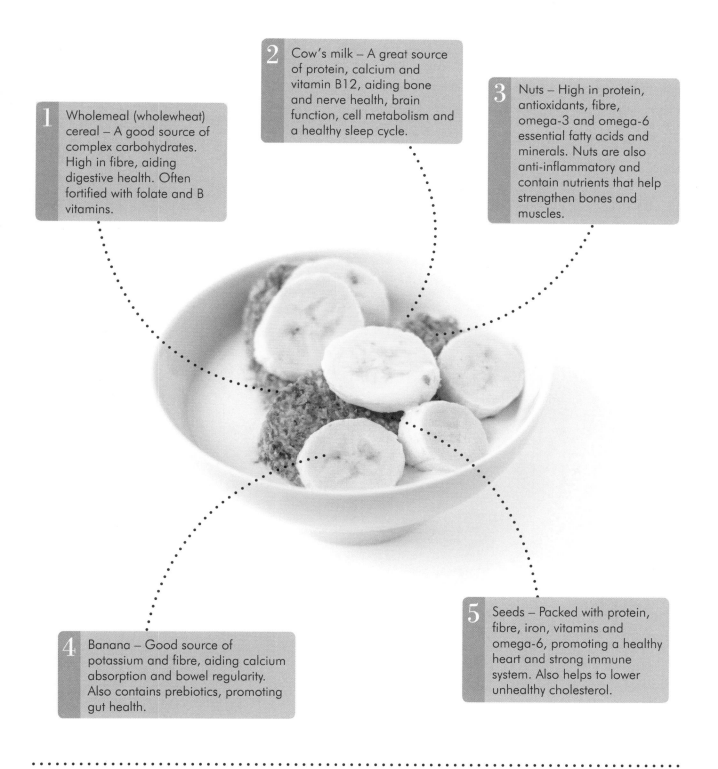

1 Wholemeal (wholewheat) cereal – A good source of complex carbohydrates. High in fibre, aiding digestive health. Often fortified with folate and B vitamins.

2 Cow's milk – A great source of protein, calcium and vitamin B12, aiding bone and nerve health, brain function, cell metabolism and a healthy sleep cycle.

3 Nuts – High in protein, antioxidants, fibre, omega-3 and omega-6 essential fatty acids and minerals. Nuts are also anti-inflammatory and contain nutrients that help strengthen bones and muscles.

4 Banana – Good source of potassium and fibre, aiding calcium absorption and bowel regularity. Also contains prebiotics, promoting gut health.

5 Seeds – Packed with protein, fibre, iron, vitamins and omega-6, promoting a healthy heart and strong immune system. Also helps to lower unhealthy cholesterol.

Bagel with Cream Cheese

A calcium-rich breakfast or lunch, providing the body with energy and minerals that support healthy bones, teeth and nails. Easily prepared and eaten at home, but equally suitable for a packed lunch out and about.

Total time: 00:05   Preparation time: 00:03   Cooking time: 00:02   Serves: 1

Ingredients

- 1 bagel
- 2 tablespoons of cream cheese

Optional: cherry tomatoes and/or spinach leaves

Equipment

- Toaster or grill (broiler)
- Tablespoon
- Knife

Instructions

1. Cut the bagel in half and place in a toaster or under the grill (broiler) (turning when necessary).
2. Remove from the toaster (or grill (broiler)) and evenly spread the cream cheese on the bagel.
   If using, slice the cherry tomatoes and add these and/or the spinach leaves over the cream cheese

Hints and tips

- Choose wholemeal (wholewheat) or seeded bagels over white varieties to benefit from additional nutrients and fibre.
- Include sliced smoked salmon or a slice of ham to add protein to this meal.
- Eating sensible meals on a regular basis will help to boost metabolism and stabilise the body, physically and emotionally.

> " My counsellor says that I should make more time to prepare and eat my food, but I find this very difficult. I'm starting with this toasted bagel because it only takes a few mintues, but hope to progress to cooking a full meal one day soon.
>
> Lisa – overcoming body-image issues

1 Bagel – A source of carbohydrate. Low in saturated fat and cholesterol. Contains thiamin, folate, iron and selenium.

2 Cream cheese – A great source of protein, aiding cell growth and repair. Contains good levels of calcium, supporting healthy bones, teeth and nails.

3 Tomatoes – Good source of potassium, which aids the reduction of water retention. Also contains vitamins C, E and beta-carotene.

Tuna Salad

A fresh salad including a variety of colourful vegetables and protein-rich fish. Easy and quick to make fresh or in advance, for a packed lunch. Include an array of colours from the salad leaves and raw vegetables to increase nutritional content.

Total time: 00:05   Preparation time: 00:05   Cooking time: 00:00   Serves: 1

Ingredients

- ½ a red pepper
- 2 spring (green) onions
- ¼ can of sweetcorn (approx. 100g/½ cup)
- ½ can of tuna (approx. 75g/2.5oz)
- 1 handful of mixed salad leaves

Optional: 1 tablespoon of mayonnaise (see page 256 for homemade mayonnaise recipe)

Equipment

- Chopping board
- Can opener
- Sharp knife
- Tablespoon

Instructions

1. Cut the red pepper and spring onions to your preferred size.
2. Open the can of sweetcorn and drain any excess liquid.
3. Open the can of tuna and drain any excess liquid.
4. Combine the tuna with a tablespoon of mayonnaise, if using.
5. Serve the mixed salad leaves, tuna and vegetables, as preferred.

Hints and tips

- Include a rainbow of colours in your diet to encourage intake of a variety of vitamins and minerals that promote good health.
- Tuna is a lean, inexpensive source of protein easily added to salads or sandwiches; however, pregnant women are advised to eat no more than 2–3 cans per week.
- See page 268 for a variety of nutritionally beneficial salad dressings.

"
Striving to eat a variety of colours in my meals has helped me to eat more vegetables. I try to eat some protein and at least one portion of fruit or veg at every meal time.

Fleur – recovering from over-eating
"

1 Tuna – An excellent source of protein, selenium, magnesium, potassium and omega-3 fatty acids. Also contains B vitamins, aiding heart health.

2 Salad leaves – Include a variety of mixed leaves to benefit from various vitamins and minerals, such as vitamin C and iron. Rich in fibre and antioxidants, aiding digestion and the immune system.

3 Red pepper – Rich in vitamin C and beta-carotene, promoting healthy skin and eyes. Contains antioxidants, boosting the immune system, reducing the risk of poor health.

4 Sweetcorn – Contains nutrients that promote eye health. High-fibre content promotes a healthy digestive tract and helps to control blood sugar levels.

5 Spring (green) onions – Contains immunity-boosting sulphur compounds, in addition to antibacterial qualities that help the body fight illness.

Pasta in Herby Tomato Sauce

Wholewheat pasta served with tomatoes and green herbs, offering numerous health benefits. See page 258 for a more nutrient-dense pizza/pasta sauce recipe, containing a variety of vegetables.

Total time: 00:15   Preparation time: 00:03   Cooking time: 00:12   Serves: 1

Ingredients

- 1 handful of fresh herbs (for example basil, oregano or thyme) or 1 teaspoon of dried mixed herbs
- Approx. 75g (2.5oz) wholewheat pasta
- ½ can of chopped tomatoes (approx. 200g/1 cup)
- Pinch of pepper

Optional: 2 tablespoons of cream cheese

Equipment

- Oven hob (stovetop)
- Non-stick saucepan
- Chopping board
- Kitchen scales
- Sharp knife
- Wooden spoon
- Colander
- Can opener

Instructions

1. Chop the fresh herbs with a sharp knife.
2. Half fill a non-stick saucepan with water and bring it to the boil.
3. Add the pasta to the water, bring back to the boil and cook for 8–10 minutes, or until cooked to preferred texture.
4. Drain the pasta in a colander and then return it to the warm saucepan.
5. Add the chopped tomatoes and fresh or dried herbs.
6. Add the cream cheese, if using.
7. Stir and heat for a further 2 minutes, or until warmed through.
8. Sprinkle with pepper, as preferred.

Hints and tips

- Choose wholewheat pasta over white varieties to benefit from additional nutrients and fibre.
- Canned chopped tomatoes can be purchased with herbs included.
- Adding the cream cheese increases the protein content of the recipe, resulting in a more balanced meal.

" This was a good recipe to introduce me to pasta. I now double the ingredients, placing one portion in the fridge for the following day, which I can eat hot or cold. Also, I've noticed tomato pasta on the menu at many restaurants, so hope that I can challenge myself to eat this meal out in the future. "

Jenni – recovering from anorexia

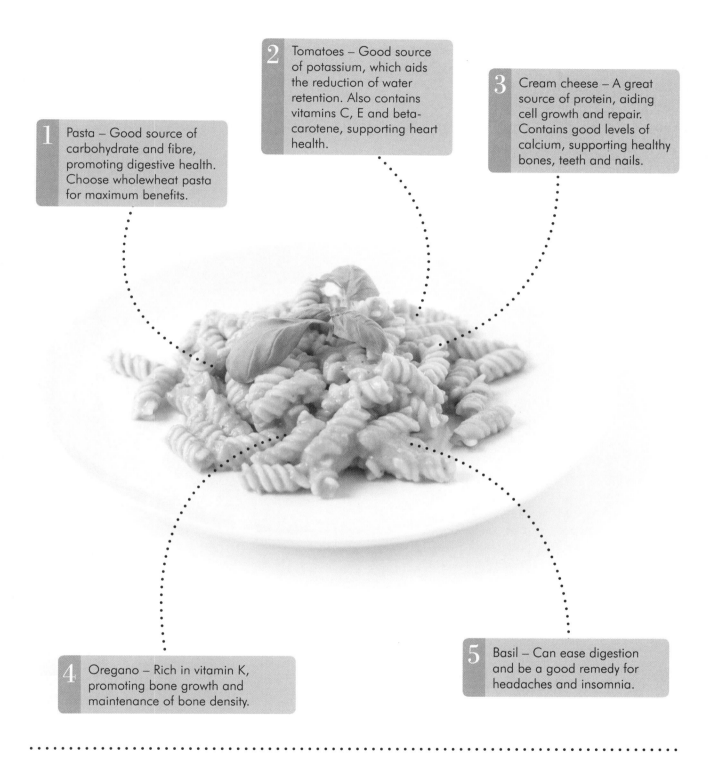

1 Pasta – Good source of carbohydrate and fibre, promoting digestive health. Choose wholewheat pasta for maximum benefits.

2 Tomatoes – Good source of potassium, which aids the reduction of water retention. Also contains vitamins C, E and beta-carotene, supporting heart health.

3 Cream cheese – A great source of protein, aiding cell growth and repair. Contains good levels of calcium, supporting healthy bones, teeth and nails.

4 Oregano – Rich in vitamin K, promoting bone growth and maintenance of bone density.

5 Basil – Can ease digestion and be a good remedy for headaches and insomnia.

Pasta with Peas and Parmesan

A simple pasta dish, providing slow-release energy, protein and fibre to aid digestion and muscle repair. Serve with a squeeze of lemon juice and a few basil leaves to enhance flavour. Suitable for lunch or dinner.

Total time: 00:15   Preparation time: 00:05   Cooking time: 00:10   Serves: 1

Ingredients

- Approx. 75g (2.5oz) spaghetti
- 3 heaped tablespoons of peas
- Approx. 30g (1oz) Parmesan
- Pinch of pepper

Optional: 1 tablespoon of olive oil

Instructions

1. Half fill a non-stick saucepan with water and bring to the boil.
2. Add the pasta to the water and cook for 4 minutes.
3. Add the peas to the water.
4. Bring back to the boil and cook for a further 4 minutes, or until cooked to preferred texture.
5. Turn off the heat.
6. Drain the pasta and peas in a colander and then return them to the warm saucepan.
7. Grate the Parmesan over the pasta.
8. Sprinkle with pepper, as preferred.
9. Add a tablespoon of olive oil, if using.
10. Stir everything together and then serve.

Equipment

- Oven hob (stovetop)
- Non-stick saucepan
- Colander
- Kitchen scales
- Grater
- Wooden spoon
- Tablespoon

Hints and tips

- Choose wholewheat pasta over white varieties to benefit from additional nutrients and fibre.
- Peas are an amazing source of protein, especially relevant if vegetarian or vegan.
- A small portion of cheese adds protein and natural fat, that will encourage a feeling of physical satisfaction, subsequently reducing the likelihood of unwanted cravings.

"
This recipe was really simple to make, using only one saucepan. My daughter is vegetarian, so it was good to learn that peas are high in protein.

Kate – supportive parent
"

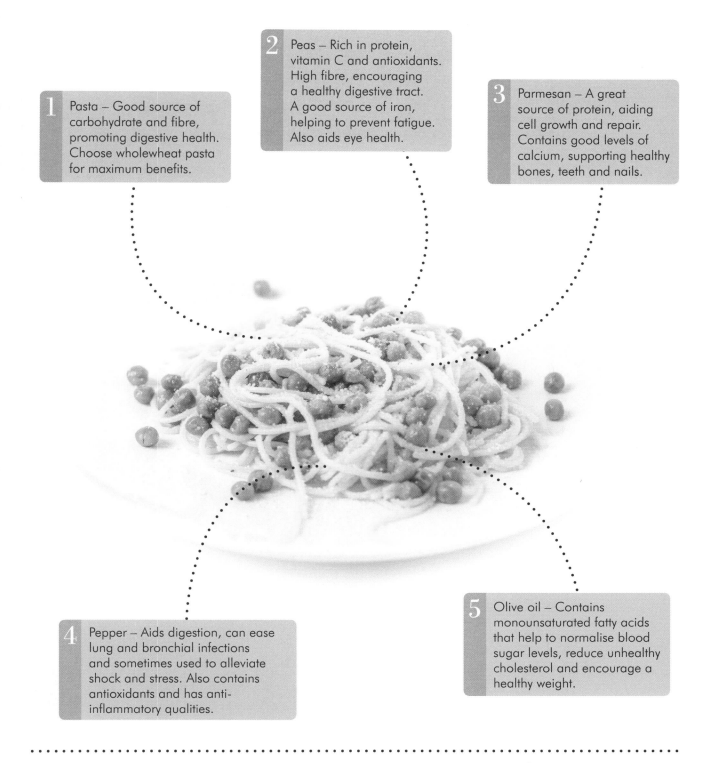

1 Pasta – Good source of carbohydrate and fibre, promoting digestive health. Choose wholewheat pasta for maximum benefits.

2 Peas – Rich in protein, vitamin C and antioxidants. High fibre, encouraging a healthy digestive tract. A good source of iron, helping to prevent fatigue. Also aids eye health.

3 Parmesan – A great source of protein, aiding cell growth and repair. Contains good levels of calcium, supporting healthy bones, teeth and nails.

4 Pepper – Aids digestion, can ease lung and bronchial infections and sometimes used to alleviate shock and stress. Also contains antioxidants and has anti-inflammatory qualities.

5 Olive oil – Contains monounsaturated fatty acids that help to normalise blood sugar levels, reduce unhealthy cholesterol and encourage a healthy weight.

Baked Potato with Beans

A healthy 'comfort' food combining carbohydrate and protein for a steady release of energy. Alternatively, serve with canned tuna or homemade coleslaw, packed with vegetables (see page 208 for recipe).

Total time: 00:50 Preparation time: 00:05 Cooking time: 00:45 Serves: 1

Ingredients

- 1 baking potato
- ½ can of baked beans (approx. 200g/ 1 cup)
- Approx. 1 teaspoon of butter

Optional: approx. 30g (1oz) cheese

Equipment

- Oven
- Oven hob (stovetop)
- Non-stick baking tray
- Non-stick saucepan
- Can opener
- Wooden spoon

Hints and tips

- To reduce preparation time, cook the baked potato in the microwave for 8–10 minutes – the skin will remain soft rather than crispy.
- This recipe can be eaten for lunch or dinner.
- Serve with a side salad to add a variety of vitamins and minerals.
- Choose low sugar/salt canned beans, mixed beans or make your own – see page 78 for a recipe that can be batch cooked.

Instructions

1. Preheat the oven to 180–200°C (350–400°F/Gas 4–6).
2. Put the baking potato on a non-stick baking tray and place in the oven.
3. Bake for 45 minutes.
4. Five minutes before serving, heat ½ a can of baked beans in a non-stick saucepan on a medium heat.
5. Remove the baking potato from the oven and open it up into two halves.
6. Add the butter and mash this into the potato using a fork.
7. Pour the beans over the potato.
8. Grate the cheese on top, if using.

"

Baked potatoes are available from almost every cafe, bar or restaurant, so introducing them to my food plan has enabled me to be more flexible about where I eat. I like mine with tuna mayonnaise, or even better... homemade chilli.

"

Helen – recovering from bulimia

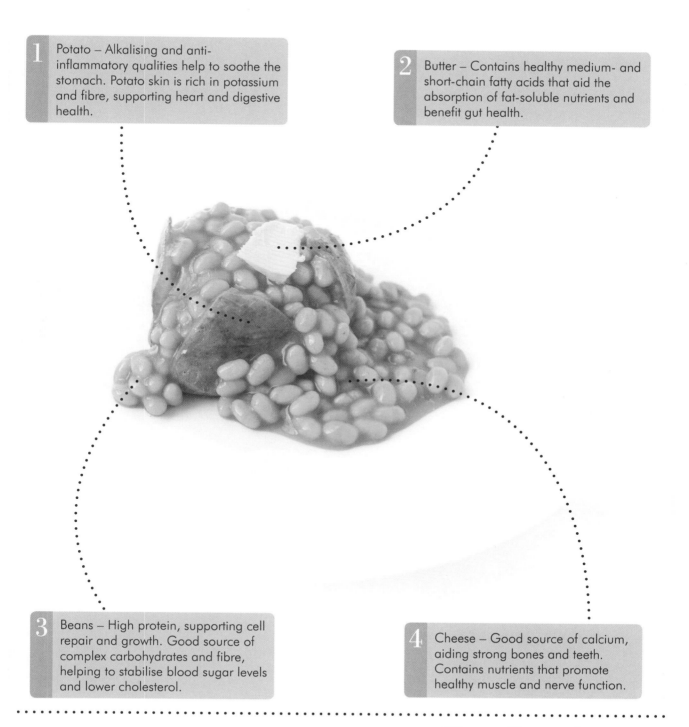

1 Potato – Alkalising and anti-inflammatory qualities help to soothe the stomach. Potato skin is rich in potassium and fibre, supporting heart and digestive health.

2 Butter – Contains healthy medium- and short-chain fatty acids that aid the absorption of fat-soluble nutrients and benefit gut health.

3 Beans – High protein, supporting cell repair and growth. Good source of complex carbohydrates and fibre, helping to stabilise blood sugar levels and lower cholesterol.

4 Cheese – Good source of calcium, aiding strong bones and teeth. Contains nutrients that promote healthy muscle and nerve function.

Simple Popcorn

A high-fibre natural snack made from 100% sweetcorn kernels, aiding digestion and steadying blood sugar levels. See page 216 for flavouring inspirations. Batch cook and store in an airtight container so ready in advance.

Total time: 00:05   Preparation time: 00:02   Cooking time: 00:03   Serves: 1

Ingredients

- 1–2 tablespoons of popcorn kernels

Optional: pinch of salt and pepper

Equipment

- Oven hob (stovetop)
- Non-stick saucepan or frying pan, with a lid (or use kitchen foil)
- Tablespoon

Hints and tips

- Allow yourself a good portion to ensure that you stimulate the metabolism.
- Don't wait for all kernels to pop before removing from the heat otherwise the popcorn may burn.
- It's normal for a few kernels to remain un-popped.

Instructions

1. Put 2–3 popcorn kernels into a non-stick saucepan or frying pan.
2. Cover with a lid (or kitchen foil) and cook on a medium-high heat, until you've heard the kernels pop.
3. Remove the 2–3 pieces of popcorn.
4. Add the rest of the kernels to the hot pan, in an even layer.
5. Shake the pan occasionally, until the sound of popping slows down (after approximately 2 minutes).
6. Remove from the heat and take the lid off the pan – this allows the steam to escape and keeps the popcorn crisp.
7. Add the salt and pepper, if using.

> " When I feel emotionally hungry I know that I am tempted to snack on crips or biscuits, so popcorn has been a lifeline. I have salt and pepper popcorn when I cannot beat the craving any more and feel that I just need to eat something. "
>
> M – recovering from over-eating

1 Popcorn kernels – Contains nutrients that promote eye health. High-fibre content promotes a healthy digestive tract and helps to control blood sugar levels.

2 Pepper – Aids digestion, can ease lung and bronchial infections and sometimes used to alleviate shock and stress. Also contains antioxidants and has anti-inflammatory qualities.

Fresh Fruit

Natural and nutritious, fruit provides an array of vitamins and minerals. Bursting with antioxidants that improve general health and vitality. Perfect for a portable snack and even more beneficial when served with protein-rich nuts or seeds.

Total time: 00:05   Preparation time: 00:05   Cooking time: 00:00   Serves: 1

Ingredients

- Choice of fruit – see opposite page

Instructions

- Wash and cut the fruit, as appropriate.

One serving would consist of 1 handful of berries, or an apple, banana or pear.

Equipment

- Optional: chopping board and sharp knife

Hints and tips

- Consider serving fruit with yoghurt and/ or nuts to benefit from the combination of natural antioxidants, healthy fat and protein.
- Fruit contains an array of vitamins that benefit health. However, some fruit is also high in natural sugar, so eat in moderation, consuming 1–2 portions every day.
- A glass of 100% fruit juice is considered to be a portion.

"

I feel comfortable eating fruit, knowing that it's natural and good for my body. Berries are my favourite. I try to eat my fruit in combination with nuts or yoghurt because I've learnt this makes a really balanced snack.

"

Nadia – overcoming low self-esteem

1 Raspberries – Aids metabolism and helps to regulate blood sugar levels. Also rich in antioxidants, boosting the immune system.

2 Apple – Improves metabolic balance by maintaining steady blood sugar levels. Fights inflammation and free-radical production. High fibre, aiding digestive health.

3 Blueberries – Rich in antioxidants. Shown to improve cognitive function and memory. Also contains properties that aid eye health.

4 Pear – Good source of fibre, aiding a healthy digestive system. Also rich in vitamin B2, vitamin C, vitamin E, copper, and potassium. Eat with the skin on for maximum benefits.

5 Banana – Good source of potassium and fibre, aiding calcium absorption and bowel regularity.

6 Strawberries – Rich in vitamin C and antioxidants, aiding good heart and immune health.

Dried Fruit and Nut Mix

A tasty mix of natural ingredients offering a variety of vitamins and minerals, protein and healthy fats, for a balanced snack. Consider adding a spoonful to cereal or yoghurt to increase the nutritional value of a simple breakfast or snack.

Total time: 00:05   **Preparation time:** 00:05   **Cooking time:** 00:00   **Serves:** 4

Ingredients

- 2 tablespoons of dried fruit (for example dates, figs, prunes, apricots, raisins or cranberries)
- 4 tablespoons of nuts (for example almonds, peanuts, cashews, pistachios or macadamias)
- 2 tablespoons of seeds (for example pumpkin seeds, sunflower seeds, flax seeds, linseeds or chia seeds)

Equipment

- Chopping board
- Sharp knife
- Tablespoon

Hints and tips

- Dried fruit is fairly high in natural sugar, so should be eaten in moderation. Combining dried fruit with nuts and seeds slows the subsequent release of energy, creating a balanced snack.
- Almonds, hazelnuts, pecans and peanuts are actually fruit seeds (rather than 'nuts')!
- Consider preparing a lunchbox of nuts and seeds ready for convenient future use.

Instructions

1. Chop the dried fruit into bite-size pieces, as preferred.
2. Combine all of the ingredients.
3. Store in an airtight container.

One serving would consist of 2 tablespoons of dried fruit and nut mix.

> "
> I double this recipe and keep it stored in a lunchbox in my cupboard. Each day I fill up a little jar of fruit and nut mix for my mid-morning snack, which keeps me satisfied until lunchtime. Now it's just part of my routine. I even look forward to it!
> "
>
> Isabelle – recovering from anorexia

1 Nuts – High in protein, antioxidants, fibre, omega-3 and omega-6 essential fatty acids and minerals. Nuts are also anti-inflammatory and contain nutrients that help strengthen bones and muscles.

2 Seeds – Packed with protein, fibre, iron, vitamins and omega-6, promoting a healthy heart and strong immune system. Also helps to lower unhealthy cholesterol.

3 Dried fruit – Helps to improve bowel regularity and enhance gut health. Contains various vitamins and minerals, but is also fairly high in natural sugar, so best eaten in combination with slow-release energy sources, such as nuts.

BREAKFAST

Homemade Granola 58
Pancakes with Fruit Compote.. 60
Porridge (Oatmeal), Apple and Walnuts 62
Blueberry Nut Muffins and Yoghurt... 64
Banana and Pecan Smoothie.. 66
Cinnamon Eggy Bread with Berries 68
Darissa – Yoghurt Granola Fruit Pot 70
Mug Muffin with Yoghurt 72

Homemade Granola

An amazing mix of heart-healthy oats, high-protein nuts and seeds combined with dried fruit for a variety of vitamins and minerals. Batch cook and keep in an airtight container for later use.

Total time: 00:50   Preparation time: 00:10   Cooking time: 00:40   Serves: 4–6

Ingredients

- 3 teaspoons of coconut oil
- 200g (1⅔ cup) chopped nuts and seeds of your choice, for example pecans, almonds, walnuts, sunflower seeds, flax seeds
- 50g (¼ cup) chopped dried fruit, for example dates, figs, apricots, cranberries, raisins
- 300g (3 cups) porridge (oatmeal)
- 50g (½ cup) desiccated (dried) coconut
- 2 teaspoons of cinnamon
- 2 egg whites
- Milk or 2–3 tablespoons of Greek yoghurt

Optional: fresh berries or sliced banana

Equipment

- Oven
- Non-stick baking tray (or tray lined with baking paper)
- Mixing bowl
- Airtight container, for storage
- Knife (or food processor, for chopping)
- Fork, for whisking
- Tablespoon
- Teaspoon

Instructions

- Preheat the oven to 110°C (225°F/Gas ¼).
- Place the coconut oil on a non-stick baking tray and place this in the oven to melt.
- Chop the nuts and dried fruit, as preferred.
- In a bowl, mix the oats, nuts, seeds, dried fruit, desiccated/dried coconut and cinnamon together.
- In a separate bowl, whisk 2 egg whites with a fork, until they go frothy. Stir these through the granola mixture.
- Add the mixture to the coconut oil on the baking tray and stir together – being careful not to burn yourself on the hot tray.
- Bake for 20 minutes, mix it up, and then bake for a further 20 minutes.
- Remove from the oven and allow the mixture to cool.
- Serve either with milk or yoghurt, or eat a handful as a nutritious, high-protein snack.
- Top with the fresh berries or sliced banana, if using.

Hints and tips

- The egg whites help to bind the mixture together.
- Dried fruit and cinnamon provide a natural sweetness.
- Adding a pinch of salt will increase flavour.
- The granola can be stored in an airtight container for up to 3 weeks.
- You can purchase nuts and seeds pre-chopped/pre-mixed.

" I always feel starving when I first wake up so need a good breakfast to keep me going until lunch. This granola provides me with a great balance of carbohydrates, protein and healthy fats, boosting my metabolism – especially relevant after a night's sleep. When I start the day off right, it helps me to continue the day with a positive mindset…breakfast really is an important meal that I couldn't do without!

Emma

1 Porridge (oatmeal) – Rich in soluble fibre. Good source of slow-release complex carbohydrates. Contains natural minerals that can help balance mood, anxiety and insomnia.

2 Nuts – High in protein, antioxidants, fibre, healthy fats and minerals. Nuts are also anti-inflammatory and contain nutrients that help strengthen bones and muscles.

3 Dried fruit – Helps to improve bowel regularity and enhance gut health. Prunes, figs and dates provide slow-release energy.

4 Seeds – Packed with protein, fibre, iron, vitamins and omega-3, promoting a healthy heart and strong immune system. Also helps to lower unhealthy cholesterol levels.

5 Cinnamon – A digestive aid that helps normalise levels of fat and sugar in the blood stream. Also known to enhance cognitive function and memory.

Pancakes with Fruit Compote

Healthy and delicious high-protein pancakes served with yoghurt and fruit, adding natural sweetness and taste contrasts that will energise your body and mind. Prepare the batter the night before use to save time in the morning.

Total time: 00:15   Preparation time: 00:08   Cooking time: 00:07   Serves: 2–3

Ingredients

- 200g (scant cup) natural yoghurt
- 100ml (scant ½ cup) milk of choice
- 1 free-range egg
- 100g (scant cup) flour of your choice
- ½ teaspoon of baking powder
- ½ teaspoon of cinnamon
- ½ teaspoon of vanilla
- 1 handful of blackberries
- 1 handful of blueberries
- Juice of ½ a lime
- Drizzle of organic honey
- 1 teaspoon of coconut oil
- 2 tablespoons of yoghurt

Equipment

- Mixing bowl
- Oven hob (stovetop)
- Non-stick saucepan
- Non-stick frying pan
- Measuring jug/cup
- Spatula
- Wooden spoon
- Fork or whisk
- Tablespoon
- Teaspoon

Instructions

1. Measure the yoghurt and milk into a bowl.
2. Add the egg and mix until fully combined.
3. Sieve the flour into the mixture.
4. Add the baking powder, cinnamon and vanilla.
5. Mix using a fork or whisk until a smooth batter.
6. The batter can be used straight away, or kept in the fridge for up to 24 hours.
7. To make the fruit compote, combine a handful of blackberries and blueberries with the juice of ½ a lime and a drizzle of honey in a non-stick saucepan.
8. Cook on a medium heat for 3–4 minutes, stirring occasionally.
9. To make the pancakes, melt a small amount of coconut oil in a non-stick frying pan, on a medium-high heat.
10. Once the pan is hot, add 2 tablespoons of batter per pancake (making 6 pancakes in total).
11. Cook for approximately 1 minute before turning over with a spatula to cook on the other side.
12. Repeat the process for as many pancakes as required.
13. Serve warm, layered with yoghurt and fruit compote, as preferred.

Hints and tips

- You could serve this with yoghurt, nuts and seeds, or lemon and honey.
- Experiment with different types of flours, like rice flour, gram flour and buckwheat flour if you follow a gluten/wheat-free diet.
- Make 1 large pancake rather than 2–3 smaller ones, if preferred.
- Prepare the batter the night before use, if helpful.

> " When I first saw this recipe I couldn't believe that it was healthy! I had to read the ingredients list at least three times before I could even consider making it. But now, I make pancakes every Sunday! I tend to make the batter the night before to make the process even easier. "
>
> Amy – recovering from an eating disorder

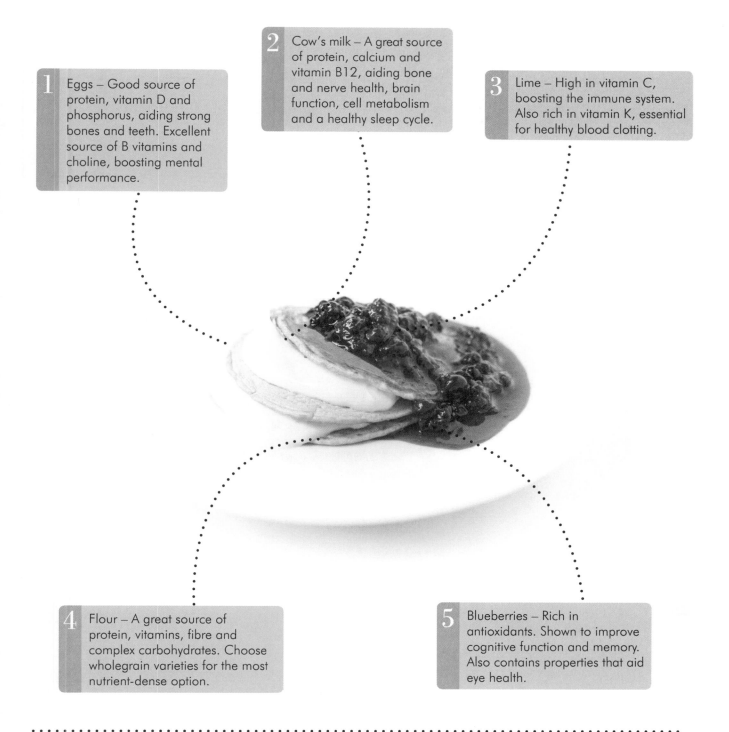

1 Eggs – Good source of protein, vitamin D and phosphorus, aiding strong bones and teeth. Excellent source of B vitamins and choline, boosting mental performance.

2 Cow's milk – A great source of protein, calcium and vitamin B12, aiding bone and nerve health, brain function, cell metabolism and a healthy sleep cycle.

3 Lime – High in vitamin C, boosting the immune system. Also rich in vitamin K, essential for healthy blood clotting.

4 Flour – A great source of protein, vitamins, fibre and complex carbohydrates. Choose wholegrain varieties for the most nutrient-dense option.

5 Blueberries – Rich in antioxidants. Shown to improve cognitive function and memory. Also contains properties that aid eye health.

Porridge (Oatmeal), Apple and Walnuts

A comforting breakfast providing slow-release energy and heart-healthy nutrients that soothe the digestive system and encourage a feeling of calm. Perfect on a cold day or when the body needs refuelling after exercise.

Total time: 00:05   Preparation time: 00:02   Cooking time: 00:03   Serves: 1

Ingredients

- 4–6 heaped tablespoons of porridge (oatmeal)
- Milk of your choice
- 1 apple
- 1 handful of walnuts
- ½ teaspoon of cinnamon

Optional: drizzle of organic honey and/or flaked almonds

Equipment

- Oven hob (stovetop)
- Non-stick saucepan (or microwave)
- Chopping board
- Sharp knife
- Wooden spoon
- Tablespoon
- Teaspoon

Hints and tips

- Use 100% natural porridge (without added sugar).
- Digesting uncooked oats will encourage bloating so always heat or bake oats before eating them.
- The skin is the most nutrient-dense part of an apple.

Instructions

If making on the hob:
1. Place the porridge in a non-stick saucepan.
2. Completely cover the oats with milk.
3. Cook on a medium heat until fully warmed through (approximately 2–3 minutes), stirring occasionally.
4. Whilst the porridge is cooking, chop the apple and walnuts to preferred size.
5. Add the cinnamon to the porridge and stir.
6. Transfer the porridge to a bowl, serving the apple and walnuts on top.
7. Add a drizzle of honey and/or a handful of almonds, if desired.

If using a microwave:
1. Place the porridge in a microwavable bowl.
2. Completely cover the oats with milk.
3. Cook on full power for 1½–2 minutes, stirring halfway through the cooking time.
4. Whilst the porridge is cooking, chop the apple and walnuts to preferred size.
5. Add the cinnamon to the porridge and stir.
6. Serve the apple and walnuts on top.
7. Add a drizzle of honey and/or a handful of almonds, if desired.

" I really love the variety of textures and flavours in this recipe. The cinnamon adds natural sweetness, but I tend to drizzle over the optional honey as well because it tastes even better. "

Fleur – recovering from over-eating

1 Porridge (oatmeal) – Good source of soluble fibre and slow-release complex carbohydrates. Contains natural minerals that have been reported to help balance mood, anxiety and insomnia.

2 Cow's milk – A great source of protein, calcium and vitamin B12, aiding bone and nerve health, brain function, cell metabolism and a healthy sleep cycle.

3 Walnuts – Rich in omega-3, helping to lower unhealthy cholesterol levels. Good source of serotonin, a chemical that can help balance mood.

4 Apple – Improves metabolic balance by maintaining steady blood sugar levels. Fights inflammation and free-radical production. High fibre, aiding digestive health.

5 Cinnamon – A digestive aid that helps normalise levels of fat and sugar in the blood stream. Also known to enhance cognitive function and memory.

Blueberry Nut Muffins and Yoghurt

Gorgeous muffins made with nutrient rich ingredients full of vitamins and minerals that promote a healthy immune system and boost mental performance. These muffins have a dense texture that contrasts with the smooth yoghurt and encourages satiety.

Total time: 00:25   Preparation time: 00:07   Cooking time: 00:18   Serves: 10–12

Ingredients

- 2–3 tablespoons of organic honey
- 100g (½ cup) almond/cashew butter
- 3 free-range eggs
- 100g (scant cup) wholemeal (wholewheat) flour
- 100g (¾ cup) ground almonds
- 50g (½ cup) desiccated (dried) coconut
- 2 tablespoons of flax seeds (preferably ground) or coconut
- ½ teaspoon of baking powder
- ½ teaspoon of cinnamon
- ½ teaspoon of nutmeg
- Pinch of salt
- 1 handful of blueberries
- 2 tablespoons of yoghurt

Instructions

1. Preheat the oven to 170–180°C (325–350°F/Gas 3–4).
2. In a mixing bowl (or food processor), fully combine the honey, almond or cashew butter and eggs, using a fork or whisk.
3. Beat for 2–3 minutes.
4. In a separate bowl, mix the wholemeal flour, ground almonds, desiccated (dried) coconut, flax seeds, baking powder, cinnamon, nutmeg and salt.
5. Add the bowl of dry ingredients to the bowl of wet ingredients and mix together thoroughly.
6. Carefully stir in the blueberries.
7. Divide the mixture between 10–12 paper muffin cases/liners.
8. Bake for 15–18 minutes, or until risen and golden.
9. Serve with yoghurt.

Equipment

- Oven
- Non-stick muffin tray
- 2 mixing bowls
- Paper muffin cases/liners
- Fork or whisk
- Tablespoon
- Teaspoon

Hints and tips

- A blueberry nut muffin makes the perfect portable snack when out and about.
- 1 handful of nuts a day can help reduce your risk of heart disease!
- Grinding flax seeds helps to release nutrients and fibre.
- The honey and coconut in this recipe provide natural sweetness.
- The muffins are suitable for freezing.

> " I make a small batch of these muffins and keep them in my fridge for breakfast or snacks. Eating a muffin feels indulgent but I can taste that it's good for me. I find it helpful to read the nutritional facts on the opposite page as this reassurance gives me the permission I need to eat them without worrying. "
>
> Becky – overcoming body-image issues

1 Eggs – Good source of protein, vitamin D and phosphorus, aiding strong bones and teeth. Excellent source of B vitamins and choline, boosting mental performance.

2 Coconut – Aids the immune system, helping to fight the common cold and flu. Healthy fats boost metabolism and reduce the risk of heart disease.

3 Nuts – High in protein, antioxidants, fibre, omega-3 and omega-6 essential fatty acids and minerals. Also anti-inflammatory and strengthen bones and muscles.

4 Nutmeg – Acts as a tonic, lifting mood when over-tired. Can soothe stomach aches, ease anti-inflammatory conditions and calm respiratory problems.

5 Flax seeds – Excellent source of omega-3 fatty acids, iron, zinc, copper, calcium, potassium, magnesium, folate and fibre.

Banana and Pecan Smoothie

A nutritious drink made with 100% natural ingredients, strengthening the heart, bones, muscles and immune system. A great high-protein breakfast but also suitable as a snack in between meals.

Total time: 00:05   Preparation time: 00:05   Cooking time: 00:00   Serves: 1

Ingredients

- ½ glass of milk of your choice
- 1 banana
- 1–2 tablespoons of natural yoghurt
- 1 teaspoon of ground flax seeds
- 1 handful of pecan nuts
- Drizzle of organic honey

Optional: 1 teaspoon of cacao powder

Equipment

- Tablespoon
- Teaspoon

Instructions

1. Place all ingredients into a food processor and blend until smooth.
2. Serve immediately.

Hints and tips

- Use whichever nuts you prefer.
- Natural Greek yoghurt provides your body with helpful probiotics that aid digestion.
- Grinding flax seeds helps to release nutrients and fibre.
- Raw cacao powder is rich in antioxidants and promotes a healthy heart.
- Add 1 handful of berries to further boost the immune system and vary the taste.

> " I make this smoothie as a quick breakfast or snack before or after training. I've learnt that it's important to fuel my body for exercise, helping it to perform and repair afterwards. I feel stronger as a result. "
>
> Lisa – overcoming body-image issues

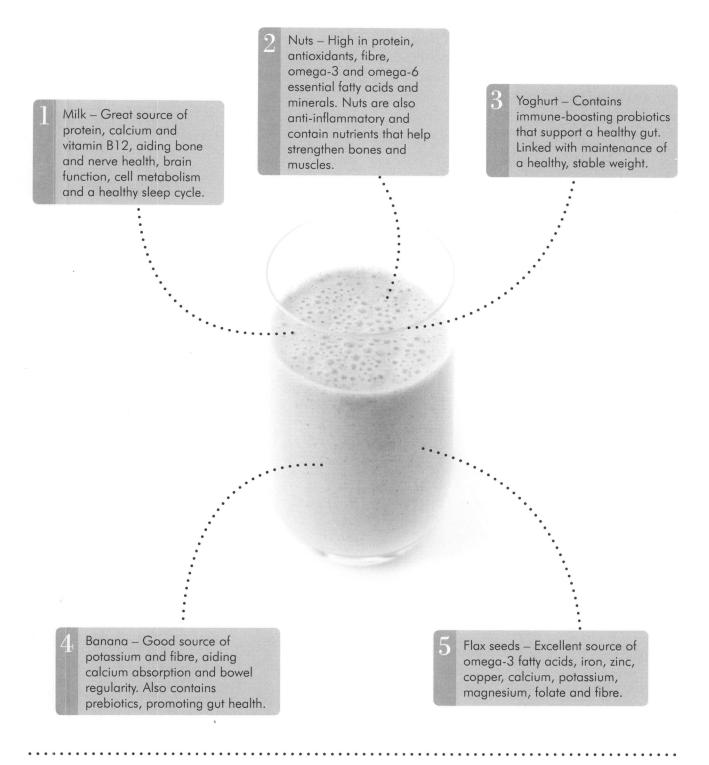

1 Milk – Great source of protein, calcium and vitamin B12, aiding bone and nerve health, brain function, cell metabolism and a healthy sleep cycle.

2 Nuts – High in protein, antioxidants, fibre, omega-3 and omega-6 essential fatty acids and minerals. Nuts are also anti-inflammatory and contain nutrients that help strengthen bones and muscles.

3 Yoghurt – Contains immune-boosting probiotics that support a healthy gut. Linked with maintenance of a healthy, stable weight.

4 Banana – Good source of potassium and fibre, aiding calcium absorption and bowel regularity. Also contains prebiotics, promoting gut health.

5 Flax seeds – Excellent source of omega-3 fatty acids, iron, zinc, copper, calcium, potassium, magnesium, folate and fibre.

Cinnamon Eggy Bread with Berries

A delicious breakfast, containing essential vitamins and minerals, boosting the metabolism and energising the body. This breakfast may feel like an indulgent treat, but actually, it offers a fantastic balance of slow-release complex carbohydrate and protein.

Total time: 00:10   Preparation time: 00:05   Cooking time: 00:05   Serves: 1

Ingredients

- 2 free-range eggs
- ½ teaspoon of cinnamon
- 2 slices of wholemeal (wholewheat) bread
- 1 handful of raspberries
- Drizzle of organic honey

Instructions

1. Carefully break the eggs into a shallow mixing bowl.
2. Add the cinnamon and whisk with a fork.
3. Place the wholemeal bread into the egg mixture, coating both sides completely.
4. Heat the frying pan to a medium heat.
5. Add the eggy bread to the heated frying pan (one slice at a time if necessary), cooking for approximately 2 minutes each side, until lightly browned.
6. Serve warm from the pan, along with the raspberries and a drizzle of honey.

Equipment

- Oven hob (stovetop)
- Non-stick frying pan
- Mixing bowl
- Fork
- Teaspoon

Hints and tips

- Research suggests that a high-protein breakfast served with some complex carbohydrate (such as wholemeal bread) is the healthiest way to start your day.
- Serve with berries of your choice.
- Replace one of the eggs with a mashed banana to add potassium to this recipe.
- The cinnamon provides natural sweetness.

> " It's really great to find a nutritious recipe that satisfies my emotional and physical hunger, especially one that takes only minutes to prepare. I'm starting to appreciate that really healthy food can fulfill my cravings. I've just had to focus on changing old habits. "
>
> Jacob – recovering from over-eating

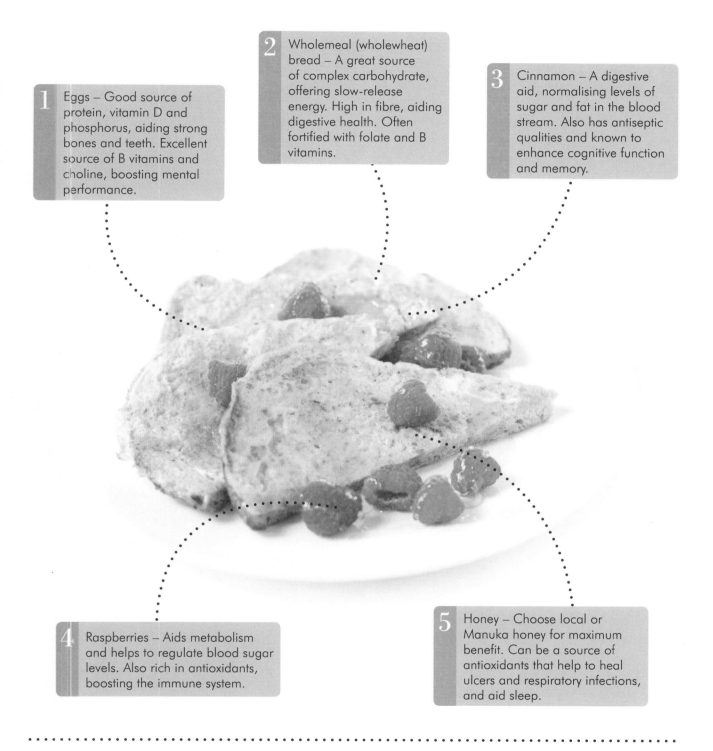

1 Eggs – Good source of protein, vitamin D and phosphorus, aiding strong bones and teeth. Excellent source of B vitamins and choline, boosting mental performance.

2 Wholemeal (wholewheat) bread – A great source of complex carbohydrate, offering slow-release energy. High in fibre, aiding digestive health. Often fortified with folate and B vitamins.

3 Cinnamon – A digestive aid, normalising levels of sugar and fat in the blood stream. Also has antiseptic qualities and known to enhance cognitive function and memory.

4 Raspberries – Aids metabolism and helps to regulate blood sugar levels. Also rich in antioxidants, boosting the immune system.

5 Honey – Choose local or Manuka honey for maximum benefit. Can be a source of antioxidants that help to heal ulcers and respiratory infections, and aid sleep.

Darissa – Yoghurt Granola Fruit Pot

A colourful breakfast, combining high-protein yoghurt, wholesome granola and immune-boosting berries. Serve in a bowl or glass, layering the ingredients as desired – consuming well-presented food encourages emotional and physical satisfaction.

Total time: 00:05   Preparation time: 00:05   Cooking time: 00:00   Serves: 1

Ingredients

- 1 handful of raspberries
- 1 handful of blueberries
- 3 tablespoons of natural yoghurt
- 3 tablespoons of homemade granola (see page 58 for recipe or use a good-quality pre-brought granola)

Optional: drizzle of organic honey

Equipment

- Tablespoon

Instructions

1. Wash the raspberries and blueberries.
2. Layer the ingredients, as preferred.
3. Drizzle with honey, if using.

Hints and tips

- Use homemade granola (page 58) or a shop-bought variety based on natural ingredients with no added sugar.
- Experiment with a variety of fruits (see page 52 for nutritional information).
- Yoghurt contains immune-boosting probiotics that support a healthy gut.
- Regular consumption of yoghurt is linked with maintenance of a healthy, stable weight.

> " My children and I enjoy making this for breakfast or dessert. It's so nice to watch them enjoying food...having fun with it! Eating with them helps me to appreciate and embrace food with a more positive attitude. They named it a 'Darissa' – they would have been very upset with me if I'd called it anything else!
>
> Emma "

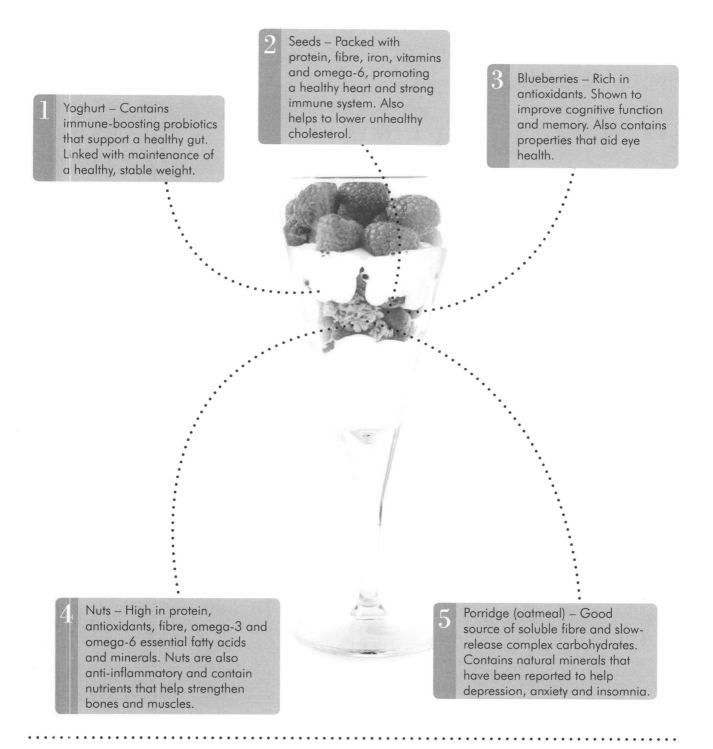

1 Yoghurt – Contains immune-boosting probiotics that support a healthy gut. Linked with maintenance of a healthy, stable weight.

2 Seeds – Packed with protein, fibre, iron, vitamins and omega-6, promoting a healthy heart and strong immune system. Also helps to lower unhealthy cholesterol.

3 Blueberries – Rich in antioxidants. Shown to improve cognitive function and memory. Also contains properties that aid eye health.

4 Nuts – High in protein, antioxidants, fibre, omega-3 and omega-6 essential fatty acids and minerals. Nuts are also anti-inflammatory and contain nutrients that help strengthen bones and muscles.

5 Porridge (oatmeal) – Good source of soluble fibre and slow-release complex carbohydrates. Contains natural minerals that have been reported to help depression, anxiety and insomnia.

Mug Muffin with Yoghurt

A high-protein breakfast bursting with antioxidants, vitamins and minerals, promoting a healthy body and mind. Made in a mug, this recipe is simple, quick and fun to create. This recipe contains nothing but healthy ingredients!

Total time: 00:05   Preparation time: 00:03   Cooking time: 00:02   Serves: 1

Ingredients

- ½ banana
- 1 free-range egg
- 1 tablespoon of almond or cashew butter
- 1 tablespoon of ground almonds
- 1 teaspoon of flax seeds (preferably ground)
- 1 teaspoon of cacao powder
- ½ teaspoon of baking powder
- 2 tablespoons of yoghurt
- 1 handful of berries

Optional: drizzle of organic honey

Instructions

1. Mash ½ a banana in a mug.
2. Add the egg, almond/cashew butter, almonds, flax seeds, cacao powder and baking powder.
3. Mix until fully combined.
4. Microwave on full power for 60–90 seconds.
5. Serve with yoghurt and berries.
6. Drizzle with honey, if using.

Equipment

- Microwave
- Microwavable mug
- Tablespoon
- Teaspoon

Hints and tips

- Unlike cocoa powder, raw cacao powder is unprocessed and therefore retains an impressive amount of antioxidants and flavanols.
- Grinding flax seeds helps to release its nutrients and fibre.
- Almonds and cashews are actually seeds rather than nuts.

" This recipe encourages 'childlike' experimentation with food, which is a healthy alternative to the serious, nervous attitude that I've had in the past. I'm trying to see cooking as an adventure rather than something to be afraid of. The more I cook, the more relaxed I seem to be feeling, so perhaps it's helping.

Rosie – overcoming low self-esteem "

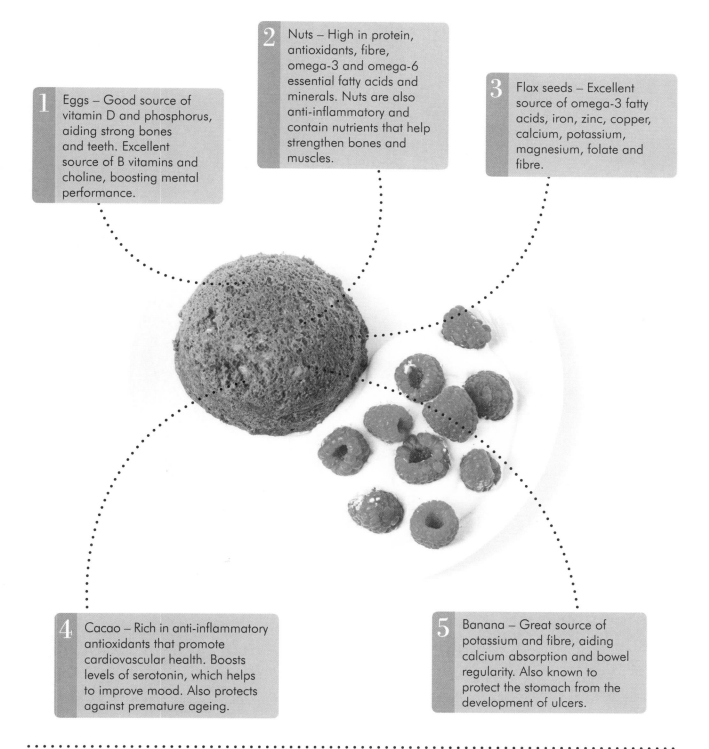

1 Eggs – Good source of vitamin D and phosphorus, aiding strong bones and teeth. Excellent source of B vitamins and choline, boosting mental performance.

2 Nuts – High in protein, antioxidants, fibre, omega-3 and omega-6 essential fatty acids and minerals. Nuts are also anti-inflammatory and contain nutrients that help strengthen bones and muscles.

3 Flax seeds – Excellent source of omega-3 fatty acids, iron, zinc, copper, calcium, potassium, magnesium, folate and fibre.

4 Cacao – Rich in anti-inflammatory antioxidants that promote cardiovascular health. Boosts levels of serotonin, which helps to improve mood. Also protects against premature ageing.

5 Banana – Great source of potassium and fibre, aiding calcium absorption and bowel regularity. Also known to protect the stomach from the development of ulcers.

BREAKFAST OR LUNCH

Scrambled Egg and Smoked Salmon.................................... 76
Homemade Baked Bean Burrito.................................... 78
Ham, Spinach and Parmesan Eggs.................................... 80
Poached Egg and Avocado on Toast 82
Cheese and Mushrooms on Toast 84
Kipper (Smoked Herring) and Spinach.................................... 86
Egg, Bacon, Lettuce and Tomato.................................... 88

Scrambled Egg and Smoked Salmon

A high-protein breakfast, accompanied by complex carbohydrates, to boost your metabolism and help you think clearly throughout the day. Wholesome and satisfying, this meal is easy to make, even for the most novice cook.

Total time: 00:10   Preparation time: 00:05   Cooking time: 00:05   Serves: 1

Ingredients

- 2 free-range eggs
- 1–2 tablespoons of milk
- 1–2 slices of smoked salmon
- 1 piece of wholemeal (wholewheat) bread
- Pinch of salt and pepper

Instructions

1. Carefully break 2 eggs into a mixing bowl, along with the milk.
2. Whisk together, using a fork.
3. Pour the mixture into a hot pan and cook over a low heat, stirring regularly, to your desired consistency.
4. In the meantime, slice the smoked salmon into bite-size pieces and toast the bread.
5. Serve the scrambled egg and smoked salmon on top of the toast, adding salt and pepper, to taste.

Equipment

- Oven hob (stovetop)
- Toaster or grill (broiler)
- Saucepan/frying pan
- Mixing bowl
- Knife and fork
- Tablespoon

Hints and tips

- Delicious served with the addition of wilted spinach or grilled asparagus.
- Research suggests that a high-protein breakfast served with some complex carbohydrate (such as wholemeal bread) is the healthiest way to start your day.
- Cook the salmon with the egg, if preferred.

> "I've had many strange ideas about breakfast: not eating it at all, only eating fruit, having to measure everything out, and so on. So to realise that having smoked salmon on toast would be good for my metabolism and general health was hard to believe. But I took a deep breath, tested the theory…and haven't looked back since.
>
> Helen – recovering from bulimia

1 Eggs – Good source of protein, vitamin D and phosphorus, aiding strong bones and teeth. Excellent source of B vitamins and choline, boosting mental performance.

2 Milk – Rich in calcium, protein and B vitamins. Promotes healthy brain and nerve function. Aids cell metabolism and encourages positive sleep cycles.

3 Wholemeal (wholewheat) bread – A great source of complex carbohydrate, offering slow-release energy. High in fibre, aiding digestive health. Often fortified with folate and B vitamins.

4 Smoked salmon – Rich in omega-3 fatty acids, which help to reduce unhealthy cholesterol levels, blood pressure and inflammation. Also thought to help prevent memory loss.

5 Pepper – Aids digestion, can ease lung and bronchial infections and sometimes used to alleviate shock and stress. Also contains antioxidants and has anti-inflammatory qualities.

Homemade Baked Bean Burrito

Heart-healthy beans combined with tomatoes, vegetables and a wholemeal (wholewheat) wrap to create a well-balanced meal that will satisfy hunger and support general health. Batch cook the homemade baked beans and store in the fridge for up to a week.

Total time: 00:15   Preparation time: 00:04   Cooking time: 00:11   Serves: 2

Ingredients

- 1 red or white onion
- 1 teaspoon of oil
- 1 can of cannellini beans (approx. 400g/14oz)
- 2 teaspoons of paprika
- ½ can of chopped tomatoes (approx. 200g/7oz)
- 1 tablespoon of tomato puree (paste)
- Pinch of salt and pepper
- 2 wholemeal (wholewheat) wraps

Optional: approx. 30g (1oz) cheese per person

Instructions

1. To make the homemade baked beans, finely chop the onion and add to the oil in a non-stick saucepan.
2. Cook the onion for 2–3 minutes, or until softened but not browned.
3. Add the cannellini beans, paprika, chopped tomatoes, tomato puree (paste), salt and pepper.
4. Cook for a further 5 minutes, stirring occasionally.
5. Heat the wholemeal wraps in a dry non-stick frying pan for 30 seconds each side, or longer for a crispier wrap.
6. Place the warm wraps on plates, add the baked beans on top and sprinkle with grated cheese, if using.
7. Fold the wraps in half and serve.

Note: The homemade baked beans can be batch cooked and stored in the freezer, but use fresh wraps when serving.

Equipment

- Oven hob (stovetop)
- Non-stick saucepan
- Non-stick frying pan
- Chopping board
- Can opener
- Sharp knife
- Wooden spoon
- Tablespoon
- Teaspoon
- Optional: grater

Hints and tips

- Use a variety of beans to maximise nutritional benefits.
- Consider adding a sprinkle of cheese for additional protein and flavour.
- Homemade baked beans could be eaten on their own as a snack, or served with poached eggs and toast for breakfast or lunch.

" I batch cook these baked beans and keep them in my fridge ready for my daughter to have on toast, in a wrap or as a side dish. Reminding her that it's just fruit, vegetable and a protein source has helped reassure her nerves and encourage her to eat. "

Thomas – supportive parent

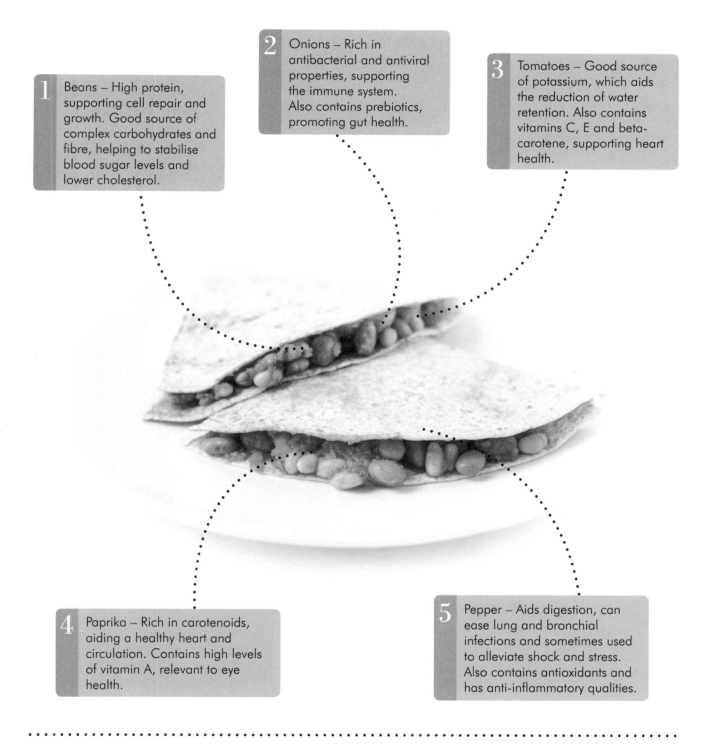

1 Beans – High protein, supporting cell repair and growth. Good source of complex carbohydrates and fibre, helping to stabilise blood sugar levels and lower cholesterol.

2 Onions – Rich in antibacterial and antiviral properties, supporting the immune system. Also contains prebiotics, promoting gut health.

3 Tomatoes – Good source of potassium, which aids the reduction of water retention. Also contains vitamins C, E and beta-carotene, supporting heart health.

4 Paprika – Rich in carotenoids, aiding a healthy heart and circulation. Contains high levels of vitamin A, relevant to eye health.

5 Pepper – Aids digestion, can ease lung and bronchial infections and sometimes used to alleviate shock and stress. Also contains antioxidants and has anti-inflammatory qualities.

Ham, Spinach and Parmesan Eggs

A quick and simple protein-rich breakfast prepared in minutes. Serve with fresh salad leaves or a side of tomatoes for further benefits and texture.

Total time: 00:05   Preparation time: 00:02   Cooking time: 00:03   Serves: 1

Ingredients

- 1 handful of fresh spinach
- 2 slices of ham
- 2 free-range eggs
- Approx. 30g (1oz) Parmesan
- Pinch of salt and pepper

Instructions

1. Chop the spinach and ham into bite-size pieces.
2. Break the eggs into a non-stick saucepan and cook on a medium heat for 1 minute, stirring continuously.
3. Add the spinach and ham to the saucepan.
4. Grate the cheese over the top.
5. Heat and stir until the eggs are cooked, as preferred.
6. Serve with salt and pepper, if desired.

If using a microwave, beat the eggs in a bowl with a fork, add the chopped spinach, ham and cheese and heat for 1 minute. Stir again with the fork and heat for a further 1–2 minutes until cooked to preference.

Equipment

- Oven hob (stovetop) or microwave
- Non-stick saucepan (or microwaveable bowl)
- Chopping board
- Grater
- Sharp knife (or kitchen scissors)
- Wooden spoon (or fork)

Hints and tips

- Consider adding a side of mixed salad leaves and red pepper – why not eat fresh greens and vegetables with breakfast! Eating at least one fruit or vegetable with each meal will encourage the consumption of a variety of nutrients.

> " When I feel in a fluster, I need a quick meal that can be ready without any fuss. I like how I only need a bowl, fork and microwave to make this recipe. It's now my 'go-to' meal when I'm not sure what to eat. "
>
> Charlie – recovering from anorexia

1 Eggs – Good source of protein, vitamin D and phosphorus, aiding strong bones and teeth. Excellent source of B vitamins and choline, boosting mental performance.

2 Ham – Contains zinc, iron and a variety of B vitamins that aid energy regulation and muscle growth and repair. High in salt, so enjoy in moderation.

3 Parmesan – A great source of protein, aiding cell growth and repair. Contains good levels of calcium, supporting healthy bones, teeth and nails.

4 Pepper – Aids digestion, can ease lung and bronchial infections and sometimes used to alleviate shock and stress. Also contains antioxidants and has anti-inflammatory qualities.

5 Spinach – Contains high levels of vitamin K, supporting healthy bones. Also rich in anti-inflammatory and anti-cancer substances.

<15

Poached Egg and Avocado on Toast

A high-protein breakfast with complex carbohydrate and healthy fats. Delicious served with a pinch of salt, pepper and fresh red chillies. Colourful and healthy. Add a handful of fresh coriander (cilantro) leaves for a flavour boost.

Total time: 00:10   Preparation time: 00:05   Cooking time: 00:05   Serves: 1

Ingredients

- ½ avocado
- 2 free-range eggs
- 1 slice of wholemeal (wholewheat) bread
- Pinch of salt and pepper

Optional: sliced fresh red chilli or dried chilli flakes

Equipment

- Oven hob (stovetop)
- Non-stick saucepan
- Toaster or grill (broiler)
- Cling film (plastic wrap)
- Chopping board
- Sharp knife

Instructions

1. Prepare the avocado by slicing it in half lengthways, remove the central seed and peel the skin away from the half being used in the recipe.
2. Wrap the other half in cling film and place this in the fridge for future use.
3. Cut the avocado half into approximately 4 slices.
4. Half fill a saucepan with water and bring to the boil.
5. Put the bread in a toaster or under the grill (turning when necessary).
6. Whilst the bread is toasting, carefully crack the eggs into the boiling water.
7. Place the avocado slices on top of the toast.
8. Remove the eggs from the hot water (when cooked to your preference), using a large spoon.
9. Place the eggs on top of the avocado.
10. Serve with salt and pepper.
11. Add the chilli flakes, if using.

Hints and tips

- An avocado is a fruit, which needs to be ripened before consumption. You can tell when it's ready to use by placing it in the palm of your hand and gently squeezing it. If the avocado yields to firm but gentle pressure, then it's ready to eat.
- Choose wholemeal bread as white breads are not considered a complex carbohydrate.

> " This is one of my favourite meals for breakfast or lunch. I've seen similar versions in my healthy cookbooks, which is reassuring. It helps to know that I'm having complex carbohydrates, healthy fats and protein all from one meal. I like it best with salt, pepper and chilli flakes. Delicious, any time of day! "
>
> Emma

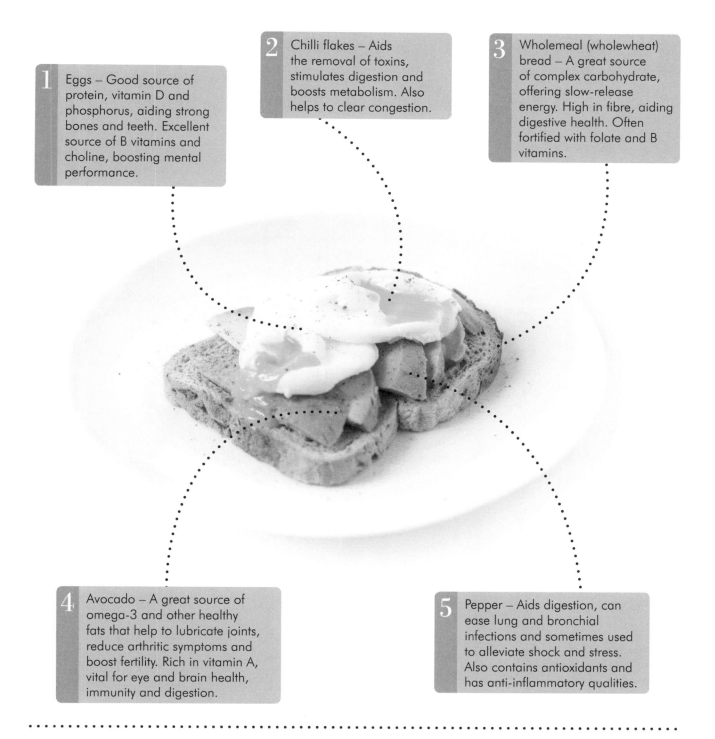

1 Eggs – Good source of protein, vitamin D and phosphorus, aiding strong bones and teeth. Excellent source of B vitamins and choline, boosting mental performance.

2 Chilli flakes – Aids the removal of toxins, stimulates digestion and boosts metabolism. Also helps to clear congestion.

3 Wholemeal (wholewheat) bread – A great source of complex carbohydrate, offering slow-release energy. High in fibre, aiding digestive health. Often fortified with folate and B vitamins.

4 Avocado – A great source of omega-3 and other healthy fats that help to lubricate joints, reduce arthritic symptoms and boost fertility. Rich in vitamin A, vital for eye and brain health, immunity and digestion.

5 Pepper – Aids digestion, can ease lung and bronchial infections and sometimes used to alleviate shock and stress. Also contains antioxidants and has anti-inflammatory qualities.

Cheese and Mushrooms on Toast

A balanced meal combining complex carbohydrate, protein and a variety of vitamins and minerals. Especially good served with goat's cheese, thyme and black pepper. Experiment with different mushroom varieties.

Total time: 00:10   Preparation time: 00:05   Cooking time: 00:05   Serves: 1

Ingredients

- 1–2 handfuls of mushrooms
- 1 slice of wholemeal (wholewheat) bread
- Approx. 30g (1oz) cheese (for example goat's cheese or cream cheese)
- Pinch of salt and pepper

Optional: ½ teaspoon of thyme

Instructions

1. Wash and dry the mushrooms.
2. Slice the mushrooms to preferred size.
3. Cook the mushrooms in a non-stick saucepan or frying pan on a medium heat for approximately 5 minutes.
4. Whilst the mushrooms cook, toast the bread.
5. Smear the toast with the soft cheese, adding the cooked mushrooms on top.
6. Season with salt and pepper (and thyme, if using).

Equipment

- Oven hob (stovetop)
- Toaster or grill (broiler)
- Non-stick saucepan or frying pan
- Chopping board
- Sharp knife
- Wooden spoon

Hints and tips

- Choose wholemeal, seeded or rye bread over white varieties to benefit from high levels of fibre, vitamins and minerals.
- Mushrooms have a high water content so ensure that you wash and dry them fully before cooking.
- Consider cooking ½ an onion or 1 handful of spinach with the mushrooms.

"
This is really nice. I think this recipe might become my new favourite! I like food to be healthy and comforting.

M – recovering from over-eating
"

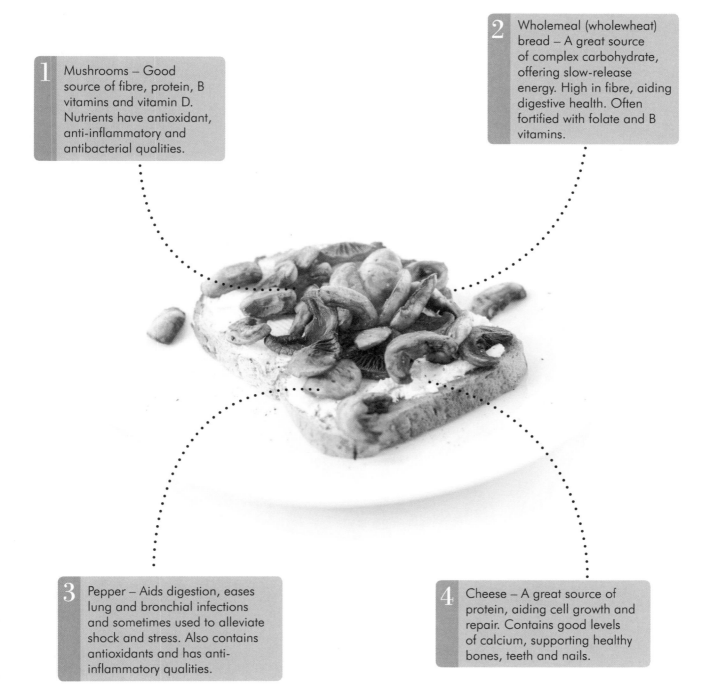

1 Mushrooms – Good source of fibre, protein, B vitamins and vitamin D. Nutrients have antioxidant, anti-inflammatory and antibacterial qualities.

2 Wholemeal (wholewheat) bread – A great source of complex carbohydrate, offering slow-release energy. High in fibre, aiding digestive health. Often fortified with folate and B vitamins.

3 Pepper – Aids digestion, eases lung and bronchial infections and sometimes used to alleviate shock and stress. Also contains antioxidants and has anti-inflammatory qualities.

4 Cheese – A great source of protein, aiding cell growth and repair. Contains good levels of calcium, supporting healthy bones, teeth and nails.

Kipper (Smoked Herring) and Spinach

Fresh fish and vitamin-rich greens which provide the body with protein to support cell repair and promote healthy bones. Consider serving with a piece of wholemeal (wholewheat) toast or a runny poached egg – delicious!

Total time: 00:05   Preparation time: 00:02   Cooking time: 00:03   Serves: 1

Ingredients

- 2 handfuls of fresh spinach
- 1 kipper (smoked herring) fillet
- Pinch of black pepper

Instructions

1. Wash and dry the spinach leaves, if necessary.
2. Place the spinach in a non-stick saucepan and cook on a medium heat until the leaves appear wilted, stirring occasionally.
3. Whilst the spinach is cooking, using strong kitchen scissors, remove the head and tail from the kipper, if necessary.
4. Place the kipper on a plate, skin side down, and cover with microwavable cling film, piercing in a few places.
5. Microwave on full power for 2½ minutes.
6. Serve the cooked fish and wilted spinach on the warm plate from the microwave.
7. Add black pepper, as preferred.

Equipment

- Oven hob (stovetop)
- Microwave
- Non-stick saucepan
- Plate
- Cling film (plastic wrap)
- Kitchen scissors or sharp knife
- Wooden spoon

Hints and tips

- Fishmongers are always happy to prepare fish for customers.
- Kippers can be brought precooked, ready to be re-heated at home.
- The very small bones found in kippers are generally safe to eat.
- If you have a little space in your garden, spinach is easy to grow at home.

> I've learnt the importance of including oily fish in my diet, especially because my joints and bones have been damaged by my eating disorder. I try to have salmon, kippers or mackerel at least once or twice a week.
>
> Isabelle – recovering from anorexia

1 Spinach – Contains high levels of vitamin K, supporting healthy bones. Also rich in anti-inflammatory and anti-cancer substances.

2 Kipper (smoked herring) – A great source of protein and omega-3 fatty acids. Rich in B vitamins, promoting a healthy digestive system and nervous system. Also contains vitamin D.

3 Pepper – Aids digestion, can ease lung and bronchial infections and sometimes used to alleviate shock and stress. Also contains antioxidants and has anti-inflammatory qualities.

Egg, Bacon, Lettuce and Tomato

A healthy 'English breakfast' prepared in just one pan, rich in vitamin B and D. Quick, easy and delicious. Serve with a slice of wholemeal (wholewheat) toast or a portion of homemade baked beans (see page 78 for recipe).

Total time: 00:10   Preparation time: 00:05   Cooking time: 00:05   Serves: 1

Ingredients

- 1 tomato
- 1 little gem or Bibb lettuce
- 1–2 pieces of bacon
- 1 free-range egg
- 1 slice of wholemeal (wholewheat) bread
- Pinch of black pepper

Instructions

1. Preheat a non-stick frying pan to a medium-high heat.
2. Slice the tomato and little gem or Bibb lettuce in half.
3. Add the bacon, lettuce and tomatoes to the pan and cook for 2 minutes each side.
4. Carefully crack the egg into the pan.
5. Cook for a further 2 minutes, or until everything is cooked to your preference.

Equipment

- Oven hob (stovetop)
- Toaster or grill (broiler)
- Non-stick frying pan
- Chopping board
- Sharp knife

Hints and tips

- Choose wholemeal, seeded or rye bread over white varieties to benefit from additional nutrients and fibre.
- Bacon is naturally high in salt so have only 1–2 pieces per serving.
- Consider adding homemade baked beans.
- You could poach the egg, if preferred, cooking the other ingredients under the grill.

"
This recipe means that I no longer need to feel guilty about having a cooked breakfast! Thank you!
"

M – recovering from over-eating

1 Bacon – Contains zinc, iron and a variety of B vitamins that aid energy regulation and muscle growth and repair. High in salt, so enjoy in moderation.

2 Lettuce – Contains a natural sedative, relaxing the nervous system and aiding sleep. High water and fibre content helps to ease digestive bloating.

3 Tomatoes – Good source of potassium, which aids the reduction of water retention. Also contains vitamins C, E and beta-carotene, supporting heart health.

4 Eggs – Good source of protein, vitamin D and phosphorus, aiding strong bones and teeth. Excellent source of B vitamins and choline, boosting mental performance.

5 Pepper – Aids digestion, can ease lung and bronchial infections and sometimes used to alleviate shock and stress. Also contains antioxidants and has anti-inflammatory qualities.

LUNCH

Tuna Pasta Salad 92
Mackerel Pâté 94
Ham and Pea Frittata 96
Turkey Sandwich 98
Mango and Feta Salad 100
Salmon and Spinach Frittata 102
Cranberry and Almond Couscous 104
Chicken and Sweetcorn Wrap 106
Sweet Potato and Red Pepper Soup 108
Red Lentil Pâté 110
Mixed Bean Salad 112
Pea Soup 114
Rainbow Salad with Hummus 116
Egg Mayo and Red Pepper Sandwich 118
Quinoa Greek Salad 120
Butternut Squash and Feta Pitta 122
Tomato, Avocado and Quinoa Salad 124
Falafel and Hummus Salad Wrap 126
Leek and Potato Soup 128
Bagel, Cream Cheese and Salmon 130
Sweet Potato with Cottage Cheese 132
Tuna Salad Pitta 134

Tuna Pasta Salad

A colourful recipe providing steady-release energy and antioxidant-rich raw vegetables. Batch cook and refrigerate for later use. Great served with salad leaves, at home or as a packed lunch out and about.

Total time: 00:15 **Preparation time: 00:05** **Cooking time: 00:10** **Serves: 1**

Ingredients

- Approx. 75g (2.5oz) pasta of choice
- ½ red pepper
- ½ can of tuna (approx. 75g/2.5oz)
- ¼ can of sweetcorn (100g/½ cup)
- 1–2 teaspoons of capers
- Pinch of pepper
- Salad dressing – see page 268

Instructions

1. Half fill a non-stick saucepan with water and bring to the boil.
2. Add the pasta to the water, bring back to the boil, and cook for a further 6–8 minutes, or until cooked to preference.
3. Whilst the pasta cooks, finely slice the red pepper.
4. Drain the pasta and combine with the red pepper, tuna, sweetcorn, capers and black pepper.
5. Add a salad dressing, as preferred.
6. Serve or store for later use.

Equipment

- Oven hob (stovetop)
- Non-stick saucepan
- Colander
- Chopping board
- Can opener
- Sharp knife
- Teaspoon

Hints and tips

- Include a rainbow of colours in your diet to encourage intake of a variety of vitamins and minerals that promote good health.
- Tuna is a lean, inexpensive source of protein easily added to salads or sandwiches; however, pregnant women are advised to eat not more than 2–3 cans per week.

> " I find that planning healthy meals in advance helps to reduce the risk of binges. I like to make this recipe at the weekend and then store it in the fridge for use at lunchtimes. Sometimes I add salad leaves too. I really like how colourful it is. "
>
> Sarah – recovering from bulimia

1 Tuna – An excellent source of protein, selenium, magnesium, potassium and omega-3 fatty acids. Also contains B vitamins, aiding heart health.

2 Sweetcorn – Contains nutrients (carotenoids) that support eye health. High-fibre content supports a healthy digestive tract and helps to control blood sugar levels.

3 Pasta – Good source of carbohydrate and fibre, promoting digestive health. Choose wholewheat pasta for maximum benefits.

4 Red pepper – Rich in vitamin C and beta-carotene, promoting healthy skin and eyes. Contains antioxidants, boosting the immune system.

5 Capers – A flower bud, rich in phytonutrients, antioxidants and vitamins essential for optimum health, including vitamin A, vitamin K, calcium, iron and copper.

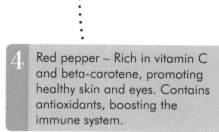

Mackerel Pâté

A delicious lunch that will help to regulate metabolism whilst supporting healthy bones, teeth, nerves and muscles. Made by combining all pâté ingredients in a food processor – couldn't be any easier. Batch cook and keep in the fridge for later use.

Total time: 00:05   Preparation time: 00:05   Cooking time: 00:00   Serves: 1

Ingredients

- 1 precooked mackerel fillet
- 2 tablespoons of natural yoghurt or cream cheese
- 1 teaspoon of horseradish
- 1 handful of parsley
- Juice of ½ a lemon
- Pinch of salt and pepper

Optional accompaniments: crusty bread and side salad

Equipment

- Food processor
- Tablespoon

Instructions

1. Remove the skin from the mackerel fillet and discard.
2. Place all ingredients into a food processor and blend until smooth.
3. Serve with fresh crusty bread and side salad.

Hints and tips

- Oily fish is rich in omega oils, relevant to a healthy heart, nervous system, metabolism and brain function.
- Omega oils cannot be stored in the body, so they should be eaten on a regular basis.
- This recipe can be prepared in advance, for convenience.

"

I really appreciate recipes that allow me to put everthing together and blitz! I want healthy, wholesome food, but need it to be quick and easy to prepare.

"

Nadia – overcoming low self-esteem

1 Yoghurt – Contains immune-boosting probiotics that support a healthy gut. Linked with maintenance of a healthy, stable weight.

2 Mackerel – Contains omega-3 fatty acids, vitamins A, B-complex, C, D, E and K, potassium, selenium and magnesium, helping to regulate metabolism and support healthy bones, teeth, nerves and muscles.

3 Parsley – Rich in antioxidants that help reduce congestion. Contains vitamin K, supporting healthy bones. Also thought to help relieve constipation.

4 Lemon – Alkalising and detoxifying, lemons aid digestion and reduce water retention.

Ham and Pea Frittata

A balanced meal containing B vitamins which boost mental performance, iron, aiding cell and muscle growth and repair, and calcium, supporting healthy bones. Double the recipe and store half in the fridge for another breakfast or lunch later in the week.

Total time: 00:10   Preparation time: 00:03   Cooking time: 00:07   Serves: 1

Ingredients

- 1–2 slices of ham
- Approx. 30g (1oz) cheese (for example cheddar cheese, feta cheese, goat's cheese)
- 2 free-range eggs
- 2 tablespoons of peas
- Pinch of salt and pepper
- 1 handful of mixed salad leaves

Instructions

1. Cut the ham and cheese into bite-size pieces.
2. Break the eggs into a mixing bowl and whisk until the egg yolk and white have combined.
3. Pour the eggs and peas into a non-stick frying pan and stir continuously, until the eggs begin to solidify a little.
4. Add the ham and stir again.
5. Add the cheese on top.
6. Put the frying pan under the grill to finish cooking the surface of the frittata.
7. Add salt and pepper, as preferred.
8. Serve with a handful of mixed salad leaves.

Equipment

- Oven hob (stovetop)
- Mixing bowl
- Fork or whisk
- Non-stick frying pan
- Spatula
- Grill (broiler)
- Sharp knife
- Chopping board
- Tablespoon

Hints and tips

- Also delicious made with the addition of spinach in the fritatta.
- Once cooked, frittata can be eaten hot or cold.
- For breakfast egg muffins, combine all the ingredients (apart from the salad) and pour into muffin cases/liners. Bake for 10–15 minutes or until cooked through and slightly browned, creating a great portable snack.

> When I was first shown how to make a frittata I couldn't believe how simple it was. I've since felt able to experiment with the use of different ingredients added to the eggs. I usually make two portions so that I have breakfast or lunch ready made for the next day.
>
> Rosie – overcoming low self-esteem

1 Eggs – Good source of protein, vitamin D and phosphorus, aiding strong bones and teeth. Excellent source of B vitamins and choline, boosting mental performance.

2 Peas – Rich in vitamin C and antioxidants. High fibre, encouraging a healthy digestive tract. A good source of iron, helping to prevent fatigue. Also aids eye health.

3 Cheese – Great source of protein, aiding cell growth and repair. Rich in calcium, supporting healthy bones, teeth and nails.

4 Ham – Contains zinc, iron and a variety of B vitamins that aid energy regulation and muscle growth and repair. High in salt, so enjoy in moderation.

5 Salad leaves – Include a variety of mixed leaves to benefit from various vitamins and minerals, such as vitamin C and iron. Rich in fibre and antioxidants, aiding digestion and the immune system.

Turkey Sandwich

A healthy sandwich that provides slow-release energy and a variety of vitamins and minerals that boost the immune system and reduce water retention. Often available as a sandwich choice when out and about, so a good recipe to familiarise yourself with.

Total time: 00:05   Preparation time: 00:05   Cooking time: 00:00   Serves: 1

Ingredients

- 1 tomato
- 5–6 cucumber slices
- Approx. 100g (3.5oz) of turkey
- 1 tablespoon of mayonnaise
- 2 slices of wholemeal (wholewheat) bread
- Pinch of salt and pepper

Equipment

- Chopping board
- Sharp knife
- Tablespoon
- Knife

Instructions

1. Slice the tomato, cucumber and turkey into bite-size pieces.
2. Spread the mayonnaise over the bread.
3. Place all ingredients between the slices of bread and serve immediately.

Hints and tips

- Choose wholemeal or seeded bread rather than white varieties for additional nutritional benefits and fibre.
- Replace the turkey with chicken, if preferred.
- See page 256 for a homemade mayonnaise recipe.
- Consider adding lettuce or other salad leaves, as preferred.

"
Rather than getting a pack of turkey, which I can find overwhelming, I get the exact portion I need from the supermarket deli counter. This way I also know it is 'just' turkey as it is carved in front of me.

Jenni – recovering from anorexia
"

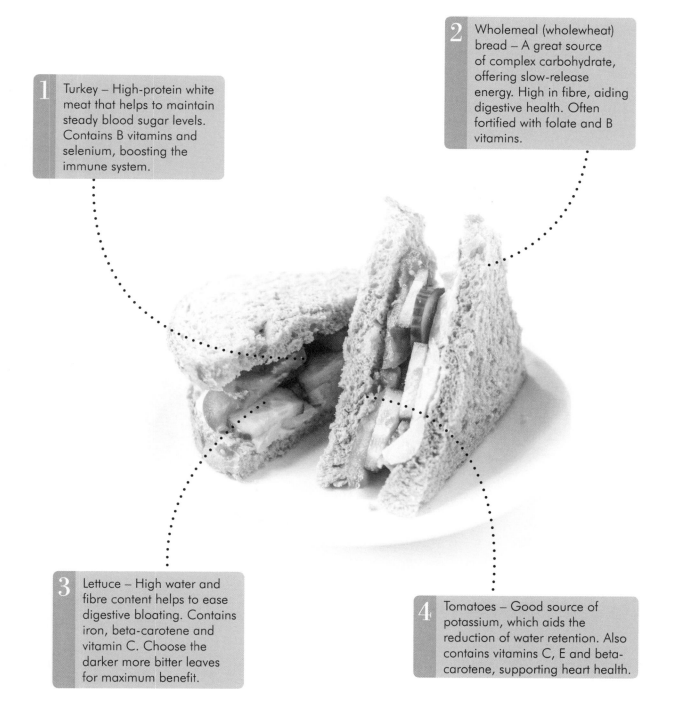

1 Turkey – High-protein white meat that helps to maintain steady blood sugar levels. Contains B vitamins and selenium, boosting the immune system.

2 Wholemeal (wholewheat) bread – A great source of complex carbohydrate, offering slow-release energy. High in fibre, aiding digestive health. Often fortified with folate and B vitamins.

3 Lettuce – High water and fibre content helps to ease digestive bloating. Contains iron, beta-carotene and vitamin C. Choose the darker more bitter leaves for maximum benefit.

4 Tomatoes – Good source of potassium, which aids the reduction of water retention. Also contains vitamins C, E and beta-carotene, supporting heart health.

Mango and Feta Salad

A fresh, colourful salad with sweet and savoury flavours. This dish is perfect as a light lunch or side salad, and is also well received by others when entertaining. Use a number of different salad leaves, of multiple colours, to maximise nutritional variety.

Total time: 00:10   **Preparation time:** 00:10   **Cooking time:** 00:00   **Serves:** 1

Ingredients

- 2 handfuls of mixed salad leaves, for example spinach, watercress, iceberg lettuce
- ½ mango
- 2–4 radishes
- Approx. 50g (1.75oz) feta cheese
- Juice of 1 lemon
- 1 teaspoon of olive oil
- Pinch of salt and pepper

Instructions

1. Wash the mixed salad leaves, shake off excess water, and place them in a bowl.
2. Cut up the flesh from ½ a mango (skin removed), into bite-size pieces.
3. Finely slice 2–4 radishes.
4. Dice the feta cheese.
5. Combine all the ingredients, including the lemon juice, olive oil, salt and pepper.
6. Serve immediately.

Equipment

- Bowl
- Sharp knife
- Chopping board

Hints and tips

- You can buy mango pieces ready prepared.
- There are various online videos showing easy ways to cut a mango.
- Wash salad leaves before eating.
- Include a variety of different salad leaves to benefit from an array of vitamins and minerals.
- See page 268 for alternative salad dressing options, adding flavour and nutrition.

> " This salad tastes so fresh and clean that it reminds me of a beautiful summer's day! The bright colours and the smell of lemon help to lift my mood. And, somehow, finding it attractive to look at makes it easier for me to eat. "
>
> Isabelle – recovering from anorexia

1 Olive oil – Contains monounsaturated fatty acids that help to normalise blood sugar levels, reduce unhealthy cholesterol and encourage a healthy weight.

2 Mango – Good source of vitamin C and beta-carotene, boosting the immune system, skin and eye health. Its high-fibre content also aids digestion.

3 Feta cheese – A low-fat, high-protein hard cheese, containing B vitamins, phosphorus and zinc.

4 Radish – Good source of potassium, vitamin C, magnesium and B vitamins. Aids the digestion of fat. Helps to fight inflammation and congestion.

5 Spinach leaves – Contain high levels of vitamin K, supporting healthy bones. Also rich in anti-inflammatory and anti-cancer substances.

Salmon and Spinach Frittata

A protein-rich meal containing a variety of essential vitamins and minerals, aiding mental performance and supporting cell growth and repair. Double the recipe and store half in the fridge for another breakfast or lunch later in the week.

Total time: 00:10   Preparation time: 00:07   Cooking time: 00:03   Serves: 1

Ingredients

- 2 slices of smoked salmon
- 1 handful of spinach leaves
- Approx. 30g (1oz) goat's cheese or feta cheese
- 2 free-range eggs
- Pinch of salt and pepper
- 1 handful of mixed salad leaves

Equipment

- Oven hob (stovetop)
- Grill (broiler)
- Non-stick frying pan
- Mixing bowl
- Sharp knife
- Chopping board
- Wooden spoon
- Fork or whisk

Instructions

1. Cut the smoked salmon, spinach leaves and cheese into bite-size pieces.
2. Break the eggs into a mixing bowl and whisk until the egg yolk and white have combined.
3. Pour the eggs into a non-stick frying pan on a medium heat.
4. Stir continuously, until the eggs begin to solidify a little.
5. Add the smoked salmon and spinach and stir again.
6. Add the cheese on top.
7. Put the frying pan under the grill to finish cooking the surface of the frittata (being careful not to heat the handle).
8. Add salt and pepper, as preferred.
9. Serve with a handful of mixed salad leave, or cool and store in the fridge for later use.

Hints and tips

- Consider adding cooked peas, cherry tomatoes or asparagus to the frittata.
- Double the recipe to cook 2 portions, saving one for the following day.
- For breakfast egg muffins, combine all the ingredients (apart from the salad) and pour into muffin cases/liners. Bake for 10–15 minutes or until cooked through and slightly browned, creating a great portable snack.

"This fritatta is so easy to make! As a novice cook, I was nervous of trying recipes at first, but now, I've even taught my little brother how to make this. I actually felt quite proud of myself.

Lisa – overcoming body-image issues"

1 Eggs – Good source of protein, vitamin D and phosphorus, aiding strong bones and teeth. Excellent source of B vitamins and choline, boosting mental performance.

2 Smoked salmon – Rich in omega-3 fatty acids, helping to reduce unhealthy cholesterol levels, blood pressure and inflammation. Also thought to help prevent memory loss.

3 Salad leaves – Include a variety of mixed leaves to benefit from various vitamins and minerals, such as vitamin C and iron. Rich in fibre and antioxidants, aiding digestion and the immune system.

4 Spinach – Contains high levels of vitamin K, supporting healthy bones. Also rich in anti-inflammatory substances.

5 Goat's cheese – Great source of protein, aiding cell growth and repair. Rich in calcium, supporting healthy bones, teeth and nails.

Cranberry and Almond Couscous

A colourful couscous salad containing a variety of raw vegetables and heart-healthy olive oil, supporting good health and vitality. Batch cook and store in the fridge for a week. Delicious served with salad, chicken or hummus.

Total time: 00:25   Preparation time: 00:10   Cooking time: 00:15   Serves: 2–4

Ingredients

- 2 teaspoons of bouillon/stock powder
- 200ml (scant cup) boiling water
- 100g (scant ½ cup) couscous
- 1 carrot
- 1 courgette (zucchini)
- 3 spring (green) onions
- 1 handful of fresh mint leaves
- 1 teaspoon of ground cumin
- 1 teaspoon of cinnamon
- Approx. 100g (½ cup) sweetcorn
- 2–3 tablespoons of dried cranberries
- 2–3 tablespoons of olive oil
- 2–3 tablespoons of red wine vinegar
- Approx. 50g (½ cup) flaked almonds

Equipment

- Measuring jug/cup
- Kettle
- Large flat dish
- Mixing bowl
- Cling film (plastic wrap)
- Grater
- Sharp knife
- Chopping board
- Tablespoon
- Teaspoon
- Fork

Instructions

1. Add the stock to the boiling water and stir until fully dissolved.
2. Evenly spread the couscous in the bottom of a large flat serving dish or bowl, in as thin a layer a possible.
3. Add the water and cover with cling film for approximately 15 minutes.
4. Whilst waiting for the couscous, grate the carrot and courgette into a mixing bowl.
5. Finely slice the spring onions and fresh mint leaves.
6. Once the water has been fully absorbed into the couscous, fluff with a fork.
7. Fully combine the couscous with all other ingredients, sprinkling the flaked almonds on top.
8. Serve warm or refrigerate for future use.

Hints and tips

- Eating fresh vegetables raw maximises the nutritional benefits of this recipe.
- Cranberry and almond couscous can be served as a main meal or side dish.
- Delicious eaten with hummus, tuna mayonnaise or cooked chicken pieces.
- Eating an array of natural colours in your diet will encourage consumption of a variety of vitamins and minerals.

"

I love this recipe. Such a variety of ingredients in just one dish. I even prepared it for a family buffet recently – I felt proud to provide a contribution that everyone liked, including me!

"

Lisa – overcoming low self-esteem

1 Couscous – Good source of carbohydrate and protein. Contains potassium, aiding heart health and water balance, and selenium, protecting against premature ageing.

2 Sweetcorn – Contains nutrients (carotenoids) that promote eye health. High-fibre content promotes a healthy digestive tract and helps to control blood sugar levels.

3 Cranberries – Contains antioxidants that help reduce receding gums, tooth decay and damage caused by free radicals. Helps protect against urinary tract infections.

4 Courgette (zucchini) – Contains high levels of water, aiding water balance and bowel regularity. Good source of vitamin C, magnesium, folate and potassium.

5 Mint – Antiseptic and antibacterial properties, reported to aid relief from indigestion and stomach upsets. Also thought to help soothe headaches.

Chicken and Sweetcorn Wrap

A convenient high-fibre lunch rich in protein, iron and potassium, helping to build strong bones and muscles. Serve with cherry tomatoes or a side of mixed salad leaves. Replace the chicken with cottage cheese for a vegetarian alternative.

Total time: 00:05   Preparation time: 00:05   Cooking time: 00:00   Serves: 1

Ingredients

- Approx. 100g (3.5oz) precooked chicken
- 2 tablespoons of sweetcorn
- 2 tablespoons of guacamole or mayonnaise
- 1 handful of mixed salad leaves
- 1 wholemeal (wholewheat) wrap
- 2–4 cherry tomatoes

Instructions

1. Place the chicken, sweetcorn, guacamole/mayonnaise and mixed salad in the wrap.
2. Slice and add the tomatoes.
3. Fold the wrap around all the ingredients.
4. Serve immediately.

Equipment

- Sharp knife
- Chopping board
- Can opener
- Tablespoon

Hints and tips

- See page 206 for a homemade guacamole recipe. See page 256 for a homemade mayonnaise recipe.
- The homemade recipes have been included in this book to provide information about the ingredients included in a food type, as well as the option of making your own. It is fine to use pre-bought alternatives. Everything in moderation, including moderation itself.

> "This is a fabulous lunch, similar to what I've seen in the shops, but even healthier. I have always felt comfortable eating chicken but this book has helped me to add nutritional accompaniments that further benefit my health.
>
> Lesley – recovering from bulimia

2 Wholemeal (wholewheat) wrap – A great source of complex carbohydrate, offering slow-release energy. High in fibre, aiding digestive health. Often fortified with folate and B vitamins.

1 Chicken – A good source of zinc, iron, potassium and phosphorus, helping to build strong bones, teeth and muscles. Also rich in B vitamins, aiding the nervous system.

3 Salad leaves – Include a variety of mixed leaves to benefit from various vitamins and minerals, such as vitamin C and iron. Rich in fibre and antioxidants, aiding digestion and the immune system.

4 Guacamole – A great source of omega-3 and other healthy fats that help to lubricate joints, reduce arthritic symptoms and boost fertility. Rich in vitamin A, vital for eye and brain health, immunity and digestion.

Sweet Potato and Red Pepper Soup

A delicious soup that helps to increase metabolism and reduce the risk of heart disease and unhealthy cholesterol. Serve with wholemeal (wholewheat) bread on the side – great for dunking! Take out in a flask for a healthy packed lunch.

Total time: 00:20   Preparation time: 00:10   Cooking time: 00:30   Serves: 2

Ingredients

- 1 sweet potato
- 1 red onion
- 1 red pepper
- 1 teaspoon of oil
- ½ can of chickpeas (approx. 200g/scant cup)
- 1 can of coconut milk (approx. 400ml/1½ cups)
- ½ can of water (approx. 200ml/scant cup)
- Pinch of salt and pepper

Optional: sliced fresh red chilli or dried chilli flakes

Equipment

- Oven hob (stovetop)
- Food processor
- Non-stick saucepan
- Can opener
- Vegetable peeler
- Sharp knife
- Chopping board
- Tablespoon
- Teaspoon

Instructions

1. Wash and dry the sweet potato, peeling as necessary.
2. Slice the red onion, red pepper and sweet potato into small pieces.
3. Heat the oil in a non-stick saucepan.
4. Add the vegetables and cook for 5 minutes.
5. Add the chickpeas and coconut milk to the pan.
6. Half fill the empty can with water and pour this into the mixture.
7. Bring to the boil and reduce to a medium-high heat, allowing the liquid to simmer for 20 minutes.
8. Add the salt, pepper and dried chilli flakes, if using.
9. Place everything into a food processor and blend until smooth.
10. Serve immediately or refrigerate after cooling, for future use.

Hints and tips

- Chickpeas are a great source of vegetarian protein.
- Sweet potatoes are thought to be more nutrient-dense than white potatoes.
- Retaining the sweet potato skin will increase the fibre and nutrients in this recipe.
- Research suggests than soup aids satiety, meaning that you feel full for longer, helping to reduce the likelihood of food cravings.

> As someone who really struggles to eat fruit and vegetables I have found soups a good way of eating vegetables without it being obvious. It's also helpful to see a photographic example of a healthy portion.
>
> M – recovering from over-eating

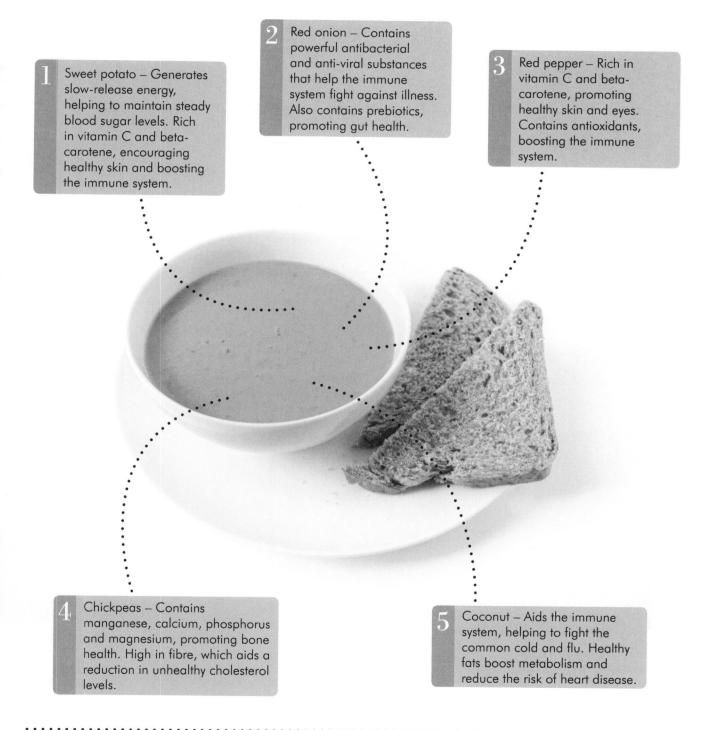

1 Sweet potato – Generates slow-release energy, helping to maintain steady blood sugar levels. Rich in vitamin C and beta-carotene, encouraging healthy skin and boosting the immune system.

2 Red onion – Contains powerful antibacterial and anti-viral substances that help the immune system fight against illness. Also contains prebiotics, promoting gut health.

3 Red pepper – Rich in vitamin C and beta-carotene, promoting healthy skin and eyes. Contains antioxidants, boosting the immune system.

4 Chickpeas – Contains manganese, calcium, phosphorus and magnesium, promoting bone health. High in fibre, which aids a reduction in unhealthy cholesterol levels.

5 Coconut – Aids the immune system, helping to fight the common cold and flu. Healthy fats boost metabolism and reduce the risk of heart disease.

Red Lentil Pâté

An immune-boosting recipe, rich in potassium, aiding healthy circulation and a steady heartbeat. Batch cook and keep in the fridge for future use with toast, pitta, sliced raw vegetables or crackers.

Total time: 00:25   Preparation time: 00:10   Cooking time: 00:15   Serves: 2–4

Ingredients

- 1 red onion
- 2 cloves of garlic (skin removed)
- 1 teaspoon of oil
- Approx. 50g (⅓ cup) pine nuts
- 1 teaspoon of tomato puree (paste)
- 1 teaspoon of ground coriander
- ½ teaspoon of cumin
- ½ teaspoon of cayenne pepper
- Pinch of salt and pepper
- Juice of ½ a lemon
- Approx. 200g (scant cup) of red lentils

Optional: sliced fresh red chilli or dried chilli flakes

Equipment

- Oven hob (stovetop)
- Food processor
- Non-stick frying pan
- Kitchen scales
- Sharp knife
- Chopping board
- Teaspoon

Instructions

1. Cut the onion and garlic cloves (skin removed) into small pieces.
2. Add the oil, chopped onion, garlic and pine nuts into a non-stick frying pan and sauté on a medium heat for 5–7 minutes.
3. Add the tomato puree (paste), coriander, cumin, cayenne pepper, salt and pepper.
4. Continue to cook for a further 3 minutes, stirring occasionally.
5. Stir in the lemon juice and red lentils and cook for an additional 5 minutes.
6. Add the chilli, if using.
7. Place the mixture into a food processor and blend until smooth.
8. Serve hot or cold, with toast, pitta, sliced raw vegetables or crackers.

Hints and tips

- Do not eat uncooked lentils – they must be soaked and cooked first.
- Canned lentils have already been cooked so can be used straight away.
- Experiment with different spices, according to your preferences.
- This recipe can be baked in an oven-proof dish, creating a firmer texture, if preferred.

" As a vegan, my sandwich fillings are limited so this recipe is a great option. I simply add a handful of salad leaves and I'm happy. "

Lucus – recovering from anorexia

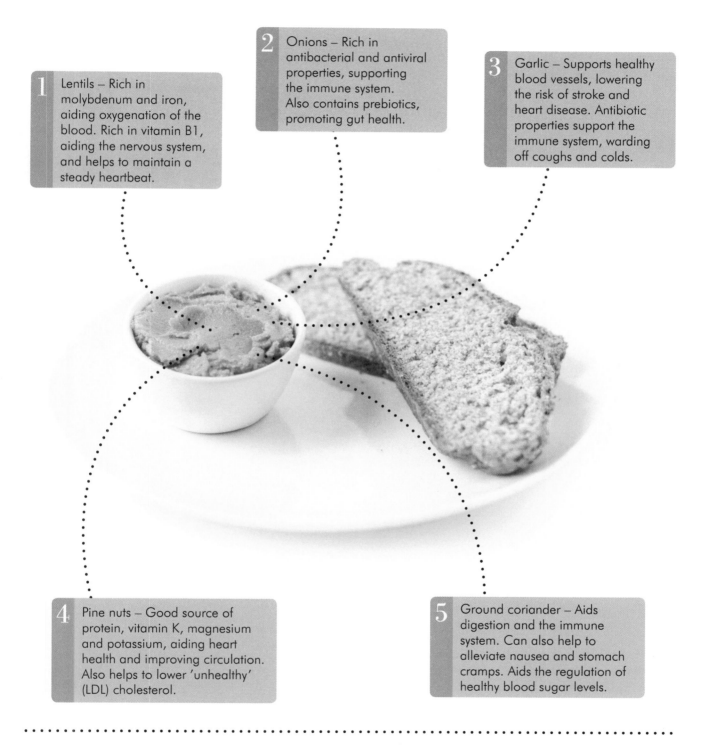

1 Lentils – Rich in molybdenum and iron, aiding oxygenation of the blood. Rich in vitamin B1, aiding the nervous system, and helps to maintain a steady heartbeat.

2 Onions – Rich in antibacterial and antiviral properties, supporting the immune system. Also contains prebiotics, promoting gut health.

3 Garlic – Supports healthy blood vessels, lowering the risk of stroke and heart disease. Antibiotic properties support the immune system, warding off coughs and colds.

4 Pine nuts – Good source of protein, vitamin K, magnesium and potassium, aiding heart health and improving circulation. Also helps to lower 'unhealthy' (LDL) cholesterol.

5 Ground coriander – Aids digestion and the immune system. Can also help to alleviate nausea and stomach cramps. Aids the regulation of healthy blood sugar levels.

Mixed Bean Salad

A high-fibre, high-protein salad that will stabilise blood sugar levels and help reduce the risk of heart disease. Eat as a main meal or serve as a side, along with mixed salad leaves, hummus or tuna, for example.

Total time: 00:05   Preparation time: 00:05   Cooking time: 00:00   Serves: 2

Ingredients

- 3 cherry tomatoes
- 3 spring (green) onions
- ½ red pepper
- ¼ cucumber
- 1 handful of parsley
- 1 can of mixed beans (approx. 400g/1¾ cups)
- ½ can of sweetcorn (approx. 200g/scant cup)
- 1 tablespoon of olive oil
- 1 tablespoon of red wine vinegar
- Pinch of salt and pepper

Optional: 1 can of tuna (approx 150g/5.5oz)

Equipment

- Mixing bowl
- Can opener
- Sharp knife
- Chopping board
- Tablespoon

Instructions

1. Cut the tomatoes, spring onions, red pepper, cucumber and parsley to the preferred size.
2. Combine with all other ingredients in a mixing bowl.
3. Serve immediately or store in the fridge for future use.

Hints and tips

- Do not eat raw/uncooked beans. Canned beans have already been cooked so can be used straight away.
- Place a portion of this recipe into an airtight container for a great portable snack or lunch.

" I make this with my young children. They like to help me wash the beans and cut the cucumber. They often snack on the ingredients as we prepare the dish, which I don't mind at all. It's just so nice to be enjoying food together. "

Emma

1 Mixed beans – High protein, supporting cell repair and growth. Good source of complex carbohydrates and fibre, stabilising blood sugar levels and cholesterol.

2 Red pepper – Rich in vitamin C and beta-carotene, promoting healthy skin and eyes. Contains antioxidants, boosting the immune system, reducing the risk of poor health.

3 Sweetcorn – Contains nutrients (carotenoids) that promote eye health. High-fibre content promotes a healthy digestive tract and helps to control blood sugar levels.

4 Olive oil – Contains monounsaturated fatty acids that help to normalise blood sugar levels, reduce unhealthy cholesterol and encourage a healthy weight.

5 Cucumber – Contains phytoestrogens that help reduce the risk of cardiovascular disease and cancer. Aids a healthy digestive tract.

Pea Soup

A tasty soup full of wholesome ingredients that will help strengthen the body, support energy levels and encourage a healthy digestive system. Batch cook so that you have a portion for another day. Serve with wholemeal (wholewheat) bread – great for dunking!

Total time: 00:30   Preparation time: 00:05   Cooking time: 00:25   Serves: 1

Ingredients

- 1 white onion
- 1 clove of garlic (skin removed)
- 1 teaspoon of oil
- Approx. 200g (scant cup) peas
- Approx. 300ml (1¼ cups) water
- 1 teaspoon of bouillon/stock powder
- Approx. 1 teaspoon of butter

Optional: 1 teaspoon of mint

Instructions

1. Slice the white onion and garlic bulb (skin removed) into small pieces.
2. Sauté the onion and garlic along with the oil in a non-stick saucepan for 5 minutes, on a medium heat.
3. Add the peas, water and stock to the pan.
4. Bring to the boil and then reduce to a medium-high heat, allowing the liquid to simmer for 15 minutes.
5. Add the butter and mint, if using.
6. Place everything into a food processor and blend until preferred consistency.
7. Serve immediately, alongside fresh bread or a roll.

Equipment

- Oven hob (stovetop)
- Food processor
- Non-stick saucepan
- Measuring jug/cup
- Sharp knife
- Chopping board
- Wooden spoon
- Teaspoon

Hints and tips

- Peas are an amazing source of protein, especially relevant if vegetarian or vegan.
- Research suggests that soup aids satiety, meaning that you feel full for longer, helping to reduce the likelihood of food cravings.
- Adding a white potato to this recipe will thicken the consistency of the soup, if preferred.

> Tasty, delicious and nutritious. Pea soup was the first meal that I ate in a public place when I began to recover from anorexia. I am fond of it for this reason.
>
> N – recovering from anorexia

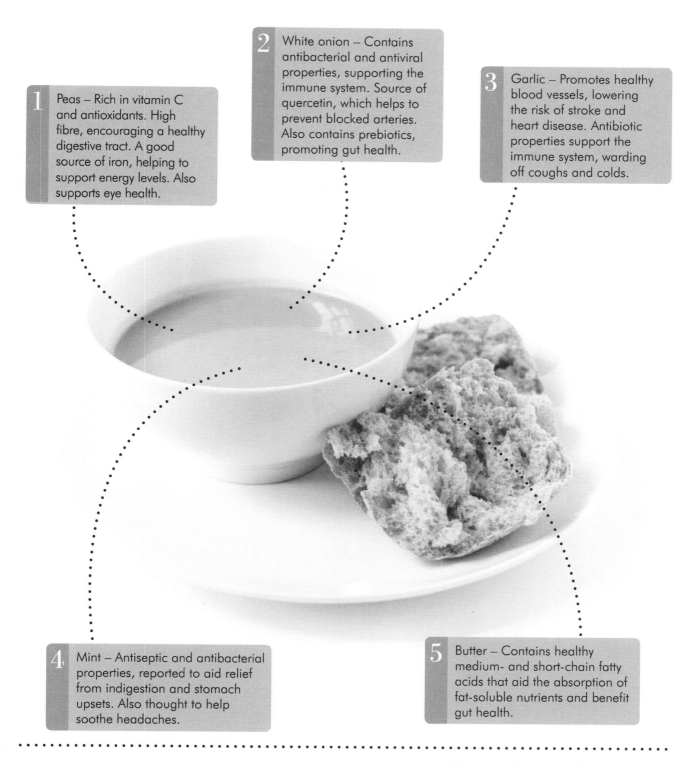

1 Peas – Rich in vitamin C and antioxidants. High fibre, encouraging a healthy digestive tract. A good source of iron, helping to support energy levels. Also supports eye health.

2 White onion – Contains antibacterial and antiviral properties, supporting the immune system. Source of quercetin, which helps to prevent blocked arteries. Also contains prebiotics, promoting gut health.

3 Garlic – Promotes healthy blood vessels, lowering the risk of stroke and heart disease. Antibiotic properties support the immune system, warding off coughs and colds.

4 Mint – Antiseptic and antibacterial properties, reported to aid relief from indigestion and stomach upsets. Also thought to help soothe headaches.

5 Butter – Contains healthy medium- and short-chain fatty acids that aid the absorption of fat-soluble nutrients and benefit gut health.

Rainbow Salad with Hummus

A high-fibre meal bursting with vitamins and minerals that aid healthy water balance and the digestive system. A great way of having a variety of vegetables in just one meal. Enjoy creating a colourful picture with your food – it may encourage satiety.

Total time: 00:05   Preparation time: 00:05   Cooking time: 00:00   Serves: 1

Ingredients

- 2 handfuls of mixed salad leaves (for example spinach, watercress, lettuce, rocket (arugula))
- 2 radishes
- 2 spring (green) onions
- ¼ can of sweetcorn (approx. 100g/½ cup)
- ½ courgette (zucchini)
- ½ carrot
- 1–2 tablespoons of salad dressing
- 3 tablespoons of hummus
- Pinch of salt and pepper

Instructions

1. Place 2 handfuls of mixed salad leaves in a serving bowl.
2. Finely slice the radishes and spring onions, adding these to the bowl, along with the sweetcorn.
3. Grate the courgette and carrot on top.
4. Add a salad dressing of your choice.
5. Add the hummus on top.
6. Add salt and pepper, as preferred and serve immediately.

Equipment

- Bowl
- Grater
- Sharp knife
- Chopping board
- Tablespoon
- Can opener

Hints and tips

- Use a pre-bought hummus or make your own – see page 192 for recipe.
- See page 268 for a variety of nutrient rich salad dressings that could be added to this recipe.
- Consider grating raw sweet potato onto the salad in addition to the courgette and carrot (but note that you cannot eat white potato raw).

> " I love all the colours in this recipe. Sometimes I also grate sweet potato on top as well. I like to add beetroot and couscous if I'm having this for dinner. "
>
> Emma

1 Hummus – Contains manganese, calcium, phosphorus and magnesium, promoting bone health. High in fibre, which aids a reduction in unhealthy cholesterol levels.

2 Salad leaves – Include a variety of mixed leaves to benefit from various vitamins and minerals, such as vitamin C and iron. Rich in fibre and antioxidants, aiding digestion and the immune system.

3 Carrots – Good source of fibre, aiding digestion and the feeling of fullness. Also helps to maintain good eyesight.

4 Sweetcorn – Contains nutrients (carotenoids) that promote eye health. High-fibre content promotes a healthy digestive tract and helps to control blood sugar levels.

5 Courgette (zucchini) – Contains high levels of water, aiding water balance and bowel regularity. Good source of vitamin C, magnesium, folate and potassium.

Egg Mayo and Red Pepper Sandwich

A simple sandwich that offers many essential vitamins and minerals alongside complex carbohydrates, helping to stabilise blood sugar levels and maintain good health. Batch cook boiled eggs for future use – see page 210 for a great snack idea.

Total time: 00:15   Preparation time: 00:05   Cooking time: 00:10   Serves: 1

Ingredients

- 2 free-range eggs
- ¼ red pepper
- 1 handful of spinach leaves
- 1 tablespoon of mayonnaise (pre-bought or see page 256 for recipe)
- 2 slices of bread
- Pinch of salt and pepper

Equipment

- Oven hob (stovetop)
- Saucepan
- Sharp knife
- Chopping board
- Fork or potato masher
- Tablespoon

Instructions

1. Half fill a saucepan with water and bring it to the boil.
2. Add the whole free-range eggs to the water.
3. Boil for 8 minutes.
4. Whilst the eggs are cooking, finely slice the red pepper and spinach leaves, as preferred.
5. When the eggs are cooked, drain the water from the saucepan and soak the eggs in cold water to cool the shell enough to handle.
6. Remove and discard the egg shell, and mash the eggs to the preferred consistency.
7. Combine the mashed eggs, red pepper, spinach leaves, mayonnaise, salt and pepper.
8. Spread the egg mixture on the bread and serve as a sandwich, cut as preferred.

Hints and tips

- Choose wholemeal (wholewheat) or seeded bread over white varieties to benefit from a slower release of energy and an increased amount of vitamins, minerals and fibre.
- Delicious with spring (green) onions.
- Use free-range eggs whenever possible.
- Adding a wedge of lemon to the boiling water when cooking boiled eggs will help the shell peel off once cooked.

" I made this sandwich at home, many times, to help me build the courage to have it from my local bakers. Now I'm able to purchase an egg mayonnaise sandwich wherever I am, helping me to feel more 'normal' with my friends. "

Charlie – recovering from anorexia

1 Eggs – Good source of protein, vitamin D and phosphorus, aiding strong bones and teeth. Excellent source of B vitamins and choline, boosting mental performance.

2 Wholemeal (wholewheat) bread – A great source of complex carbohydrate, offering slow-release energy. High in fibre, aiding digestive health. Often fortified with folate and B vitamins.

3 Spinach – Contains high levels of vitamin K, supporting healthy bones. Also rich in anti-inflammatory substances.

4 Pepper – Aids digestion, can ease lung and bronchial infections and sometimes used to alleviate shock and stress. Also contains antioxidants and has anti-inflammatory qualities.

5 Red pepper – Rich in vitamin C and beta-carotene, promoting healthy skin and eyes. Contains antioxidants, boosting the immune system, reducing the risk of poor health.

Quinoa Greek Salad

A fresh, vibrant salad full of antioxidants, complete proteins, fibre and healthy fats, aiding the immune system and discouraging bloating. Beautiful and satisfying. Batch cook and keep in the fridge for future use, as a main meal or side salad.

Total time: 00:25   Preparation time: 00:10   Cooking time: 00:15   Serves: 1

Ingredients

- 100g (heaped ½ cup) quinoa
- 200ml (scant cup) water
- 1 teaspoon of bouillon/stock powder
- 6–8 black olives
- 2–4 cherry tomatoes
- ½ yellow pepper
- ¼ red onion
- ¼ cucumber
- 1 small romaine lettuce

Instructions

1. Put the quinoa in a colander and thoroughly rinse under cold water.
2. Place the quinoa into a non-stick saucepan, along with the water and stock.
3. Bring to the boil and then turn the heat down allowing the water to simmer for 15 minutes, stirring occasionally.
4. Whilst the quinoa is cooking, slice the olives, tomatoes, yellow pepper, red onion and cucumber into bite-size pieces.
5. Cut the end off the romaine lettuce and wash, as necessary.
6. Once the quinoa is cooked and all the water has been absorbed, leave the grain to stand for 5 minutes before fluffing it up with a fork.
7. Combine the quinoa with all other ingredients.
8. Add a salad dressing of your choice (see page 268)

Equipment

- Colander
- Oven hob (stovetop)
- Non-stick saucepan
- Kitchen scales
- Measuring jug/cup
- Mixing bowl
- Sharp knife
- Chopping board
- Wooden spoon

Hints and tips

- Quinoa is a complete protein source suitable for vegetarians and vegans.
- Dried quinoa flakes are also great in breakfast cereals (available from health food shops and some major supermarkets).
- Eating an array of colours will encourage consumption of a variety of vitamins and minerals.

" It's really good to know that I can fill myself up on this dish. I like to combine it with the honey and mustard dressing on page 268.

Alex – recovering from over-eating "

1 Quinoa – An easily digested complete protein containing all essential amino acids. Good source of anti-inflammatory, monounsaturated and omega-3 fatty acids, aiding heart health.

2 Lettuce – High water and fibre content helps to ease digestive bloating. Contains iron, beta-carotene and vitamin C. Choose the darker more bitter leaves for maximum benefit.

3 Olives – Contain healthy fats that help to reduce risk of heart disease. Also a source of fibre, vitamin E and antioxidants.

4 Yellow pepper – Rich in vitamin C and beta-carotene, promoting healthy skin and eyes. Contains antioxidants, boosting the immune system, reducing the risk of poor health.

5 Red onion – Contains powerful antibacterial and anti-viral substances that help the immune system fight against illness. Also contains prebiotics, promoting gut health.

Butternut Squash and Feta Pitta

A warm and comforting meal, rich in antioxidant and anti-inflammatory properties. Batch cook the butternut squash for future use in salads, stews or soups. Can be served hot or cold.

Total time: 00:40   Preparation time: 00:10   Cooking time: 00:30   Serves: 1

Ingredients

- ½ butternut squash
- 1 tablespoon of oil
- 1 tablespoon of turmeric
- Pinch of salt and pepper
- 1 wholemeal (wholewheat) pitta
- ½ can of sweetcorn (approx. 200g/scant cup)
- Approx. 30g (1oz) feta cheese
- 1 handful of mixed salad leaves

Optional: sliced fresh red chilli or dried chilli flakes

Equipment

- Oven
- Non-stick baking tray
- Toaster or grill (broiler)
- Cling film (plastic wrap)
- Sharp knife
- Chopping board
- Can opener
- Tablespoon

Instructions

1. Preheat the oven to 170–180°C (324–350°F/Gas 3–4).
2. Cut the butternut squash in half. Remove the central seeds, using a tablespoon, and cut off each end.
3. Wrap one half of the squash in cling film and store in the fridge for later use.
4. Slice the rest of the butternut squash into bite-size pieces (leaving the skin on).
5. Combine the butternut squash, oil, turmeric, salt and pepper in the baking tray.
6. Sprinkle with the chilli, if using.
7. Place the baking tray in the oven for 25 minutes, or until the butternut squash is soft.
8. Once the butternut squash has been cooked, heat a pitta in the toaster or grill to make it easier to open the bread pocket.
9. Cut the pitta in half and fill with the butternut squash, sweetcorn, cheese and mixed salad leaves, as preferred.

Hints and tips

- Either leave the butternut squash skin on, or remove the skin with a vegetable peeler, if preferred.
- Orange-coloured vegetables are rich in beta-carotene – a precursor to vitamin A.
- Experiment with the use of different herbs and spices, according to your preferences.

> " This is one of my favourite recipes in the book. I like to make twice as much butternut squash so that I have an extra serving to eat with salad the next day. Delicious hot or cold. "
>
> Nadia – overcoming low self-esteem

1 Butternut squash – Antioxidant and anti-inflammatory properties. Contains vitamins and minerals that aid the cardiovascular system.

2 Wholemeal (wholewheat) pitta – A great source of complex carbohydrate, offering slow-release energy. High in fibre, aiding digestive health. Often fortified with folate and B vitamins.

3 Salad leaves – Include a variety of mixed leaves to benefit from various vitamins and minerals, such as vitamin C and iron. Rich in fibre and antioxidants, aiding digestion and the immune system.

4 Cheese – Good source of calcium, aiding strong bones and teeth. Contains nutrients that promote healthy muscle and nerve function.

Tomato, Avocado and Quinoa Salad

An amazing combination of ingredients rich in omega-3, aiding a healthy heart, reducing inflammation and boosting fertility. Eat fresh or prepare for later use. Serve as a main meal or side dish.

Total time: 00:25   Preparation time: 00:10   Cooking time: 00:15   Serves: 2

Ingredients

- 100g (heaped ½ cup) quinoa
- 200ml (scant cup) water
- 1 teaspoon of bouillon/stock powder
- 4 tomatoes
- 1 avocado
- 1 can of cannellini beans (approx. 400g/ 1¾ cups)
- Pinch of salt and pepper

Optional: sliced fresh red chilli or dried chilli flakes

Equipment

- Colander
- Oven hob (stovetop)
- Non-stick saucepan
- Measuring jug/cup
- Cling film (plastic wrap)
- Can opener
- Sharp knife
- Chopping board
- Wooden spoon
- Fork

Instructions

1. Put the quinoa in a colander and thoroughly rinse with cold water.
2. Place the quinoa into a non-stick saucepan, along with 150ml of cold water and the stock.
3. Bring to the boil and then turn down the heat, allowing the water to simmer for 15 minutes, stirring occasionally.
4. Whilst the quinoa is cooking, slice the tomatoes into bite-size pieces.
5. Prepare the avocado by slicing it in half lengthways, remove the central seed and peel the skin away from the half being used in the recipe.
6. Wrap the other half in cling film and place this in the fridge for future use.
7. Cut the avocado into bite sized pieces.
8. Once the quinoa is cooked and all the water has been absorbed, remove the pan from the heat and leave the grain to stand for 5 minutes, before fluffing it up with a fork.
9. Combine the quinoa, tomatoes, avocado and cannellini beans.
10. Add salt and pepper, as preferred.
11. Sprinkle with chilli, if using.

Hints and tips

- Quinoa is a complete protein source suitable for vegetarians and vegans.
- Dried quinoa flakes are also great in breakfast cereals (available from health food shops and some major supermarkets).
- Experiment with the use of different canned beans, as preferred.

> " This recipe feels so fresh and clean. My daughter likes to eatl natural, wholesome foods, so this is something I make for her at least once a week. "
>
> Thomas – supportive parent

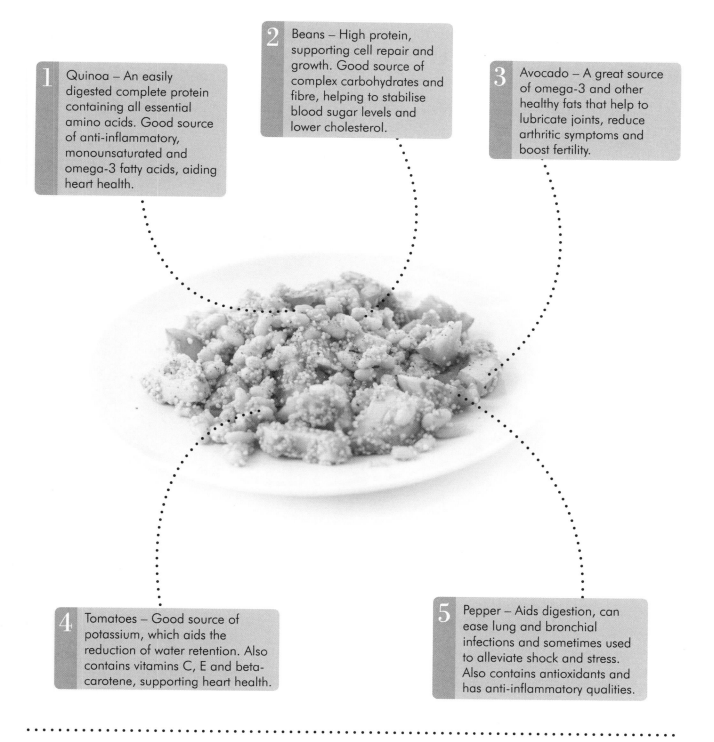

1 Quinoa – An easily digested complete protein containing all essential amino acids. Good source of anti-inflammatory, monounsaturated and omega-3 fatty acids, aiding heart health.

2 Beans – High protein, supporting cell repair and growth. Good source of complex carbohydrates and fibre, helping to stabilise blood sugar levels and lower cholesterol.

3 Avocado – A great source of omega-3 and other healthy fats that help to lubricate joints, reduce arthritic symptoms and boost fertility.

4 Tomatoes – Good source of potassium, which aids the reduction of water retention. Also contains vitamins C, E and beta-carotene, supporting heart health.

5 Pepper – Aids digestion, can ease lung and bronchial infections and sometimes used to alleviate shock and stress. Also contains antioxidants and has anti-inflammatory qualities.

Falafel and Hummus Salad Wrap

A high-fibre, high-protein lunch that stimulates the metabolism and aids digestive health. Easily made at home and wrapped in foil as a packed lunch. See page 192 for a homemade hummus recipe.

Total time: 00:05   Preparation time: 00:05   Cooking time: 00:00   Serves: 1

Ingredients

- 3 pre-bought falafels
- 3 tablespoons of hummus
- 1 handful of mixed salad leaves
- 1 wholemeal (wholewheat) wrap

Optional: sliced fresh red chilli or dried chilli flakes

Instructions

1. Break the falafels into smaller pieces and place with the hummus and mixed salad in the wrap.
2. Add the dried chilli flakes, if using.
3. Fold the wrap around all of the ingredients.
4. Serve immediately.

Equipment

- Tablespoon

Hints and tips

- Falafels are made from chickpeas and spices. If you feel adventurous, consider researching a recipe to make your own.
- You could use homemade or pre-brought hummus – see page 192 for recipe.
- Combine mashed sweet potato with hummus to create a deliciously nutritious spread/dip.

> " I buy ready-made falafels and hummus so that I can prepare this lunch easily. I add as many different salad leaves as I can, knowing that I'm giving my body goodness that will help me heal, from the inside out. "
>
> Sarah – recovering from bulimia

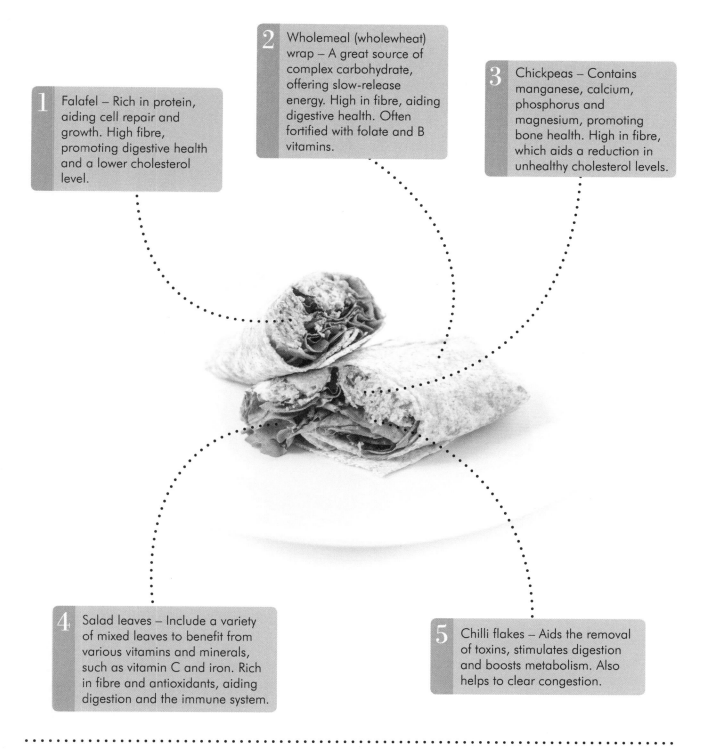

1 Falafel – Rich in protein, aiding cell repair and growth. High fibre, promoting digestive health and a lower cholesterol level.

2 Wholemeal (wholewheat) wrap – A great source of complex carbohydrate, offering slow-release energy. High in fibre, aiding digestive health. Often fortified with folate and B vitamins.

3 Chickpeas – Contains manganese, calcium, phosphorus and magnesium, promoting bone health. High in fibre, which aids a reduction in unhealthy cholesterol levels.

4 Salad leaves – Include a variety of mixed leaves to benefit from various vitamins and minerals, such as vitamin C and iron. Rich in fibre and antioxidants, aiding digestion and the immune system.

5 Chilli flakes – Aids the removal of toxins, stimulates digestion and boosts metabolism. Also helps to clear congestion.

Leek and Potato Soup

A soothing soup with anti-inflammatory properties, promoting good heart and digestive health. Create a chunky or smooth soup, according to your preference. Serve with wholemeal (wholewheat) bread on the side – great for dunking!

Total time: 00:30   Preparation time: 00:05   Cooking time: 00:25   Serves: 1

Ingredients

- 1 white onion
- 2 leeks
- 1 white potato
- 150ml (¾ cup) water
- 1 teaspoon of bouillon/stock powder
- 2 tablespoons of cream cheese

Instructions

1. Peel and cut the potato into small pieces.
2. Place the potato, water and stock into a saucepan.
3. Bring to the boil and then reduce to a medium-high heat, allowing the liquid to simmer for 18 minutes.
4. While the water is simmering, cut the white onion and leeks into small pieces.
5. Sauté in a non-stick saucepan for 5 minutes, on a medium heat.
6. Add the cream cheese and continue to cook until the cheese has melted and combined.
7. Place everything into a food processor and blend until preferred consistency.
8. Serve immediately, alongside fresh bread.

Equipment

- Oven hob (stovetop)
- Saucepan
- Non-stick saucepan
- Measuring jug/cup
- Wooden spoon
- Vegetable peeler
- Sharp knife
- Chopping board
- Food processor
- Tablespoon
- Teaspoon

Hints and tips

- Skip instruction 6 to serve the soup chunky.
- Choose wholemeal (wholewheat) or seeded bread over white varieties to benefit from additional nutrients and fibre.
- Research suggests that soup aids satiety, meaning that you feel full for longer, helping to reduce the likelihood of food cravings.

"
I really liked this soup as a child so it made sense to try and make it during my recovery. I was surprised at how easy it was to follow the recipe instructions and the finished product tasted really good.

Lesley – recovering from bulimia
"

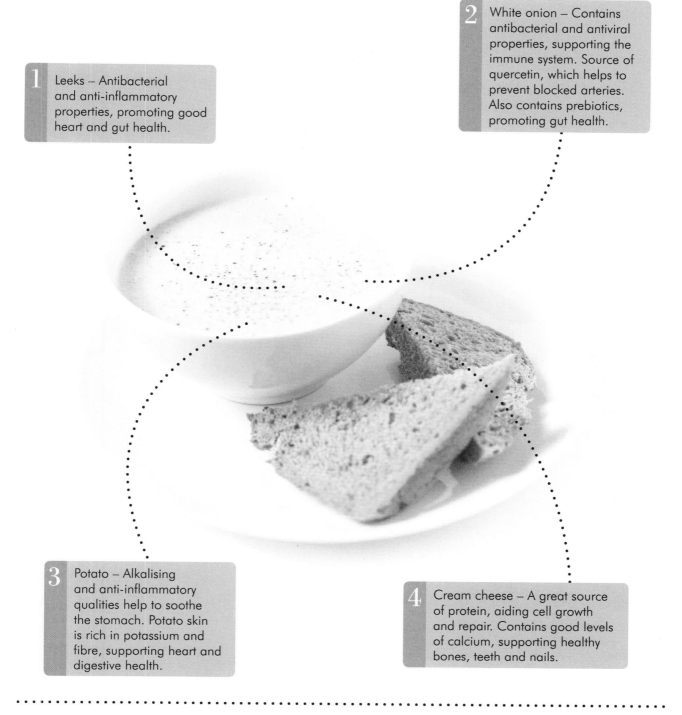

1 Leeks – Antibacterial and anti-inflammatory properties, promoting good heart and gut health.

2 White onion – Contains antibacterial and antiviral properties, supporting the immune system. Source of quercetin, which helps to prevent blocked arteries. Also contains prebiotics, promoting gut health.

3 Potato – Alkalising and anti-inflammatory qualities help to soothe the stomach. Potato skin is rich in potassium and fibre, supporting heart and digestive health.

4 Cream cheese – A great source of protein, aiding cell growth and repair. Contains good levels of calcium, supporting healthy bones, teeth and nails.

Bagel, Cream Cheese and Salmon

A quick and convenient lunch rich in omega-3, vitamins and minerals which can help to reduce cholesterol and inflammation levels. Also suitable as a breakfast option. Add spinach leaves for a boost of iron.

Total time: 00:05   Preparation time: 00:03   Cooking time: 00:02   Serves: 1

Ingredients

- 1 bagel
- 2 tablespoons of cream cheese
- 2 slices of smoked salmon
- 1 tomato

Instructions

1. Cut the bagel in half and toast under the grill or in the toaster.
2. Evenly spread the cream cheese on the bagel.
3. Add the smoked salmon and sliced tomato.

Equipment

- Toaster or grill (broiler)
- Sharp knife
- Chopping board
- Tablespoon

Hints and tips

- Choose seeded or wholemeal (wholewheat) bagels rather than white varieties to benefit from additional nutrients and fibre.
- If the bagel does not come pre-sliced, ensure that you cut it in half before placing it under the grill (broiler) or in the toaster.
- Consider serving alongside a portion of mixed salad leaves.

"

I usually have these ingredients in my cupboard because the whole family like to have bagels for breakfast or lunch. We also enjoy bagels with tuna and melted cheese.

"

Kate – supportive parent

1 Bagel – A source of carbohydrate. Low in saturated fat and cholesterol. Contains thiamin, folate, iron and selenium.

2 Smoked salmon – Rich in omega-3 fatty acids, helping to reduce unhealthy cholesterol levels, blood pressure and inflammation. Also thought to help prevent memory loss.

3 Tomatoes – Good source of potassium, which aids the reduction of water retention. Also contains vitamins C, E and beta-carotene, supporting heart health.

4 Cream cheese – A great source of protein, aiding cell growth and repair. Contains good levels of calcium, supporting healthy bones, teeth and nails.

Sweet Potato with Cottage Cheese

A comforting meal rich in protein, antioxidants and calcium, supporting a healthy immune system and strong bones, teeth and nails. Also good served with the addition of tuna or homemade coleslaw (see page 208 for recipe).

Total time: 00:55   Preparation time: 00:10   Cooking time: 00:45   Serves: 1

Ingredients

- 1 sweet potato
- 2 spring (green) onions
- 3 cherry tomatoes
- ¼ can of sweetcorn (approx. 100g/½ cup)
- 2–3 tablespoons of cottage cheese
- 1 handful of mixed salad leaves

Optional: sliced fresh red chilli or dried chilli flakes

Instructions

1. Preheat the oven to 180–200°C (350–400°F/Gas 4–6).
2. Thoroughly wash and dry the sweet potato.
3. Place the sweet potato on the baking tray and put in the oven for approximately 45 minutes.
4. Slice the spring onions and tomatoes, as preferred.
5. Serve the baked potato with the sweetcorn, cottage cheese and spring onions, along with a side salad of mixed leaves.
6. Sprinkle with chilli, is using.

Equipment

- Oven
- Baking tray
- Sharp knife
- Chopping board
- Tablespoon
- Can opener

Hints and tips

- You could use a white baking potato, if preferred.
- To save time, the potato could be cooked in the microwave for 8–10 minutes instead of baking it in the oven.
- Consider baking more than one potato so that you can place one in the fridge for later use (reheating in the microwave when needed).

"
When I started to cook regularly, I realised that creating wholesome recipes at home helped me not to count calories. Eating 'real' food has helped me to feel 'safe' when eating.
"

Jenni – recovering from anorexia

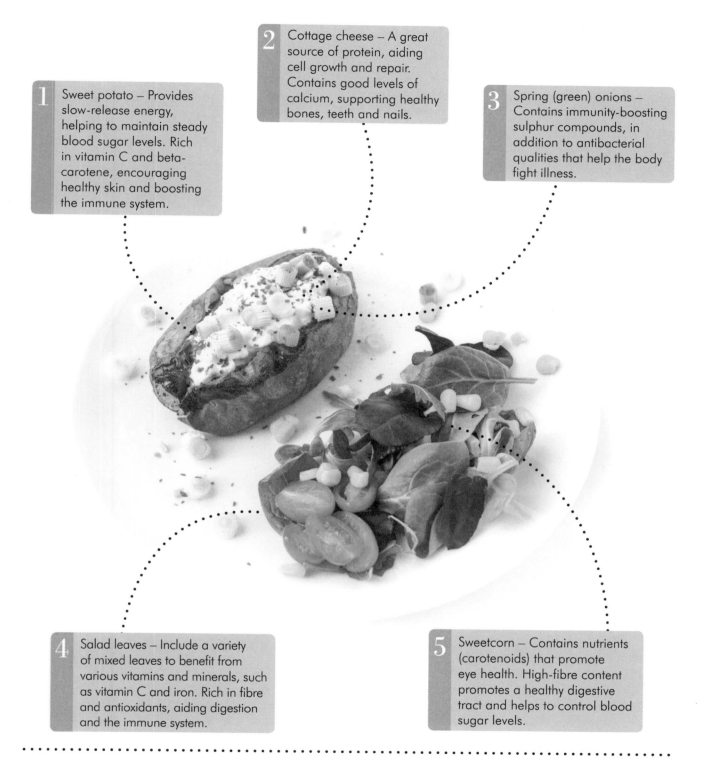

1 Sweet potato – Provides slow-release energy, helping to maintain steady blood sugar levels. Rich in vitamin C and beta-carotene, encouraging healthy skin and boosting the immune system.

2 Cottage cheese – A great source of protein, aiding cell growth and repair. Contains good levels of calcium, supporting healthy bones, teeth and nails.

3 Spring (green) onions – Contains immunity-boosting sulphur compounds, in addition to antibacterial qualities that help the body fight illness.

4 Salad leaves – Include a variety of mixed leaves to benefit from various vitamins and minerals, such as vitamin C and iron. Rich in fibre and antioxidants, aiding digestion and the immune system.

5 Sweetcorn – Contains nutrients (carotenoids) that promote eye health. High-fibre content promotes a healthy digestive tract and helps to control blood sugar levels.

Tuna Salad Pitta

A well-balanced high-fibre lunch, which promotes a healthy digestive system. Rich in vitamins that can boost skin and eye health and antioxidants that help fight illness. Consider adding fresh red chillies or capers for a burst of flavour.

Total time: 00:05   Preparation time: 00:04   Cooking time: 00:01   Serves: 1

Ingredients

- ½ red pepper
- 1 handful of fresh spinach
- ½ can of tuna (approx. 75g/2.5oz)
- ¼ can of sweetcorn (approx. 100g/½ cup)
- 1 tablespoon of mayonnaise
- Pinch of pepper
- 1 wholemeal (wholewheat) pitta bread
- 5–6 cucumber slices

Equipment

- Toaster or grill (broiler)
- Can opener
- Sharp knife
- Chopping board
- Tablespoon

Instructions

1. Finely slice the red pepper and spinach leaves.
2. Combine the tuna, red pepper, spinach, sweetcorn, mayonnaise and pepper in a bowl.
3. Heat the pitta bread in a toaster or under a grill.
4. Slice the pitta in half, filling it with the tuna mixture.
5. Serve with cucumber slices.

Hints and tips

- Include a rainbow of colours in your diet to encourage intake of a variety of vitamins and minerals that promote good health.
- Tuna is a lean, inexpensive source of protein easily added to salads or sandwiches; however, pregnant women are advised to eat not more than 2–3 cans per week.
- Choose wholemeal (wholewheat) pitta to benefit from more fibre.

> "I find wholemeal pitta less daunting than a sandwich made from bread. I tend to add various vegetables to my tuna, such as sweetcorn or grated carrot and courgette. I also add capers for extra taste. This satisfies my hunger and any emotional cravings.
>
> Amy – recovering from an eating disorder

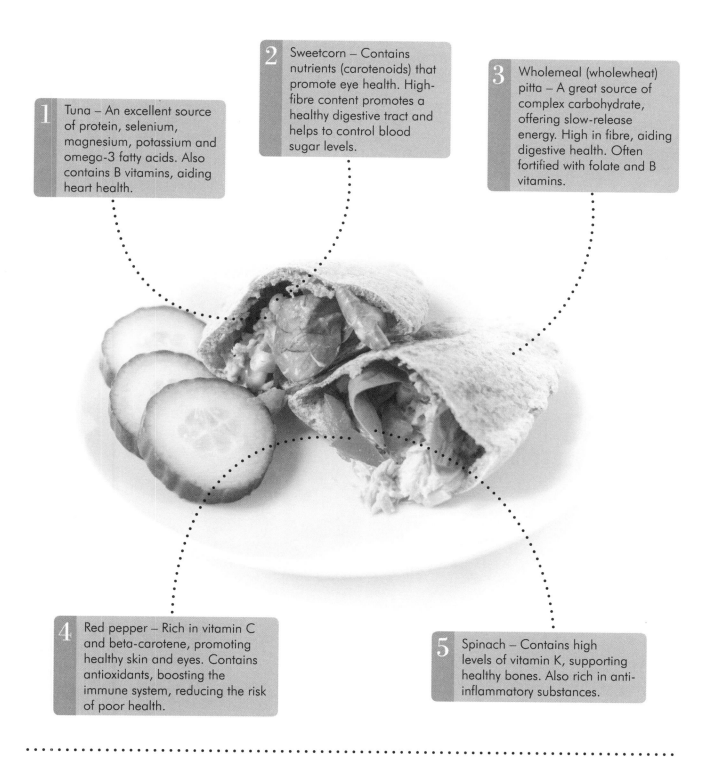

1 Tuna – An excellent source of protein, selenium, magnesium, potassium and omega-3 fatty acids. Also contains B vitamins, aiding heart health.

2 Sweetcorn – Contains nutrients (carotenoids) that promote eye health. High-fibre content promotes a healthy digestive tract and helps to control blood sugar levels.

3 Wholemeal (wholewheat) pitta – A great source of complex carbohydrate, offering slow-release energy. High in fibre, aiding digestive health. Often fortified with folate and B vitamins.

4 Red pepper – Rich in vitamin C and beta-carotene, promoting healthy skin and eyes. Contains antioxidants, boosting the immune system, reducing the risk of poor health.

5 Spinach – Contains high levels of vitamin K, supporting healthy bones. Also rich in anti-inflammatory substances.

DINNER

Chilli Con Carne and Rice 138
Lentil Cottage Pie 140
Pesto Pasta with Chicken 142
Chickpea and Sweet Potato Stew 144
Chicken and Roast Veg Tray Bake 146
Simple Spaghetti Carbonara.. 148
Cosy Beef Stew.. 150
Asian Style Salmon with Veg Rice 152
Tuna, Sweetcorn and Broccoli Bake.. 154
Lemon, Basil and Pea Spaghetti 156
Veg Stir-Fried Noodles with Prawns 158
Sweetcorn Salsa with Chicken.. 160
Pitta Pizza 162
Avocado, Egg, Salmon and Lentils 164
Veg Couscous with Spiced Chicken 166
Beef Burrito.. 168
Sweet Potato, Chicken and Spinach 170
Sea Bass, New Potatoes and Kale 172
Spaghetti and Meatballs 174
Lentil Stuffed Peppers 176
Grilled Lamb Burger with Salad 178
Roasted Veg with Garlic Chicken 180
Salmon, New Potatoes and Broccoli.. 182
Quinoa, Sundried Tomato and Feta 184
Fish Pie and Peas... 186

Chilli Con Carne and Rice

A versatile dish that can be served with rice, jacket potatoes, wholemeal (wholewheat) pitta, seeded wraps or inside baked red peppers. Includes a wide variety of vegetables, along with vitamin-rich meat and heart-healthy beans. Batch cook and freeze for up to three months.

Total time: 00:40   Preparation time: 00:10   Cooking time: 00:30   Serves: 4

Ingredients

- Approx. 300g (1½ cups) brown rice
- 1 red onion
- 1 courgette (zucchini)
- 1 red pepper
- 1 carrot
- 2 cloves of garlic (skin removed)
- 2 tablespoons of oil
- 1–2 teaspoons of cumin powder
- 1–2 teaspoons of chilli powder
- Approx. 400g (14oz) minced (ground) meat
- 1 can of red kidney beans (approx. 400g/1¾ cups)
- 2 cans of chopped tomatoes (approx. 800g/3½ cups)
- 3 tablespoons of tomato puree (paste)
- Salt and pepper, to taste

Optional: sliced fresh red chilli or dried chilli flakes

Equipment

- Oven hob (stovetop)
- 2 large non-stick saucepans
- Can opener
- Sieve
- Chopping board
- Sharp knife
- Wooden spoon
- Tablespoon
- Teaspoon

Hints and tips

- You can use any type of minced meat you prefer, including vegetarian mince. Alternatively, use mixed beans instead.
- The flavour of this recipe improves with time, so it will taste even better the day after it's made.
- This recipe makes enough for four servings, so you can refrigerate or freeze portions for future use.

Instructions

1. Half fill a non-stick saucepan with water and bring to the boil.
2. Add the brown rice, bring back to the boil and then simmer for 25 minutes (or as stated by the packet).
3. Chop the red onion, courgette, red pepper, carrot and garlic cloves into small pieces.
4. Gently heat the oil in a large non-stick saucepan.
5. Add the chopped vegetables and garlic, along with the cumin and chilli powder.
6. Stir continuously for 3–5 minutes, or until the vegetables soften.
7. Add the meat and stir until browned all over.
8. Add the kidney beans, tomatoes and tomato puree (paste).
9. Gently simmer on a medium heat for a minimum of 20 minutes, stirring occasionally. If you have more time, cook for up to 40 minutes to intensify flavours.
10. Add salt and pepper to taste.
11. Drain the rice and serve alongside the chilli con carne.
12. Add sliced fresh red chilli or dried chilli flakes, if desired.

> " I like the fact that I can batch cook this recipe. One night I have it with rice, and the next in a wrap, freezing the other two portions for the week after. It helps me to know I have a healthy dinner choice ready for me as soon as I get home from work. And I don't have to worry about feeling guilty after eating... It's just lean meat with healthy vegetables and beans. "
>
> Lisa – overcoming body-image issues

1 Beef – Rich source of protein and B vitamins. Great source of iron, helping to protect against anaemia.

2 Courgette (zucchini) – Contains high levels of water, aiding water balance and bowel regularity. Good source of vitamin C, magnesium, folate and potassium.

3 Tomatoes – Good source of potassium, which aids the reduction of water retention. Also contains vitamins C, E and beta-carotene, supporting heart health.

4 Red kidney beans – High protein, supporting cell repair and growth. Good source of complex carbohydrates and fibre, stabilising blood sugar levels and cholesterol.

5 Carrots – Good source of fibre, aiding digestion and the feeling of fullness. Also helps to maintain good eyesight.

<45

Lentil Cottage Pie

A comforting recipe which aids digestion and promotes a healthy heart. Batch cook and freeze portions for later use. Serve as a meal in one, or with the addition of broccoli or peas.

Total time: 00:30   Preparation time: 00:05   Cooking time: 00:25   Serves: 2

Ingredients

- 2 potatoes or sweet potatoes
- 2 carrots
- 1 red onion
- 1–2 cloves of garlic (skin removed)
- 1 tablespoon of oil
- 1 can of precooked lentils (approx. 400g/1¾ cups)
- 1 can of chopped tomatoes/passata/tomato sauce (approx. 400g/1¾ cups)
- Pinch of salt and pepper

Optional: approx. 60g (2oz) cheese

Equipment

- Oven
- Oven hob (stovetop)
- Non-stick saucepan
- Non-stick frying pan
- Colander
- Oven-proof dish
- Chopping board
- Can opener
- Sharp knife
- Tablespoon
- Vegetable peeler
- Potato masher

Instructions

1. Preheat the oven to 170–180°C (325–350°F/Gas 3–4).
2. Half fill a non-stick saucepan with water and bring to the boil.
3. Peel and finely chop the potatoes, adding them to the saucepan to simmer for 10 minutes.
4. Whilst the potatoes are cooking, finely chop the carrots, red onion and garlic.
5. Heat the oil in a non-stick frying pan.
6. Add the carrots, red onion and garlic and sauté for 5 minutes, or until softened but not browned.
7. Add the precooked lentils and tomatoes/passata/tomato sauce to the frying pan and simmer for a further 2 minutes.
8. Drain and mash the potatoes, adding the salt and pepper as preferred.
9. Place the lentil and tomato mixture into an oven-proof dish.
10. Cover with the mashed potato.
11. Grate the cheese on top, if using.
12. Bake in the oven for 10 minutes to add texture and melt the cheese.
13. Serve immediately or cool and refrigerate/freeze for later use.

Hints and tips

- Do not eat uncooked lentils – they must be soaked and cooked first.
- Canned lentils have already been cooked so can be used straight away.
- Add peas to the carrot, onion and garlic mix, if desired.
- Double the recipe to cook enough for 4 portions, allowing for guests or ready-made meals that can be frozen for future use.

> As a vegetarian, I can't have traditional cottage pie and am not keen on meat substitutes, so this recipe is a definite favourite. Absolutely delicious!
>
> E – recovering from an eating disorder

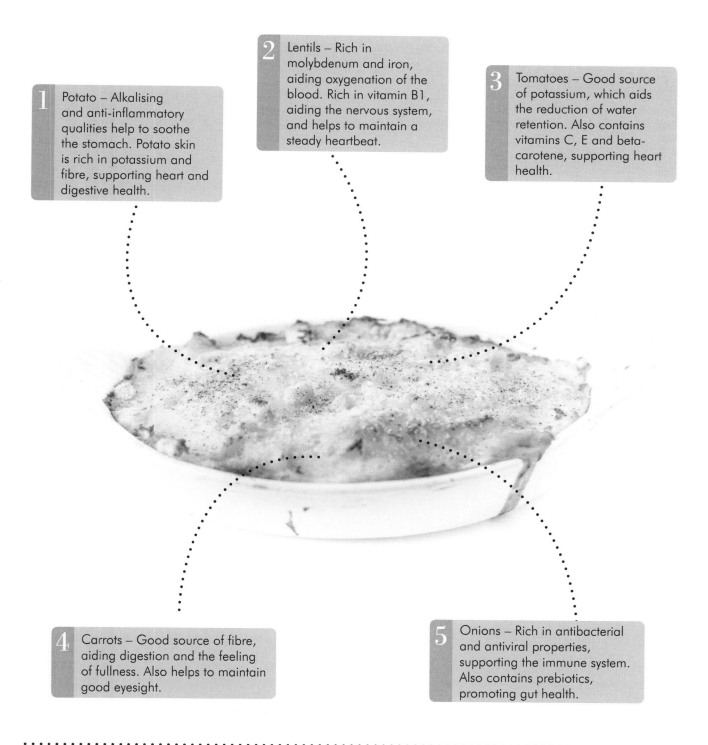

1 Potato – Alkalising and anti-inflammatory qualities help to soothe the stomach. Potato skin is rich in potassium and fibre, supporting heart and digestive health.

2 Lentils – Rich in molybdenum and iron, aiding oxygenation of the blood. Rich in vitamin B1, aiding the nervous system, and helps to maintain a steady heartbeat.

3 Tomatoes – Good source of potassium, which aids the reduction of water retention. Also contains vitamins C, E and beta-carotene, supporting heart health.

4 Carrots – Good source of fibre, aiding digestion and the feeling of fullness. Also helps to maintain good eyesight.

5 Onions – Rich in antibacterial and antiviral properties, supporting the immune system. Also contains prebiotics, promoting gut health.

Pesto Pasta with Chicken

A well-balanced meal delicious hot or cold. The combination of complex carbohydrate and protein provides slow-release energy, reducing the likelihood of cravings. See page 262 for a homemade pesto sauce recipe.

Total time: 00:20   Preparation time: 00:05   Cooking time: 00:15   Serves: 1

Ingredients

- Approx. 75g (2.5oz) wholewheat pasta
- 1 chicken breast
- 2 tablespoons of pesto sauce (see page 262)
- 3 cherry tomatoes

Optional: Parmesan cheese and fresh basil leaves

Instructions

1. Half fill a non-stick saucepan with water and bring to the boil.
2. Add the pasta, bring back to the boil and then simmer for 8–10 minutes, or until the pasta is cooked to preference.
3. Whilst the pasta is simmering, cut the chicken into bite sized pieces.
4. Cook the chicken on the grill or non-stick frying pan for 3–4 minutes each side, or until cooked through.
5. Drain the pasta, placing it back in the warm saucepan afterwards.
6. Add the pesto sauce and stir through.
7. Serve the pesto pasta and chicken along with the tomatoes and Parmesan and basil, if using.

Equipment

- Oven hob (stovetop)
- Grill (broiler) or non-stick frying pan
- Non-stick saucepan
- Chopping board
- Sharp knife
- Colander
- Wooden spoon
- Tablespoon

Hints and tips

- See page 262 for a pesto sauce recipe or buy a pre-made sauce, if preferred. Cooking at home enables you to understand the ingredients included and avoid unnecessary additives or preservatives, but it would be emotionally unhealthy if you felt unable to eat pre-made food bought out and about. Everything in moderation, including moderation itself!

> " I've made this pasta dish with homemade pesto sauce, but also used shop-bought pesto for convenience. Sometimes I also add sweetcorn or artichokes to increase my vegetable intake. This is a popular dish with the whole family. "
>
> Jacob – recovering from over-eating

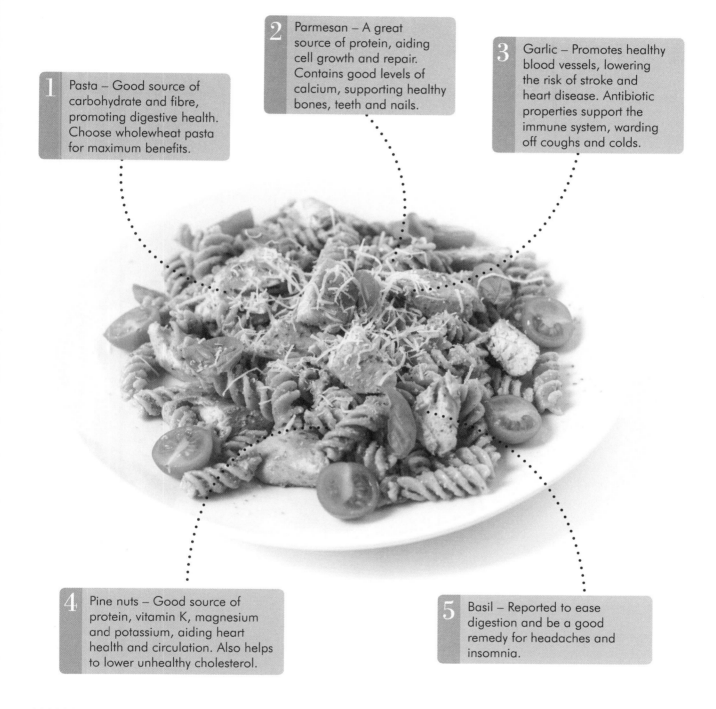

1 Pasta – Good source of carbohydrate and fibre, promoting digestive health. Choose wholewheat pasta for maximum benefits.

2 Parmesan – A great source of protein, aiding cell growth and repair. Contains good levels of calcium, supporting healthy bones, teeth and nails.

3 Garlic – Promotes healthy blood vessels, lowering the risk of stroke and heart disease. Antibiotic properties support the immune system, warding off coughs and colds.

4 Pine nuts – Good source of protein, vitamin K, magnesium and potassium, aiding heart health and circulation. Also helps to lower unhealthy cholesterol.

5 Basil – Reported to ease digestion and be a good remedy for headaches and insomnia.

Chickpea and Sweet Potato Stew

A heartwarming vegetarian stew full of wholesome ingredients. Also delicious with the addition of butter beans or sliced red peppers. Batch cook and freeze in portions for later use – simple and convenient.

Total time: 00:60   Preparation time: 00:10   Cooking time: 00:50   Serves: 2

Ingredients

- 1 tablespoon of oil
- 1 onion
- 2 cloves of garlic (skin removed)
- 2 sweet potatoes
- 1 carrot (or red pepper)
- 1 teaspoon of turmeric
- 1 teaspoon of curry powder
- ½ teaspoon of cumin powder
- 1 can of chickpeas (400g/1¾ cups)
- 1 can of chopped tomatoes (approx. 400g/1¾ cups)
- 2 teaspoons of bouillon/stock powder
- 1 can of water
- 1 tablespoon of tomato puree (paste)
- 1 handful fresh spinach leaves

Equipment

- Oven hob (stovetop)
- Non-stick saucepan
- Chopping board
- Sharp knife
- Wooden spoon
- Tablespoon
- Teaspoon
- Can opener
- Optional: vegetable peeler

Instructions

1. Heat the oil in a non-stick saucepan.
2. Finely slice the onion and garlic cloves, adding these to the saucepan.
3. Sauté on a medium heat for 5 minutes.
4. Wash and dry the sweet potatoes and carrots (peel if preferred), then dice into small chunks.
5. Add the turmeric, curry powder and cumin powder into the saucepan and stir for 1 minute.
6. Add the sweet potato, carrot, chickpeas, tomatoes, stock and water to the saucepan.
7. Simmer for at least 40 minutes.
8. Add the tomato puree (paste) and spinach leaves for the last 5 minutes, stirring through.
9. Serve with wholemeal (wholewheat) bread or couscous.

Hints and tips

- Chickpeas are a great source of vegetarian protein.
- Combining turmeric and black pepper increases the absorption of curcumin – the active anti-inflammatory nutrient in turmeric.
- A great dish to prepare in a slow cooker.
- Tastes even better the day after cooking.

> " I make this recipe in my slow cooker. I simply add all the ingredients into the slow cooker before work and come home to a delicious, healthy dinner. I don't feel afraid of any of the individual ingredients so why should I fear the meal? I shouldn't! "
>
> Emma

1 Chickpeas – Contains manganese, calcium, phosphorus and magnesium, promoting bone health. High in fibre, which aids a reduction in unhealthy cholesterol levels.

2 Sweet potato – Provides slow-release energy. Rich in vitamin C and beta-carotene, encouraging healthy skin and boosting the immune system.

3 Spinach – Contains high levels of vitamin K, supporting healthy bones. Also rich in anti-inflammatory substances.

4 Turmeric – Contains powerful anti-inflammatory properties. Also a good digestive aid, supporting liver and gallbladder function.

5 Carrots – Good source of fibre, aiding digestion and the feeling of fullness. Also helps to maintain good eyesight.

Chicken and Roast Veg Tray Bake

Roasted Mediterranean vegetables baked with herby chicken, providing protein, vitamins and minerals that benefit heart and digestive health. Double the recipe and reserve a portion to be eaten cold the next day.

Total time: 00:30   Preparation time: 00:05   Cooking time: 00:25   Serves: 2

Ingredients

- 10 new potatoes
- 1 red pepper
- 1 red onion
- 1 handful of cherry tomatoes
- 1 handful of black olives
- 2 tablespoons of olive oil
- 1 tablespoon of mixed herbs
- 1 teaspoon of paprika
- Juice of ½ a lemon
- 2 free-range chicken thighs
- 1 handful of basil leaves

Equipment

- Oven
- Oven hob (stovetop)
- Saucepan
- Oven-proof dish
- Colander
- Chopping board
- Sharp knife
- Mixing bowl

Instructions

1. Preheat the oven to 180–200°C (350–400°F/Gas 4–6).
2. Half fill a saucepan with water and bring to the boil.
3. Thickly slice the potatoes then add them to the saucepan.
4. Bring back to the boil and simmer for 8 minutes (until part cooked).
5. Slice the red pepper, red onion, tomatoes and olives as preferred.
6. Drain the potatoes.
7. In an oven-proof dish, mix the part-boiled new potatoes, red pepper, red onion, cherry tomatoes and olives.
8. Combine the olive oil, mixed herbs, paprika and lemon juice in a mixing bowl.
9. Drizzle half the marinade over the vegetables.
10. Place the chicken thighs on top of the vegetables, covering them with the other half of the marinade.
11. Bake for 15–20 minutes, or until the chicken is browned and cooked through.
12. Serve with fresh basil leaves.

Hints and tips

- Including a variety of colours in your diet encourages the consumption of numerous vitamins and minerals.
- Chicken is a great source of lean protein – choose free-range varieties whenever possible.
- Ensure that the chicken is fully cooked through before serving. It is dangerous to eat uncooked chicken.

> Chicken and vegetables feel like 'safe' foods to me. I like eating fresh produce, especially when so simple to prepare and cook. I tend to double the recipe for my partner and me so that we have a second helping ready for the next day.
>
> Lesley – recovering from bulimia

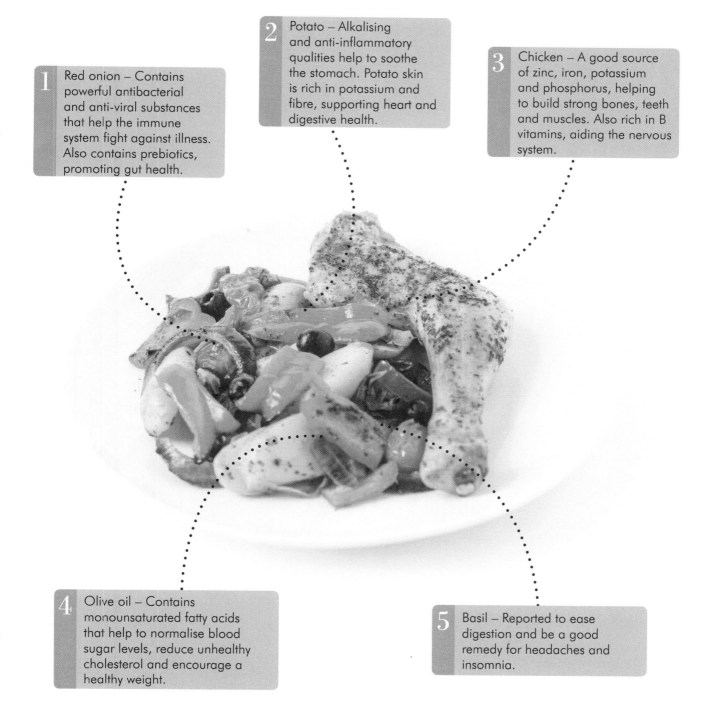

1 Red onion – Contains powerful antibacterial and anti-viral substances that help the immune system fight against illness. Also contains prebiotics, promoting gut health.

2 Potato – Alkalising and anti-inflammatory qualities help to soothe the stomach. Potato skin is rich in potassium and fibre, supporting heart and digestive health.

3 Chicken – A good source of zinc, iron, potassium and phosphorus, helping to build strong bones, teeth and muscles. Also rich in B vitamins, aiding the nervous system.

4 Olive oil – Contains monounsaturated fatty acids that help to normalise blood sugar levels, reduce unhealthy cholesterol and encourage a healthy weight.

5 Basil – Reported to ease digestion and be a good remedy for headaches and insomnia.

Simple Spaghetti Carbonara

A quick main meal combining complex carbohydrates and protein for a slow release of energy. As a calcium-rich recipe, this dish supports healthy bones, teeth and nails.

Total time: 00:15   Preparation time: 00:05   Cooking time: 00:10   Serves: 1

Ingredients

- Approx. 75g (2.5oz) spaghetti
- Approx. 50g (¼ cup) peas
- 1 teaspoon of oil
- ½ onion
- 1 clove of garlic (skin removed)
- 2 slices of ham
- 4 tablespoons of cream cheese
- ¼ glass of milk
- 1 handful of fresh flat leaf parsley

Instructions

1. Half fill a saucepan with water and bring to the boil.
2. Add the spaghetti, bring back to the boil and then simmer for 8–10 minutes.
3. Add the peas to the spaghetti for the last few minutes of cooking.
4. Whilst the pasta is cooking, heat the oil in a non-stick frying pan.
5. Finely slice the onion and garlic and add these to the frying pan, cooking for 2 minutes, or until soft but not browned.
6. Cut the ham into small pieces.
7. Add the cream cheese, milk and ham to the onion and garlic, stirring until fully combined.
8. Drain the spaghetti.
9. Combine all ingredients in the frying pan.
10. Serve immediately, sprinkled with flat leaf parsley.

Equipment

- Oven hob (stovetop)
- Non-stick frying pan
- Non-stick saucepan
- Colander
- Measuring jug/cup
- Chopping board
- Sharp knife
- Teaspoon
- Tablespoon

Hints and tips

- Choose wholewheat pasta, or experiment with rice or millet pastas.
- The milk and cheese in this recipe add valuable protein to the dish.
- Use one rasher of bacon (per serving) instead of ham, if preferred.

"My kids absolutely love this recipe, to the extent that my daughter kisses the photograph! Involving them in the cooking process reminds me that food is supposed to be enjoyed and shared. I'm grateful to them.

Emma

1 Pasta – Good source of carbohydrate and fibre, promoting digestive health. Choose wholewheat pasta for maximum benefits.

2 Ham – Contains zinc, iron and a variety of B vitamins that aid energy regulation and muscle growth and repair. High in salt, so enjoy in moderation.

3 Cream cheese – A great source of protein, aiding cell growth and repair. Contains good levels of calcium, supporting healthy bones, teeth and nails.

4 Garlic – Promotes healthy blood vessels, lowering the risk of stroke and heart disease. Antibiotic properties support the immune system, warding off coughs and colds.

Cosy Beef Stew

A comforting recipe, perfect on a cold winter's day. Batch cook and freeze for later use. Slow cook for a few hours for maximum flavour. Wholesome and nutritious.

Total time: 00:60   Preparation time: 00:10   Cooking time: 00:50   Serves: 2

Ingredients

- Approx. 200g (7oz) beef
- 1 tablespoon of oil
- 1 red onion
- 1 clove of garlic (skin removed)
- 1 white potato or sweet potato
- 1 carrot
- 3 tablespoons of peas
- 1 can of chopped tomatoes (approx. 400g/1¾ cups)
- 2 teaspoons of bouillon/stock powder
- 1 can of water
- 1 teaspoon of thyme
- 1 tablespoon of tomato puree (paste)

Instructions

1. Chop the beef into bite-size pieces.
2. Heat the oil in a non-stick saucepan.
3. Cook the beef for 5 minutes, until browned.
4. Finely slice the red onion and garlic clove, adding these to the saucepan.
5. Sauté for 8–10 minutes.
6. In the meantime, chop the potatoes and carrot into small chunks.
7. Add the potatoes, carrot, peas, chopped tomatoes, stock, water and thyme.
8. Cook on a low-medium heat for at least 40 minutes.
9. Add the tomato puree (paste) and stir.
10. Serve with wholemeal (wholewheat) bread or couscous.

Equipment

- Oven hob (stovetop)
- Non-stick saucepan
- Chopping board
- Sharp knife
- Tablespoon
- Teaspoon
- Can opener

Hints and tips

- A great dish to prepare in a slow cooker, meaning that it could be cooking whilst you are at work and ready for when you get home.
- Tastes even better the day after.
- Consider batch cooking so that you can freeze portions for future use.

" I've modified this recipe by cooking it in my slow cooker over a five- to six-hour period. The finished product is so comforting and tasty. Sometimes we have it with rice and other times with wholemeal bread and butter. "

Thomas – supportive parent

1 Potato – Alkalazing and anti-inflammatory qualities help to soothe the stomach. Potato skin is rich in potassium and fibre, supporting heart and digestive health.

2 Beef – Rich source of protein and B vitamins. Great source of iron, helping to protect against anaemia.

3 Peas – Rich in vitamin C and antioxidants. High fibre, encouraging a healthy digestive tract. A good source of iron, helping to prevent fatigue. Also aids eye health.

4 Tomatoes – Good source of potassium, which aids the reduction of water retention. Also contains vitamins C, E and beta-carotene, supporting heart health.

5 Carrots – Good source of fibre, aiding digestion and the feeling of fullness. Also helps to maintain good eyesight.

Asian Style Salmon with Veg Rice

A delicious recipe offering slow-release energy, which may help to reduce food cravings later in the day. Batch cook and reheat or serve cold another day. Consider serving with the addition of broccoli or sweetcorn, if desired.

Total time: 00:40   **Preparation time:** 00:10   **Cooking time:** 00:30   **Serves:** 1

Ingredients

- 1 clove of garlic (skin removed)
- 1 sliced fresh red chilli/½ teaspoon of dried chilli flakes
- 1 tablespoon of organic honey
- 1cm fresh ginger or 1 teaspoon of ginger powder
- Pinch of black pepper
- 1 tablespoon of soy sauce
- 1 salmon fillet
- Approx. 75g (⅓ cup) brown rice
- 3 spring (green) onions
- 1 handful of kale
- 1 teaspoon of oil

Equipment

- Oven
- Oven hob (stovetop)
- Non-stick baking tray
- Non-stick frying pan
- Non-stick saucepan
- Sieve
- Sharp knife
- Chopping board
- Kitchen foil
- Wooden spoon
- Tablespoon
- Optional: garlic crusher

Hints and tips

- Salmon is rich in omega oils, which cannot be stored in the body, so should be consumed on a regular basis.
- The vegetable rice could be batch cooked for later use, serving it with fish or chicken, as preferred.
- The vegetables could be served separate to the brown rice, if preferred.

Instructions

1. Preheat the oven to 180–200°C (350–400°F/Gas 4–6).
2. Half fill a non-stick saucepan with water and bring to the boil.
3. Peel and crush or finely slice the garlic clove and add this to the red chilli, honey, ginger, black pepper and soy sauce.
4. Marinate the salmon in the mixture for at least 5 minutes.
5. Add the brown rice to the water, bring back to the boil and then simmer for 25 minutes.
6. Wrap the salmon and excess marinade in foil and place in the oven for 18–20 minutes.
7. Whilst the rice and salmon are cooking, finely slice the kale and spring onions.
8. Heat the oil in a non-stick frying pan.
9. Add the spring onions and kale and cook for 5 minutes.
10. Drain the cooked brown rice and mix this with the kale and spring onions.
11. Serve with the cooked salmon, drizzled with excess marinade.

"
I cooked this recipe for friends. I felt so proud being able to serve a delicious meal that I also felt comfortable eating myself. Perhaps there's life after an eating disorder after all!

E – recovering from an eating disorder
"

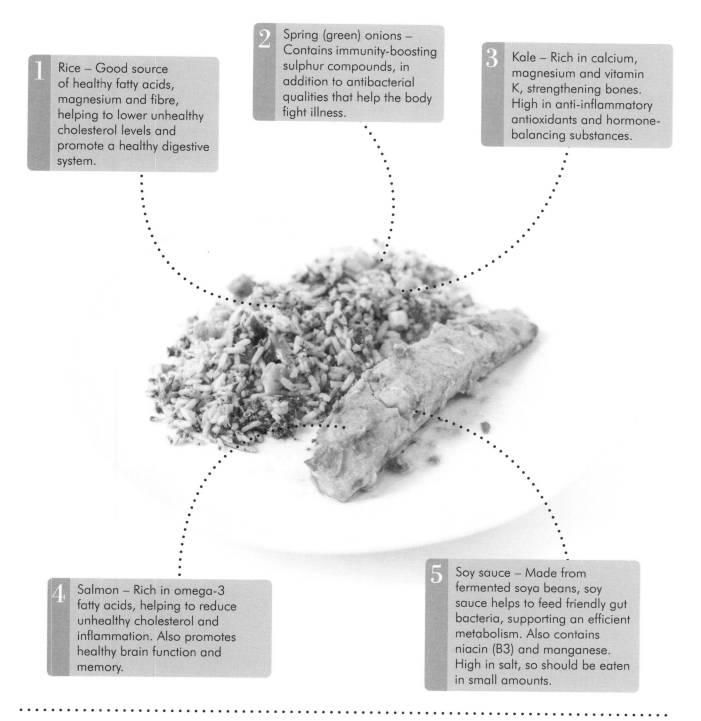

1 Rice – Good source of healthy fatty acids, magnesium and fibre, helping to lower unhealthy cholesterol levels and promote a healthy digestive system.

2 Spring (green) onions – Contains immunity-boosting sulphur compounds, in addition to antibacterial qualities that help the body fight illness.

3 Kale – Rich in calcium, magnesium and vitamin K, strengthening bones. High in anti-inflammatory antioxidants and hormone-balancing substances.

4 Salmon – Rich in omega-3 fatty acids, helping to reduce unhealthy cholesterol and inflammation. Also promotes healthy brain function and memory.

5 Soy sauce – Made from fermented soya beans, soy sauce helps to feed friendly gut bacteria, supporting an efficient metabolism. Also contains niacin (B3) and manganese. High in salt, so should be eaten in small amounts.

Tuna, Sweetcorn and Broccoli Bake

A comforting, wholesome bake that aids healthy digestion, cell growth and repair. A great recipe to batch cook and store for later use, served hot or cold.

Total time: 00:30   Preparation time: 00:05   Cooking time: 00:25   Serves: 4

Ingredients

- Approx. 300g (10.5oz) wholewheat pasta
- 1 head of broccoli
- 1 can of sweetcorn (approx. 200g/scant cup)
- 1 can of tuna (approx 150g/5.5oz)
- Approx. 200ml (scant cup) milk of your choice
- 8–10 tablespoons of cream cheese
- Pinch of salt and pepper
- 1–2 slices of bread
- 1 clove of garlic (skin removed)

Equipment

- Oven
- Oven hob (stovetop)
- Non-stick saucepan
- Food processor
- Colander
- Baking dish
- Kitchen scales
- Measuring jug/cup
- Chopping board
- Can opener
- Sharp knife
- Wooden spoon

Instructions

1. Preheat the oven to 180–200°C (350–400°F/Gas 4–6).
2. Half fill a non-stick saucepan with water and bring to the boil.
3. Add the pasta to the water and cook on a medium-high heat for 6 minutes.
4. Cut the broccoli into individual florets, adding these to the water.
5. Cook for a further 2 minutes.
6. Drain the pasta and broccoli and place into a baking dish, along with the sweetcorn and tuna.
7. Place the milk, cream cheese, salt and pepper into the hot saucepan and heat through, stirring continuously until combined.
8. Add the sauce to the baking dish and stir everything together.
9. Place the bread and garlic in a food processor and blend into breadcrumbs.
10. Sprinkle the breadcrumbs on top of the other ingredients and bake for 10 minutes.
11. Remove from the oven and serve immediately.

Hints and tips

- Choose wholewheat pasta, or experiment with rice or millet pastas.
- A great meal containing a variety of ingredients, and therefore nutrients, in one dish.
- Add cooked peas before baking, if desired.

> " I really like this meal. It's great to find a recipe that makes it easy to include vegetables and fish. I've cooked this for the whole family, and even the kids like it. I feel satisfied after I've eaten it, which means that I'm less likely to reach for extra food later in the evening. "
>
> Jacob – recovering from over-eating

1 Pasta – Good source of carbohydrate and fibre, promoting digestive health. Choose wholewheat pasta for maximum benefits.

2 Sweetcorn – Contains nutrients that promote eye health. High-fibre content promotes a healthy digestive tract and helps to control blood sugar levels.

3 Tuna – An excellent source of protein, selenium, magnesium, potassium and omega-3 fatty acids. Also contains B vitamins, aiding heart health.

4 Cream cheese – A great source of protein, aiding cell growth and repair. Contains good levels of calcium, supporting healthy bones, teeth and nails.

5 Broccoli – High in vitamin C and beta-carotene, aiding good skin and a healthy immune system.

Lemon, Basil and Pea Spaghetti

A refreshing high-fibre pasta dish, rich in protein and complex carbohydrates. Naturally flavoured with lemon, basil and Parmesan.

Total time: 00:15   Preparation time: 00:03   Cooking time: 00:12   Serves: 1

Ingredients

- Approx. 75g (2.5oz) wholewheat spaghetti
- 3 heaped tablespoons of peas
- 1 teaspoon of olive oil
- Pinch of salt and pepper
- Juice of ½ lemon
- Approx. 30g (1oz) Parmesan cheese
- 1 handful of fresh basil leaves

Equipment

- Oven hob (stovetop)
- Non-stick saucepan
- Colander
- Cling film (plastic wrap)
- Chopping board
- Grater
- Sharp knife
- Wooden spoon
- Teaspoon
- Tablespoon

Hints and tips

- Choose wholewheat pasta over white varieties to benefit from a slower release of energy and additional nutrients and fibre.
- Enthusiastic cooks may like to add spiralised courgette (zucchini) to this recipe.

Instructions

1. Half fill a non-stick saucepan with water and bring to the boil.
2. Add the spaghetti, bring back to the boil, and simmer for 4–5 minutes.
3. Add the peas, bring back to the boil and simmer for a further 4–5 minutes, or until the pasta is cooked to preference.
4. Drain the pasta and peas, placing it back in the warm saucepan afterwards.
5. Cut the lemon in half. Wrap one half in cling film and place in the fridge for later use.
6. Add the olive oil, salt and pepper to the pasta, along with the juice of half the lemon, and stir through.
7. Serve on a plate or pasta bowl.
8. Grate the Parmesan on top.
9. Sprinkle with fresh basil leaves.

> "When I'm cooking, I play relaxing music to help distract my thoughts. Sometimes I listen to the radio or even watch TV. I know that some people would argue that I should be paying more attention to my food, but for the moment, I need the mental distractions. One step at a time.
>
> S – overcoming body-image issues"

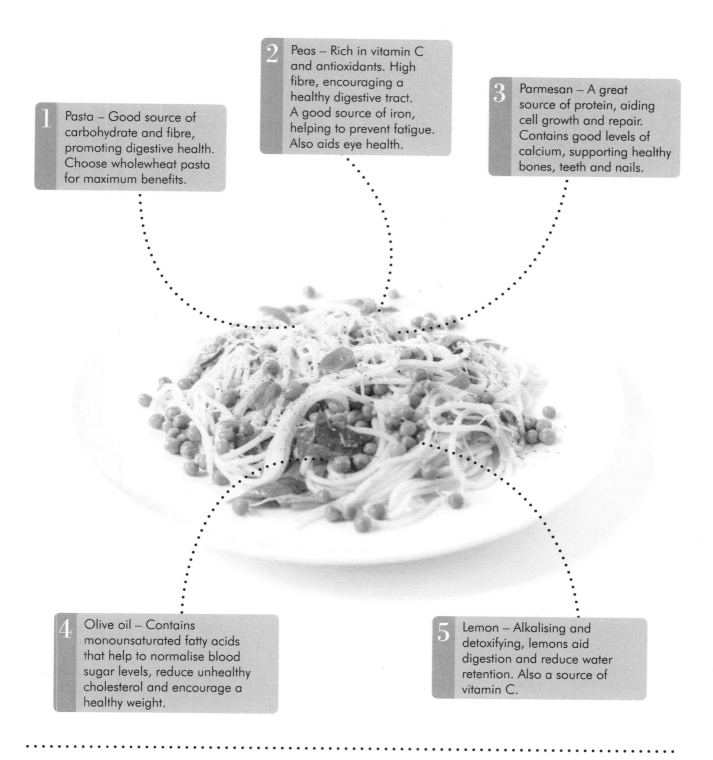

1 Pasta – Good source of carbohydrate and fibre, promoting digestive health. Choose wholewheat pasta for maximum benefits.

2 Peas – Rich in vitamin C and antioxidants. High fibre, encouraging a healthy digestive tract. A good source of iron, helping to prevent fatigue. Also aids eye health.

3 Parmesan – A great source of protein, aiding cell growth and repair. Contains good levels of calcium, supporting healthy bones, teeth and nails.

4 Olive oil – Contains monounsaturated fatty acids that help to normalise blood sugar levels, reduce unhealthy cholesterol and encourage a healthy weight.

5 Lemon – Alkalising and detoxifying, lemons aid digestion and reduce water retention. Also a source of vitamin C.

Veg Stir-Fried Noodles with Prawns

A quick and easy meal full of colourful ingredients, bursting with vitamins and minerals. Simple to prepare and cook, ready in just minutes. Experiment with a variety of stir-fry vegetables, according to your preference.

Total time: 00:15   Preparation time: 00:05   Cooking time: 00:10   Serves: 2

Ingredients

- 1 yellow pepper
- 1 courgette (zucchini)
- ½ red onion
- ½ head of broccoli
- 2 cloves of garlic (skin removed)
- Approx. 150g (5.5oz) egg or rice noodles
- 1 tablespoon of oil
- Approx. 100g (3.5oz) mangetout (snow peas)
- Approx. 150g (5.5oz) precooked prawns (shrimps)
- 1–2 tablespoons of soy sauce

Optional: sesame seeds and/or sliced fresh red chilli or dried chilli flakes

Equipment

- Oven hob (stovetop)
- Non-stick wok or frying pan
- Kettle
- Kitchen scales
- Colander
- Mixing bowl
- Chopping board
- Sharp knife
- Tablespoon

Instructions

1. Chop the yellow pepper, courgette, red onion, broccoli and garlic into thin strips.
2. Place the noodles into a mixing bowl, cover with boiling water and leave to soak for 5 minutes.
3. Heat the oil in a large wok or non-stick frying pan on a high heat.
4. Add the sliced vegetables, mangetout and garlic to the oil.
5. Stir-fry for 2–3 minutes, or until the vegetables are cooked to preference.
6. Drain the noodles.
7. Add the prawns, noodles and soy sauce to the wok/frying pan and stir-fry for a further 2–3 minutes.
8. Add the sesame seeds and/or chilli, if using.
9. Serve immediately.

Hints and tips

- Alternatively, cook chicken with the stir-fry rather than prawns.
- Eating an array of colours in your diet encourages the consumption of a variety of vitamins and minerals, promoting good health.

> "When I was restricting, I would eat a basic stir-fried vegetable dish quite often. I've learnt that including a protein and carbohydrate source will actually help to re-establish a healthy metabolism and maintain some muscle tone. So now I add prawns or chicken and some noodles too, knowing that they are good for my body."
>
> Isabelle – recovering from anorexia

1　Rice noodles – Good source of healthy fatty acids, magnesium and fibre, helping to lower unhealthy cholesterol levels and promote a healthy digestive system.

2　Courgette (zucchini) – Contains high levels of water, aiding water balance and bowel regularity. Good source of vitamin C, magnesium, folate and potassium.

3　Prawns – A complete protein, containing all nine essential amino acids. Also include omega-3 and omega-6, associated with a lowered risk of heart disease.

4　Soy sauce – Made from fermented soya beans, soy sauce helps to feed friendly gut bacteria, supporting an efficient metabolism. Also contains niacin (B3) and manganese.

5　Broccoli – High in vitamin C and beta-carotene, aiding good skin and a healthy immune system.

Sweetcorn Salsa with Chicken

A high-fibre flavoursome dinner, which is a great source of zinc, potassium, iron and B vitamins. Batch cook and store the salsa for later use, either hot or cold. Colourful and nutritious.

Total time: 00:15   Preparation time: 00:05   Cooking time: 00:10   Serves: 1

Ingredients

- ½ courgette (zucchini)
- 1 sweet potato
- 3 spring (green) onions
- 1 red chilli
- 1 handful of fresh coriander (cilantro) leaves
- ½ can of sweetcorn (approx. 200g/scant cup)
- Pinch of salt and pepper
- Zest and juice of a lime
- 1 chicken breast
- 1 teaspoon of oil
- ½ teaspoon of paprika

Instructions

1. Grate the courgette and sweet potato into a mixing bowl.
2. Finely slice the spring onion, red chilli pepper and coriander leaves, adding these to the mixing bowl.
3. Add the sweetcorn, salt and pepper and zest and juice of a lime.
4. Transfer the mixture to a non-stick saucepan and cook on a low-medium heat for 3–4 minutes.
5. Coat the chicken breast in the oil and paprika.
6. Cook the chicken in a non-stick frying pan for approximately 4–5 minutes each side, or until fully cooked through to the centre.
7. Serve the chicken and salsa straight away or refrigerate for later use.

Equipment

- Oven hob (stovetop)
- Non-stick frying pan
- Non-stick saucepan
- Mixing bowl
- Chopping board
- Can opener
- Grater
- Fine grater/zester
- Sharp knife
- Teaspoon

Hints and tips

- The sweetcorn salsa is also delicious served with fish.
- Experiment with a variety of spices, according to your preference.
- Canned and frozen vegetables retain vitamins and minerals well.

> " I am actually really scared of carbohydrates, especially in the form of bread, rice, pasta and potatoes. I know that vegetables contain carbohydrate too, but somehow they are less scary. I'm trying to introduce sweet potatoes into my diet, so this recipe is helpful – grating the sweet potato makes it less daunting. I know I need to introduce even more variety, and I will try. "
>
> B – recovering from anorexia

1 Chicken – A good source of zinc, iron, potassium and phosphorus, helping to build strong bones, teeth and muscles. Also rich in B vitamins, aiding the nervous system.

2 Sweetcorn – Contains nutrients that promote eye health. High-fibre content promotes a healthy digestive tract and helps to control blood sugar levels.

3 Red chilli – Aids the removal of toxins, stimulates digestion and boosts metabolism. Also helps to clear congestion.

4 Coriander (cilantro) – Aids digestion and the immune system. Can also help to alleviate nausea and stomach cramps. Aids the regulation of healthy blood sugar levels.

5 Sweet potato – Provides slow-release energy. Rich in vitamin C and beta-carotene, encouraging healthy skin and boosting the immune system.

Pitta Pizza

A simple meal made using either passata/tomato sauce or homemade pizza/pasta sauce –
see page 258 for recipe details. Serve with mixed salad leaves and the addition of extra pizza
toppings, as preferred.

Total time: 00:10   Preparation time: 00:05   Cooking time: 00:05   Serves: 1

Ingredients

- 1 wholemeal (wholewheat) pitta
- 3 tablespoons of pizza/pasta sauce (see page 258) or passata/tomato sauce
- 2 tablespoons of sweetcorn
- Approx. 30g (1oz) cheese
- 1 handful of mixed salad leaves
- 3 cherry tomatoes

Optional: portion of fish or meat on top of the pitta pizza (for example anchovies, tuna, ham)

Instructions

1. Preheat the grill to a medium heat.
2. Grill one side of the pitta bread.
3. Add the pizza/pasta sauce (or passata/tomato sauce) on the untoasted side of the pitta bread.
4. Add the sweetcorn evenly.
5. Add optional toppings, if using.
6. Grate the cheese on top.
7. Return to the grill to melt the cheese.
8. Serve with a handful of mixed salad leaves and a few cherry tomatoes.

Equipment

- Grill (broiler)
- Grater
- Tablespoon

Hints and tips

- Choose wholemeal pitta rather than white varieties to benefit from additional nutrients and fibre.
- Personalise the pitta pizza topping according to your preferences – try to include an element of protein, for example meat, fish or dairy.
- The homemade pizza/pasta sauce mentioned on page 258 includes a variety of vegetables.

> "Such a quick, simple idea. I keep some of the pizza/pasta sacue in the fridge ready to add to pasta or pitta breads. I like to add a topping of red pepper and olives. This weekend, a friend is coming over to support me in making a whole pizza, using the simple quick bread recipe on page 252. I'm nervous but also hope it'll be kind of fun.
>
> Jenni – recovering from anorexia

1 Pizza/pasta sauce – Contains a variety of high fibre, antioxidant-rich vegetables, tomato and herbs – see page 258 for recipe.

2 Wholemeal (wholewheat) pitta – A great source of complex carbohydrate, offering slow-release energy. High in fibre, aiding digestive health. Often fortified with folate and B vitamins.

3 Mixed salad – Include a variety of mixed leaves to benefit from various vitamins and minerals, such as vitamin C and iron. Rich in fibre and antioxidants, aiding digestion and the immune system.

4 Cheese – A great source of protein, aiding cell growth and repair. Contains good levels of calcium, supporting healthy bones, teeth and nails.

5 Sweetcorn – Contains nutrients that promote eye health. High-fibre content promotes a healthy digestive tract and helps to control blood sugar levels.

Avocado, Egg, Salmon and Lentils

A wonderful salad rich in omega-3 and B vitamins. Batch cook and store extra portions in the fridge for later use. See page 268 for a selection of salad dressings that would enhance the flavour and nutritional value of this dish.

Total time: 00:15   Preparation time: 00:05   Cooking time: 00:10   Serves: 1

Ingredients

- 2 free-range eggs
- ½ avocado
- 1 precooked salmon fillet
- Approx. 75g (⅓ cup) precooked puy lentils
- 1 handful of mixed salad leaves (for example spinach, watercress, rocket (arugula))
- 1 teaspoon of olive oil
- Juice of ½ lemon
- Pinch salt and pepper

Equipment

- Oven hob (stovetop)
- Saucepan
- Cling film (plastic wrap)
- Chopping board
- Sharp knife
- Teaspoon

Instructions

1. Half fill a saucepan with water and bring to the boil.
2. Place the eggs into the water and boil for 8 minutes.
3. Drain the eggs and cover with cold water (to cool the shell enough to handle).
4. Peel and discard the shell and slice the eggs into quarters.
5. Prepare the avocado by slicing it in half lengthways, remove the central seed and peel the skin away from the half being used in the recipe. Place the other half in the fridge, wrapped in cling film for later use.
6. Finally, cut the avocado lengthways, into approximately 4 slices.
7. Tear the salmon into bite sized pieces.
8. Combine the puy lentils, salmon, avocado and mixed salad leaves.
9. Add the hard-boiled egg quarters on top.
10. Combine the olive oil, lemon, salt and pepper, and drizzle over everything else to serve.

Hints and tips

- Organic free-range eggs contain higher levels of vitamin A, omega-3 and vitamin E than other varieties.
- Do not eat uncooked lentils – they must be soaked and cooked first.
- Canned and pouched lentils have already been cooked so can be used straight away.
- Use whichever lentils and salad leaves you prefer.

"

This is one of my favourite meals. Everything about the dish feels fresh, natural and satisfying. I add a dressng of olive oil and lemon and make extra boiled eggs for use the next day. Delicious.

"

Becky – overcoming body-image issues

1 Smoked salmon – Rich in omega-3 fatty acids, helping to reduce unhealthy cholesterol levels, blood pressure and inflammation. Also thought to help prevent memory loss.

2 Eggs – Good source of protein, vitamin D and phosphorus, aiding strong bones and teeth. Excellent source of B vitamins and choline, boosting mental performance.

3 Puy lentils – Rich in molybdenum and iron, aiding oxygenation of the blood. Rich in vitamin B1, aiding the nervous system, and helps to maintain a steady heartbeat.

4 Avocado – A great source of omega-3 and other healthy fats that help to lubricate joints, reduce arthritic symptoms and boost fertility. Rich in vitamin A, vital for eye and brain health, immunity and digestion.

5 Mixed salad – Include a variety of mixed leaves to benefit from various vitamins and minerals, such as vitamin C and iron. Rich in fibre and antioxidants, aiding digestion and the immune system.

Veg Couscous with Spiced Chicken

A comforting meal, delicious hot or cold, combining chicken, pulses and vegetables for an array of nutritional benefits. Prepared in just 10 minutes, plus cooking time.

Total time: 00:45   Preparation time: 00:10   Cooking time: 00:35   Serves: 2

Ingredients

- 1 courgette (zucchini)
- 1 red onion
- 1 sweet potato
- 1 tablespoon of oil
- 2 chicken breasts
- 3 tablespoons of plain/Greek yoghurt
- 1 teaspoon of cayenne pepper
- 2 teaspoons of bouillon/stock powder
- 200ml (scant cup) water
- 100g (heaped ½ cup) couscous
- ½ can of chickpeas (approx. 200g/scant cup)
- 1 handful of parsley
- Pinch of salt and pepper

Equipment

- Oven
- Non-stick baking tray
- Kettle
- Mixing bowl
- Cling film (plastic wrap)
- Chopping board
- Can opener
- Sharp knife
- Tablespoon
- Teaspoon
- Measuring jug/cup
- Large serving dish

Hints and tips

- Enjoy full-fat, natural and plain probiotic yoghurts for maximum benefit.
- Chickpeas are a great source of vegetarian protein.
- Ensure the chicken is fully cooked through before eating it. Uncooked chicken can be dangerous.

Instructions

1. Preheat the oven to 180–200°C (350–400°F/Gas 4–6).
2. Chop the courgette, red onion and sweet potato (skin on or off, according to your preference) into bite-size pieces.
3. Add the oil and chopped vegetables to a baking tray, stirring to ensure a light covering of oil.
4. Bake in the oven for 15 minutes.
5. Whilst the vegetables are cooking, marinate the chicken breasts in the yoghurt and cayenne pepper for 10 minutes.
6. Remove the baking tray from the oven, add the chicken and continue cooking for a further 20–25 minutes (or until the chicken is cooked through).
7. Whilst the chicken and vegetables are cooking, boil with the water, and combine with the stock in a measuring jug/cup.
8. Evenly spread the couscous and chickpeas in the bottom of a large serving dish, in as thin a layer a possible.
9. Add the water and cover with cling film for approximately 15 minutes.
10. Once the water has been absorbed, fluff the couscous with a fork.
11. Sprinkle a handful of parsley over the couscous, adding the baked vegetables and chicken on top.
12. Add salt and pepper, as preferred.
13. Serve warm or refrigerate for future use.

> It helps to remind myself that a plate full of rainbow colours provides a variety of vitamins and minerals. I keep telling myself that eating protein will help me to build strong, lean muscles.
>
> M – recovering from over-eating

1 Chicken – A good source of zinc, iron, potassium and phosphorus, helping to build strong bones, teeth and muscles. Also rich in B vitamins, aiding the nervous system.

2 Chickpeas – Contains manganese, calcium, phosphorus and magnesium, promoting bone health. High in fibre, which aids a reduction in unhealthy cholesterol levels.

3 Couscous – Good source of carbohydrate and protein. Contains potassium, aiding heart health and water balance, and selenium, protecting against premature ageing.

4 Yoghurt – Contains immune-boosting probiotics that support a healthy gut. Linked with maintenance of a healthy, stable weight.

5 Parsley – Rich in antioxidants that help reduce congestion. Contains vitamin K, supporting healthy bones. Also thought to help relieve constipation.

Beef Burrito

A heart-healthy recipe balancing macro- and micro-nutrients rich in iron and B vitamins. Suitable for breakfast, lunch or dinner, served with mixed salad leaves. Consider using a mixture of beans to further enhance the nutritional benefits of this recipe.

Total time: 00:25   Preparation time: 00:05   Cooking time: 00:20   Serves: 2

Ingredients

- 1 teaspoon of oil
- Approx. 200g (7oz) minced (ground) beef (or vegetarian mince)
- 1 red onion
- 1 red pepper
- 1 carrot
- 1 fresh red chilli/1 teaspoon of dried chilli flakes
- 2 cloves of garlic (skin removed)
- 1 can of chopped tomatoes (approx. 400g/1¾ cups)
- 1 can of red kidney beans (approx. 400g/1¾ cups)
- Pinch of salt and pepper
- 2 wholemeal (wholewheat) wraps
- Approx. 60g (2oz) cheese

Equipment

- Oven hob (stovetop)
- Non-stick saucepan
- Non-stick frying pan
- Kitchen scales
- Chopping board
- Sharp knife
- Teaspoon
- Can opener

Instructions

1. Heat the oil in a non-stick saucepan.
2. Add the minced meat and cook for 5 minutes, or until sealed/browned.
3. Chop the red onion, red pepper, carrot, red chilli and garlic cloves, adding these to the meat and cooking for a further 5 minutes.
4. Add the chopped tomatoes and red kidney beans and cook for 10 minutes.
5. Add salt and pepper, as preferred.
6. Warm the wraps in a dry non-stick frying pan or the microwave.
7. Place the wraps on 2 plates and share the mixture onto the wraps.
8. Grate the cheese on top, fold or roll the wraps and serve.

Hints and tips

- The filling can be batch cooked and stored in the freezer, but use fresh wraps when serving.
- A great recipe to make in a slow cooker.
- Add additional vegetables or spices to the meat mix, as preferred.
- For a vegetarian option, replace the meat with quinoa or mixed beans.

"Sometimes beans and onions can make my tummy feel bloated. I have to remind myself that this is just a natural reaction to some foods and that the bloating will soon subside. I just keep breathing and allow myself time to digest and relax.

E – recovering from an eating disorder"

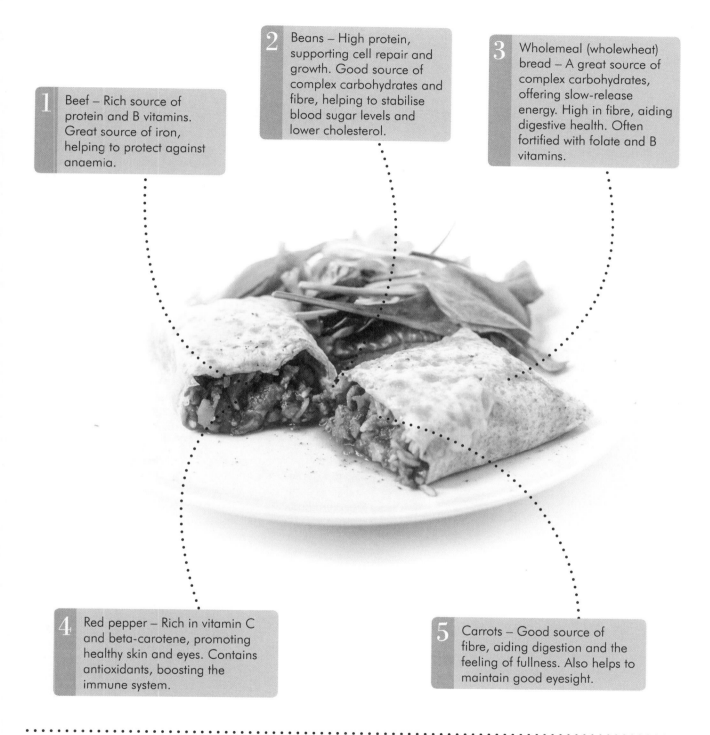

1 Beef – Rich source of protein and B vitamins. Great source of iron, helping to protect against anaemia.

2 Beans – High protein, supporting cell repair and growth. Good source of complex carbohydrates and fibre, helping to stabilise blood sugar levels and lower cholesterol.

3 Wholemeal (wholewheat) bread – A great source of complex carbohydrates, offering slow-release energy. High in fibre, aiding digestive health. Often fortified with folate and B vitamins.

4 Red pepper – Rich in vitamin C and beta-carotene, promoting healthy skin and eyes. Contains antioxidants, boosting the immune system.

5 Carrots – Good source of fibre, aiding digestion and the feeling of fullness. Also helps to maintain good eyesight.

Sweet Potato, Chicken and Spinach

A well-balanced meal providing slow-release energy from protein, healthy fats and garlicky vitamin-rich leaves. Replace the chicken with fish, if preferred.

Total time: 00:30   Preparation time: 00:10   Cooking time: 00:20   Serves: 1

Ingredients

- 1 potato/sweet potato
- 1 chicken breast
- 1 free-range egg
- 1–2 tablespoons of ground almonds
- 1 teaspoon of paprika
- Pinch of salt and pepper
- 1 clove of garlic (skin removed)
- 1–2 handfuls of spinach
- Approx. 1 teaspoon of butter

Optional: black onion seeds

Equipment

- Oven
- Oven hob (stovetop)
- Grill (broiler)
- 2 non-stick saucepans
- 2 mixing bowls
- Vegetable peeler
- Fork
- Teaspoon
- Sharp knife
- Chopping board
- Colander
- Potato masher

Hints and tips

- The process used to coat the chicken can also be used to coat fish or tofu.
- Also delicious served with peas or broccoli, if preferred.
- Keep the sweet potato skin on the mash for additional nutrients and fibre.
- Ensure the chicken is fully cooked through before eating (it is dangerous to eat raw chicken).

Instructions

1. Half fill a non-stick saucepan with water and bring to the boil.
2. Peel and then chop the potato into bite-size pieces, adding these to the water.
3. Simmer on a medium-high heat for 15 minutes, or until soft enough to mash.
4. Whilst the potato is cooking, cut the chicken into bite-size pieces.
5. Break the egg into a mixing bowl and beat with a fork.
6. Combine the ground almonds, paprika, salt and pepper (and black onion seeds, if using) in a separate mixing bowl.
7. Mix the chicken pieces in the egg.
8. Remove the chicken from the egg and place in the almond mixture, ensuring they are completely coated.
9. Place the individual chicken pieces under the grill on a medium heat, for 10 minutes, turning halfway through cooking time.
10. While the potato and chicken are cooking, remove the skin from a garlic clove and finely chop.
11. Add the garlic and spinach to a non-stick saucepan on a medium heat.
12. Stir continuously, until the leaves are wilted and warm.
13. Drain and mash the potato with the butter, salt and pepper.
14. Serve with the chicken bites and wilted garlic spinach.

"
This recipe was really fun to make. I'd never thought of using eggs and almonds to coat my chicken or fish. The kids enjoyed taking part in the cooking too. I'll be doing this again!
"

Helen – recovering from bulimia

1 Eggs – Good source of protein, vitamin D and phosphorus, aiding strong bones and teeth. Excellent source of B vitamins and choline, boosting mental performance.

2 Chicken – A good source of zinc, iron, potassium and phosphorus, helping to build strong bones, teeth and muscles. Also rich in B vitamins, aiding the nervous system.

3 Sweet potato – Provides slow-release energy. Rich in vitamin C and beta-carotene, encouraging healthy skin and boosting the immune system.

4 Spinach – Contains high levels of vitamin K, supporting healthy bones. Also rich in anti-inflammatory substances.

5 Almonds – High in protein and a variety of minerals that support brain, cardiovascular and respiratory health.

Sea Bass, New Potatoes and Kale

A delicious meal that can be part-prepared in advance, and then baked altogether in one oven dish. This recipe is rich in omega-3 and potassium, aiding a healthy heart.

Total time: 00:30   Preparation time: 00:10   Cooking time: 00:20   Serves: 2

Ingredients

- 10 new potatoes
- 1 teaspoon of oil
- 1 handful of mushrooms
- ½ red onion
- 1 handful of kale
- 1 clove of garlic (skin removed)
- ½ teaspoon of fresh or dried thyme
- 2 sea bass fillets
- Zest and juice of ½ lemon
- ½ teaspoon fresh or dried rosemary
- Pinch of salt and pepper

Equipment

- Oven
- Oven hob (stovetop)
- Oven-proof dish
- Non-stick saucepan
- Non-stick frying pan
- Colander
- Chopping board
- Sharp knife
- Teaspoon
- Fine grater/zester

Instructions

1. Preheat the oven to 180–200°C (350–400°F/Gas 4–6).
2. Half fill a non-stick saucepan with water and bring to the boil.
3. Add the new potatoes and cook for 8 minutes, or until half cooked through.
4. Whilst the potatoes are boiling, heat the oil in a non-stick frying pan.
5. Slice the mushrooms, red onion, kale and garlic, adding these to the frying pan to sauté for 2–3 minutes, or until soft but not browned.
6. Drain the potatoes and then thickly slice them lengthways.
7. Place the potatoes, mushrooms, red onion, kale, garlic and thyme into an oven-proof dish.
8. Add the sea bass fillets, skin side up, on top of the vegetables.
9. Add the zest and juice of ½ the lemon on top of everything, along with the rosemary, salt and pepper, as preferred.
10. Bake for 8–10 minutes.
11. Serve immediately.

Hints and tips

- Buy sea bass frozen and thaw on the day of use.
- Alternatively, use a different white fish fillet, according to your preference and budget.
- New potatoes are thought to release energy slowly, making them a good choice.
- Fishmongers, within supermarkets or at farmers markets, are always happy to give you advice and prepare fish for you.

"

Whenever life is overwhelming, I feel flustered about food choices. My go-to 'safe foods' include fish and vegetables so this recipe is perfect for me.

"

E – overcoming body-image issues

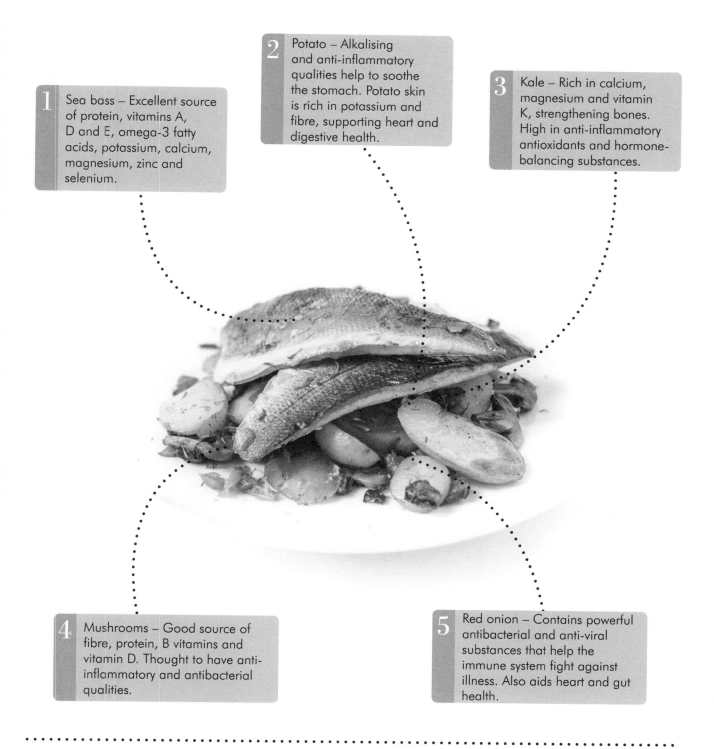

1 Sea bass – Excellent source of protein, vitamins A, D and E, omega-3 fatty acids, potassium, calcium, magnesium, zinc and selenium.

2 Potato – Alkalising and anti-inflammatory qualities help to soothe the stomach. Potato skin is rich in potassium and fibre, supporting heart and digestive health.

3 Kale – Rich in calcium, magnesium and vitamin K, strengthening bones. High in anti-inflammatory antioxidants and hormone-balancing substances.

4 Mushrooms – Good source of fibre, protein, B vitamins and vitamin D. Thought to have anti-inflammatory and antibacterial qualities.

5 Red onion – Contains powerful antibacterial and anti-viral substances that help the immune system fight against illness. Also aids heart and gut health.

Spaghetti and Meatballs

A simple, fun recipe requiring hands-on cooking, encouraging tactile experimentation with food. Ideally, the meatballs are served in a homemade pizza/pasta sauce containing a variety of vegetables – see page 258 for recipe.

Total time: 00:30   Preparation time: 00:10   Cooking time: 00:20   Serves: 2

Ingredients

- 1 clove of garlic (skin removed)
- Approx. 200g (7oz) minced (ground) beef or lamb
- 1 free-range egg
- Approx. 50g (1/3 cup) ground almonds
- Pinch of salt and pepper
- ½ teaspoon of dried parsley
- Approx. 150g (4.5oz) spaghetti
- 5 tablespoons of pizza/pasta sauce (see page 258) or passata/tomato sauce
- 1 teaspoon of olive oil

Optional: approx. 30g (1oz) Parmesan

Equipment

- Oven
- Oven hob (stovetop)
- Non-stick baking tray
- 2 non-stick saucepans
- Kitchen scales
- Mixing bowl
- Chopping board
- Sharp knife
- Tablespoon
- Teaspoon

Instructions

1. Preheat the oven to 180–200°C (350–400°F/Gas 4–6).
2. Finely chop the garlic.
3. Combine the meat, egg, ground almonds, garlic, parsley, salt and pepper in a mixing bowl.
4. Make 10 balls of the mixture using your hands.
5. Place the uncooked meatballs on a non-stick baking tray.
6. Bake for 15–18 minutes, or until cooked through.
7. Whilst the meatballs are cooking, half fill a non-stick saucepan with water and bring to the boil.
8. Add the spaghetti to the water, bring back to the boil and then simmer for 8–10 minutes.
9. Heat the pizza/pasta sauce in a separate saucepan for 2–3 minutes, or until warmed through.
10. Add the cooked meatballs to the pizza/pasta sauce.
11. Drain the cooked spaghetti and coat with olive oil.
12. Serve the meatballs in tomato sauce on top of the spaghetti and sprinkle with Parmesan, if using.

Hints and tips

- Choose wholewheat pasta, or experiment with rice or millet pastas.
- This recipe encourages hands-on cooking – being tactile with food might actually help you to feel more comfortable experimenting with it.
- Use whichever herbs you prefer.
- Consider adding sautéd onion to the meatballs before cooking.

"
I love getting my hands dirty in the kitchen and this recipe gives me permission to play with food! I buy quality meat from my local butcher and add extra garlic. Such fun to make and eat.
"

D – overcoming low self-esteem

1 Pasta – Good source of carbohydrate and fibre, promoting digestive health. Choose wholewheat pasta for maximum benefits.

2 Tomatoes – Good source of potassium, which aids the reduction of water retention. Also contains vitamins C, E and beta-carotene, supporting heart health.

3 Beef – Rich source of protein and B vitamins. Great source of iron, helping to protect against anaemia.

4 Parsley – Rich in antioxidants that help reduce congestion. Contains vitamin K, supporting healthy bones. Also thought to help relieve constipation.

5 Almonds – High in protein and a variety of minerals that support brain, cardiovascular and respiratory health.

Lentil Stuffed Peppers

A colourful dish including complementary flavours and texture that will excite taste buds. Delicious served with sweetcorn, or mixed salad leaves, as a lunch or dinner. This recipe can be cooked and eaten hot or cold.

Total time: 00:30   Preparation time: 00:05   Cooking time: 00:25   Serves: 1

Ingredients

- 1 red pepper
- 5 sundried tomatoes (from a jar/can)
- 2–3 artichoke hearts (from a jar/can)
- Approx. 30g (1oz) feta cheese
- 1 handful of fresh basil leaves
- Approx. 75g (1/3 cup) precooked puy lentils
- 2 tablespoons of balsamic vinegar
- 1 teaspoon of oil

Optional: sliced fresh red chilli or dried chilli flakes

Instructions

1. Preheat the oven to 180–200°C (350–400°F/Gas 4–6).
2. Cut the red pepper in half lengthways, removing the seeds with a tablespoon.
3. Place the red pepper (open side up) on a non-stick baking tray and bake for 10 minutes.
4. Whilst the red pepper is cooking, chop the sundried tomatoes, artichokes, feta and basil.
5. Combine with the puy lentils, balsamic vinegar, oil and chilli, if using.
6. Remove the red pepper halves from the oven and fill them with the lentil mixture.
7. Return to the oven to bake for a further 15 minutes.
8. Serve hot from the oven, or let it cool and eat later.

Equipment

- Oven
- Non-stick baking tray
- Mixing bowl
- Chopping board
- Sharp knife
- Tablespoon
- Teaspoon
- Can opener

Hints and tips

- Delicious accompanied by crisp sweetcorn and a side salad.
- Do not eat uncooked lentils – they must be soaked and cooked first.
- Canned or pouched lentils have already been cooked so can be used straight away.
- Also suitable as a lunch or side dish.

" Vegetarian, healthy food shouldn't have to be bland. This recipe is so tasty and really easy to make. I usually have the ingredients in my fridge and cupboard, so I return to this recipe again and again. If I make too much filling I simply store it in the fridge to have with salad the next day. "

E – recovering from an eating disorder

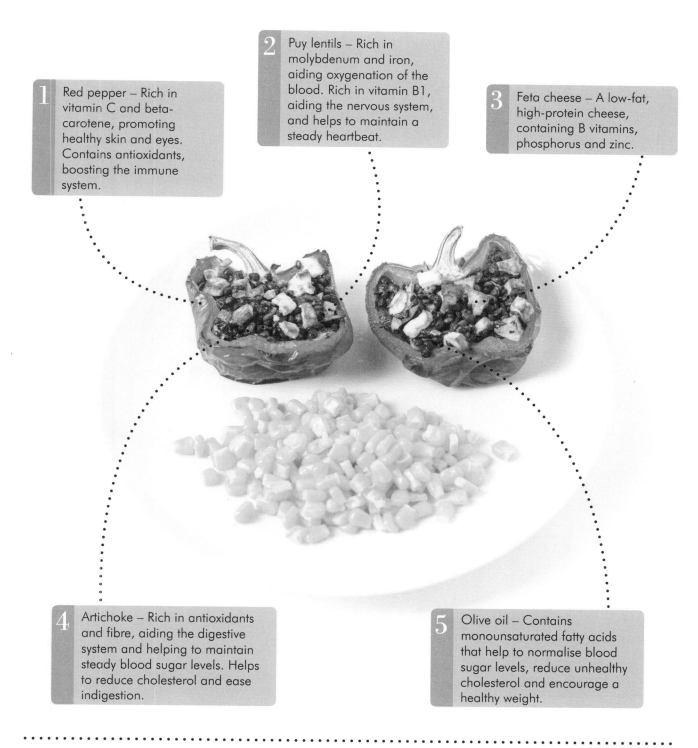

1 Red pepper – Rich in vitamin C and beta-carotene, promoting healthy skin and eyes. Contains antioxidants, boosting the immune system.

2 Puy lentils – Rich in molybdenum and iron, aiding oxygenation of the blood. Rich in vitamin B1, aiding the nervous system, and helps to maintain a steady heartbeat.

3 Feta cheese – A low-fat, high-protein cheese, containing B vitamins, phosphorus and zinc.

4 Artichoke – Rich in antioxidants and fibre, aiding the digestive system and helping to maintain steady blood sugar levels. Helps to reduce cholesterol and ease indigestion.

5 Olive oil – Contains monounsaturated fatty acids that help to normalise blood sugar levels, reduce unhealthy cholesterol and encourage a healthy weight.

Grilled Lamb Burger with Salad

A simple homemade burger served with a side salad and poached egg, challenging common misconceptions about healthy eating. Freshly made burgers can be frozen for later use, so batch cook extra portions for a convenient meal another time.

Total time: 00:15   **Preparation time:** 00:05   **Cooking time:** 00:10   **Serves:** 2

Ingredients

- 1 clove of garlic (skin removed)
- Approx. 200g (7oz) minced (ground) lamb
- 1 teaspoon of Dijon mustard
- 1 teaspoon of dried parsley
- 2 free-range eggs
- 2 wholemeal (wholewheat) rolls
- 2 handfuls of mixed salad leaves
- 6 cherry tomatoes
- Pinch of salt and pepper

Instructions

1. Peel and crush the garlic.
2. Combine the minced lamb, garlic, Dijon mustard and parsley.
3. Form the mixture into two burger patties (not too thick).
4. Cook the burgers on a non-stick frying pan or grill pan for 3–5 minutes each side, or until cooked through.
5. Whilst the burgers are cooking, half fill a non-stick saucepan with water and bring to the boil.
6. Carefully crack the free-range eggs into the water and poach until cooked to your preference.
7. Serve the lamb burgers in the wholemeal rolls, along with the eggs and a side of mixed salad leaves and tomatoes.
8. Add salt and pepper, as preferred.

Equipment

- Oven hob (stovetop)
- Non-stick frying pan/grill pan
- Non-stick saucepan
- Chopping board
- Mixing bowl
- Sharp knife
- Teaspoon

Hints and tips

- Uncooked lamb burgers can be stored in the fridge for use the next day, or stored in the freezer for up to a month.

> " Why go to a fast-food restaurant for a processed burger when you can make a much nicer, healthy version at home, personalised to your own likes and dislikes? I love the fact that I can enjoy a burger at home without any guilt! "
>
> Helen – recovering from bulimia

1 Mixed salad – Include a variety of mixed leaves to benefit from various vitamins and minerals, such as vitamin C and iron. Rich in fibre and antioxidants, aiding digestion and the immune system.

2 Wholemeal (wholewheat) bread – A great source of complex carbohydrates, offering slow-release energy. High in fibre, aiding digestive health. Often fortified with folate and B vitamins.

3 Eggs – Good source of protein, vitamin D and phosphorus, aiding strong bones and teeth. Excellent source of B vitamins and choline, boosting mental performance.

4 Parsley – Rich in antioxidants that help reduce congestion. Contains vitamin K, supporting healthy bones. Also thought to help relieve constipation.

5 Lamb – Rich in protein, B vitamins and folate, boosting the central nervous system and helping to protect against heart disease, mood disorders and dementia.

Roasted Veg with Garlic Chicken

Heartwarming root vegetables baked in tasty herbs, served with protein-rich garlic chicken and peas. This recipe is prepared in just 10 minutes, plus cooking time. Delicious served with gravy or horseradish sauce.

Total time: 00:45   Preparation time: 00:10   Cooking time: 00:35   Serves: 2

Ingredients

- 2 sweet potatoes
- 1 parsnip
- 1 carrot
- 1 onion
- 1½ tablespoons of oil
- ½ teaspoon of rosemary
- ½ teaspoon of thyme
- 2 chicken breasts
- ½ teaspoon of garlic powder
- 6 tablespoons of peas
- Pinch of salt and pepper

Equipment

- Oven
- Oven hob (stovetop)
- Non-stick baking tray
- Saucepan
- Chopping board
- Kitchen foil
- Sharp knife
- Tablespoon
- Teaspoon
- Colander
- Optional: vegetable peeler

Instructions

1. Preheat the oven to 180–200°C (350–400°F/Gas 4–6).
2. Peel the vegetables, if preferred.
3. Chop the sweet potato, parsnip, carrot and onion into bite-size pieces.
4. Add these to the baking tray, along with 1 tablespoon of oil, rosemary and thyme.
5. Bake in the oven for 30–35 minutes.
6. Whilst the vegetables are cooking, cover the chicken breasts with a little oil and garlic powder.
7. Wrap the chicken in kitchen foil.
8. Once the vegetables have cooked for 10–15 minutes, add the chicken to the oven to cook for 20 minutes, or until cooked through.
9. Ten minutes before the chicken and vegetables are ready, half fill a saucepan with water and bring to the boil.
10. Add the peas to the water, return to the boil, and simmer for 2–3 minutes.
11. Drain the peas and serve alongside the roasted vegetables and garlic chicken.
12. Add salt and pepper, as preferred.

Hints and tips

- Ensure that the chicken is fully cooked through before consuming.
- Also delicious served with broccoli.
- Add gravy, if desired.

" I find it easier to ask the butcher for one chicken breast rather than choosing one myself from the supermarket chiller. This way I avoid looking at the packaging, and so on. "

Alex – recovering from over-eating

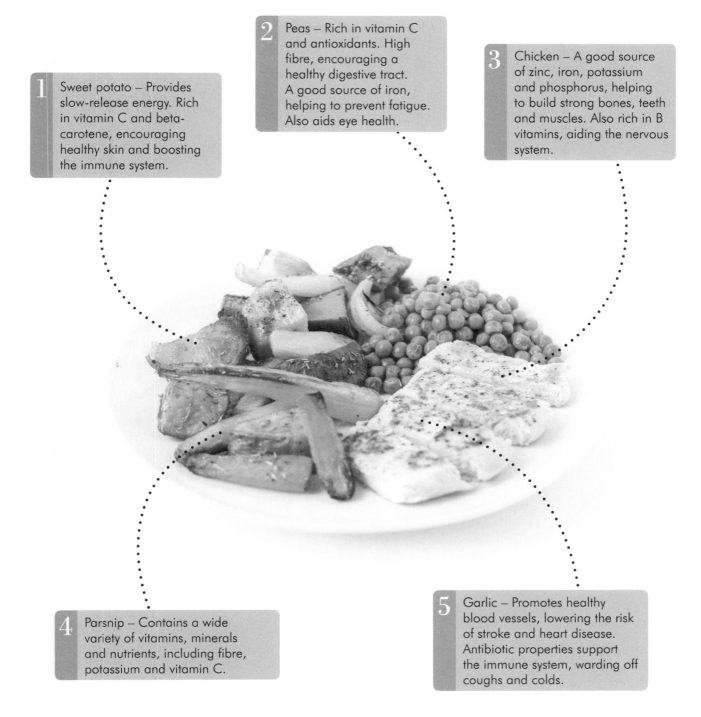

1 Sweet potato – Provides slow-release energy. Rich in vitamin C and beta-carotene, encouraging healthy skin and boosting the immune system.

2 Peas – Rich in vitamin C and antioxidants. High fibre, encouraging a healthy digestive tract. A good source of iron, helping to prevent fatigue. Also aids eye health.

3 Chicken – A good source of zinc, iron, potassium and phosphorus, helping to build strong bones, teeth and muscles. Also rich in B vitamins, aiding the nervous system.

4 Parsnip – Contains a wide variety of vitamins, minerals and nutrients, including fibre, potassium and vitamin C.

5 Garlic – Promotes healthy blood vessels, lowering the risk of stroke and heart disease. Antibiotic properties support the immune system, warding off coughs and colds.

Salmon, New Potatoes and Broccoli

A well-balanced meal served with a herby sauce made from crème fraîche/sour cream, basil, chives, parsley and lemon. This meal will aid digestion, promotes a healthy heart and support the immune system. Nutritious and delicious!

Total time: 00:30   Preparation time: 00:05   Cooking time: 00:25   Serves: 1

Ingredients

- 1 salmon fillet
- 5 new potatoes
- ½ head of broccoli
- ¼ can of sweetcorn (100g/½ cup)
- 1 handful of fresh chives
- 1 handful of fresh basil
- 1 handful of fresh parsley
- 3 tablespoons of crème fraîche/sour cream
- Juice of ½ a lemon
- Pinch of salt and pepper

Instructions

1. Preheat the oven to 180–200°C (350–400°F/Gas 4–6).
2. Wrap the salmon in a kitchen foil parcel, allowing some space around the fish.
3. Place the parcel in the oven and bake for 20–25 minutes.
4. In the meantime, half fill a steamer/non-stick saucepan with water and bring to the boil.
5. Cut the new potatoes to bite-size pieces and add to the water to cook for 10 minutes.
6. Cut the broccoli head into individual florets.
7. Cook the broccoli and sweetcorn in the steamer over the potatoes (or a separate saucepan half full of boiling water) for 4–5 minutes.
8. Finely chop the herbs.
9. Combine the crème fraîche/sour cream, herbs, lemon juice, salt and pepper.
10. Serve the fish, vegetables and herby sauce immediately.

Equipment

- Oven
- Oven hob (stovetop)
- Non-stick baking tray
- Kitchen steamer or 2 non-stick saucepans
- Mixing bowl
- Chopping board
- Kitchen foil
- Can opener
- Sharp knife
- Tablespoon

Hints and tips

- New potatoes are thought to release energy more slowly than other potatoes, making them a good choice.
- Salmon is a good source of omega oils, which can be stored in the body, but can't be synthesised, so should be consumed regularly.

> " Once I started to eat healthy meals and portion sizes I began to feel hungry every few hours. At first, this made me feel nervous and scared of eating too much. But now I feel reassured when my body tells me that it's hungry because this indicates that my metabolism is working well, helping me to stabilise my weight, health and emotions. "
>
> E – recovering from an eating disorder

1 Salmon – Rich in omega-3 fatty acids, helping to reduce unhealthy cholesterol and inflammation. Also promotes healthy brain function and memory.

2 Potato – Alkalising and anti-inflammatory qualities help to soothe the stomach. Potato skin is rich in potassium and fibre, supporting heart and digestive health.

3 Broccoli – High in vitamin C and beta-carotene, aiding good skin and a healthy immune system.

4 Sweetcorn – Contains nutrients that promote eye health. High-fibre content promotes a healthy digestive tract and helps to control blood sugar levels.

5 Basil – Reported to ease digestion and be a good remedy for headaches and insomnia.

Quinoa, Sundried Tomato and Feta

A high-protein recipe suitable for lunch or dinner. Also well received as a side dish alongside buffet-style foods. Batch cook and store in the fridge for later use.

Total time: 00:25   Preparation time: 00:10   Cooking time: 00:15   Serves: 1

Ingredients

- 100g (heaped ½ cup) quinoa
- 200ml (scant cup) water
- 1 teaspoon of bouillon/stock powder
- 6–8 sundried tomatoes
- Approx. 30g (1oz) feta cheese
- 1 handful of fresh basil leaves

Instructions

1. Thoroughly rinse the quinoa under cold water.
2. Place the quinoa into a non-stick saucepan, along with the water and stock.
3. Bring to the boil and then turn the heat down allowing the water to simmer for 15 minutes, stirring occasionally.
4. Whilst the quinoa is cooking, cut the sundried tomatoes and feta into bite-size pieces.
5. Once the quinoa is cooked and all the water has been absorbed, leave the grain to stand for 5 minutes before fluffing it up with a fork.
6. Combine the quinoa with the sundried tomatoes, feta and basil.

Equipment

- Oven hob (stovetop)
- Non-stick saucepan
- Kitchen scales
- Measuring jug/cup
- Mixing bowl
- Sharp knife
- Chopping board
- Wooden spoon
- Fork

Hints and tips

- Quinoa is a complete protein source suitable for vegetarians and vegans.
- Dried quinoa flakes are also great in breakfast cereals (available from health food shops and some major supermarkets).
- Experiment with different fresh herbs, according to your preference.
- Fresh herbs can be frozen for later use.

> " I'd heard that quinoa was a high-protein grain so I was intrigued to try this recipe. Adding the tomatoes, basil and feta gave the dish great taste and a variety of textures. I really like it! Eating this recipe makes me feel like I'm taking good care of myself, which is a skill I need to master.
>
> Nadia – overcoming low self-esteem

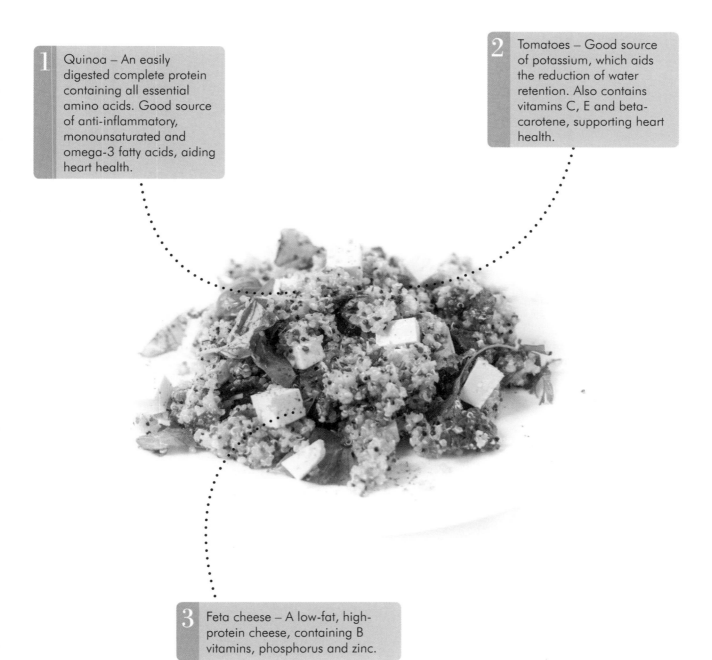

1 Quinoa – An easily digested complete protein containing all essential amino acids. Good source of anti-inflammatory, monounsaturated and omega-3 fatty acids, aiding heart health.

2 Tomatoes – Good source of potassium, which aids the reduction of water retention. Also contains vitamins C, E and beta-carotene, supporting heart health.

3 Feta cheese – A low-fat, high-protein cheese, containing B vitamins, phosphorus and zinc.

Fish Pie and Peas

This wholesome recipe includes six different vegetables in one dish! The high water content in the courgette (zucchini) and cabbage helps to create a healthy fish sauce below the tasty sweet potato mash. Delicious served with protein-rich peas or broccoli.

Total time: 00:50   Preparation time: 00:10   Cooking time: 00:40   Serves: 2

Ingredients

- 2 large sweet potatoes
- 1 leek
- ½ white cabbage
- 1 tablespoon of butter
- ½ can of sweetcorn (200g/scant cup)
- 1 courgette (zucchini)
- 1 carrot
- 2 tablespoons of cream cheese
- Approx. 325g (12oz) mixed fish, for example salmon, smoked haddock, cod or haddock
- 1 teaspoon of parsley
- Pinch of salt and pepper
- 1 tablespoon of milk
- 2 tablespoons of peas

Equipment

- Oven
- Oven hob (stovetop)
- Oven dish
- Saucepan
- Non-stick frying pan
- Grater
- Can opener
- Sharp knife
- Chopping board
- Wooden spoon
- Tablespoon
- Teaspoon
- Colander
- Potato masher
- Optional: vegetable peeler

Hints and tips

- This recipe is a great way of consuming numerous vegetables in one dish.
- Mixed fish chunks can be bought from supermarkets ready to cook.
- Use white potato mash, if preferred.
- Sprinkle with cheese before baking, if desired.
- Also delicious served with broccoli.

Instructions

1. Preheat the oven to 180–200°C (350–400°F/Gas 4–6).
2. Half fill a saucepan with water and bring to the boil.
3. Peel the sweet potatoes, as preferred.
4. Chop the sweet potatoes into small pieces and add these to the water.
5. Bring back to the boil and simmer for 12–14 minutes.
6. Whilst the potatoes are cooking, finely slice the leek and cabbage.
7. Heat the butter in a non-stick frying pan on a medium heat.
8. Add the leek, cabbage and sweetcorn to the butter and cook for 2–3 minutes.
9. Grate the courgette and carrot on top of the cabbage and leeks.
10. Add the cream cheese and stir until fully combined and starting to melt.
11. Transfer the vegetables into an oven dish.
12. Add the uncooked fish, parsley, salt and pepper and stir.
13. Drain and mash the sweet potatoes with the milk.
14. Spread the sweet potato mash on top of the fish and vegetables.
15. Bake for 25 minutes.
16. Refill the saucepan with water and boil the peas for 5 minutes before serving.

> " I make this recipe with my children on a regular basis. It's really fun to mix the fish and vegetables and mash the potato. Ultimately, this recipe combines fish and vegetables, which are my favourite foods. Healthy comfort food! "
>
> Emma

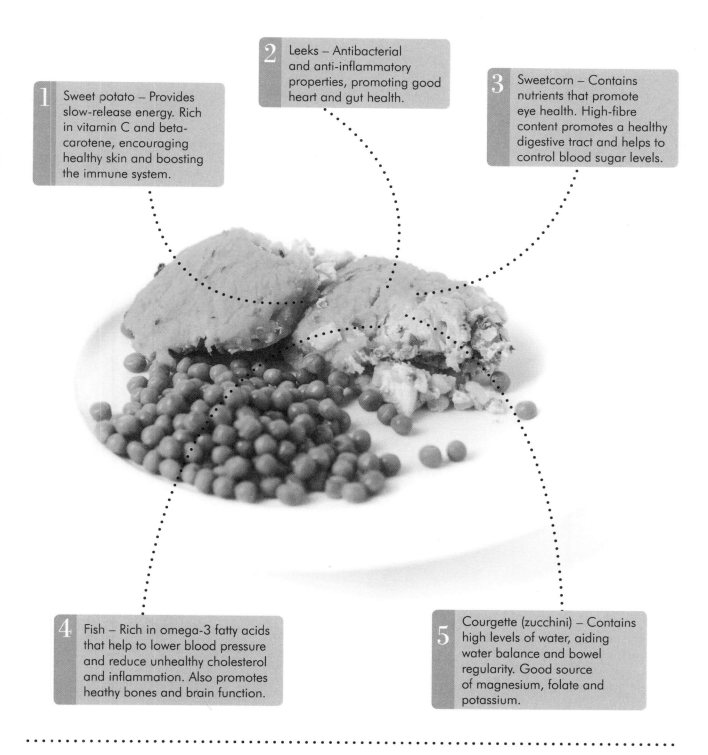

1 Sweet potato – Provides slow-release energy. Rich in vitamin C and beta-carotene, encouraging healthy skin and boosting the immune system.

2 Leeks – Antibacterial and anti-inflammatory properties, promoting good heart and gut health.

3 Sweetcorn – Contains nutrients that promote eye health. High-fibre content promotes a healthy digestive tract and helps to control blood sugar levels.

4 Fish – Rich in omega-3 fatty acids that help to lower blood pressure and reduce unhealthy cholesterol and inflammation. Also promotes heathy bones and brain function.

5 Courgette (zucchini) – Contains high levels of water, aiding water balance and bowel regularity. Good source of magnesium, folate and potassium.

SAVOURY SNACKS

Beetroot and Walnut Dip.. 190
Homemade Hummus with Crudités 192
Green Smoothie... 194
Artichoke and Cumin Dip... 196
Ratatouille 198
Pistachio Dukka.. 200
Smoked Salmon Stuffed Celery 202
Seeded Crackers 204
Guacamole 206
Rainbow Coleslaw 208
Boiled Egg and Tomato... 210
Root Vegetable Crisps 212
Lime and Pepper Cashew Nuts 214
Homemade Popcorn.. 216

Beetroot and Walnut Dip

A bright and delicious dip, perfect served with salad, crackers or vegetable crudités.
An excellent recipe to store in the fridge for snack times, also well received by guests. Made by placing all ingredients in a food processor, this recipe couldn't be much easier to make.

Total time: 00:10   Preparation time: 00:10   Cooking time: 00:00   Serves: 4

Ingredients

- 4–6 pre-cooked beetroots in natural juices
- Approx. 50g (⅓ cup) walnuts (or mixed seeds)
- Approx. 30g (1oz) feta cheese
- 1 tablespoon of red wine vinegar
- 1 tablespoon of olive oil
- 1 handful of fresh coriander (cilantro) leaves
- 1 handful of fresh parsley
- Pinch of salt and pepper

Optional: 1–2 cloves of garlic (skin removed)

Instructions

1. Place all of the ingredients into a food processor and blend until combined.
2. Serve immediately or store in the fridge for future use.

Equipment

- Food processor
- Tablespoon

Hints and tips

- The inclusion of nuts increases the amount of protein in this recipe.
- You can add natural Greek yoghurt instead of or as well as the nuts and feta, creating a creamier texture with a more subtle flavour.
- Some studies have suggested that beetroot can enhance the body's ability to uptake oxygen, relevant to sports performance.

> " This recipe couldn't be much easier to prepare and keeps really well in the fridge. It's great with salad or in a warm pitta bread. "
>
> Kate – supportive parent

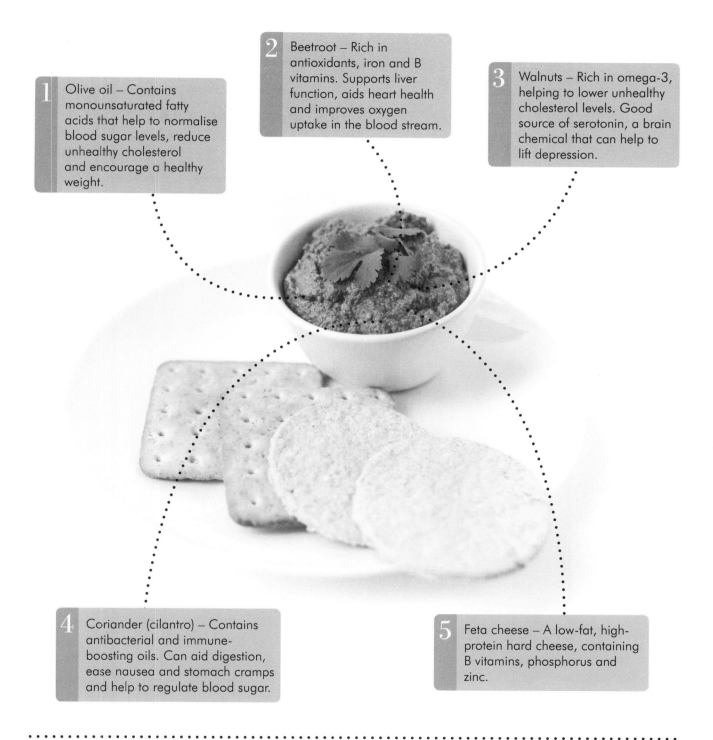

1 Olive oil – Contains monounsaturated fatty acids that help to normalise blood sugar levels, reduce unhealthy cholesterol and encourage a healthy weight.

2 Beetroot – Rich in antioxidants, iron and B vitamins. Supports liver function, aids heart health and improves oxygen uptake in the blood stream.

3 Walnuts – Rich in omega-3, helping to lower unhealthy cholesterol levels. Good source of serotonin, a brain chemical that can help to lift depression.

4 Coriander (cilantro) – Contains antibacterial and immune-boosting oils. Can aid digestion, ease nausea and stomach cramps and help to regulate blood sugar.

5 Feta cheese – A low-fat, high-protein hard cheese, containing B vitamins, phosphorus and zinc.

Homemade Hummus with Crudités

A wholesome chickpea dip bursting with ingredients that boost heart health and help to normalise blood sugar levels. Made from only natural ingredients, there is every reason to enjoy this snack on a regular basis.

Total time: 00:05   Preparation time: 00:05   Cooking time: 00:00   Serves: 2-4

Ingredients

- Juice and zest of ½ a lemon
- 1 can of chickpeas
- 3 tablespoons of olive oil
- 3 tablespoons of natural yoghurt
- 2 tablespoons of tahini
- 1–2 cloves of garlic (skin removed)
- Pinch of salt

Optional: spice of choice (for example cumin, cayenne pepper, paprika)

Instructions

1. Grate the zest of the lemon into a food processor.
2. Add the lemon juice.
3. Add all other ingredients and blend until smooth.
4. Serve with crudités/sliced raw vegetables, crackers or salad.

Equipment

- Food processor
- Can opener
- Chopping board
- Sharp knife
- Tablespoon
- Fine grater/zester

Hints and tips

- This recipe provides the information needed to make your own hummus, but it is equally fine for you to buy pre-made hummus. It would be emotionally unhealthy if you felt unable to eat food made by others so you should challenge yourself to have a variety of foods, from a variety of sources and venues. Everything in moderation, including moderation itself.

> Learning how to make hummus at home has made me feel comfortable to buy it from the shops. I regularly add it to salads and couscous dishes, but also like it with roasted vegetables in a sandwich.
>
> Charlie – recovering from anorexia

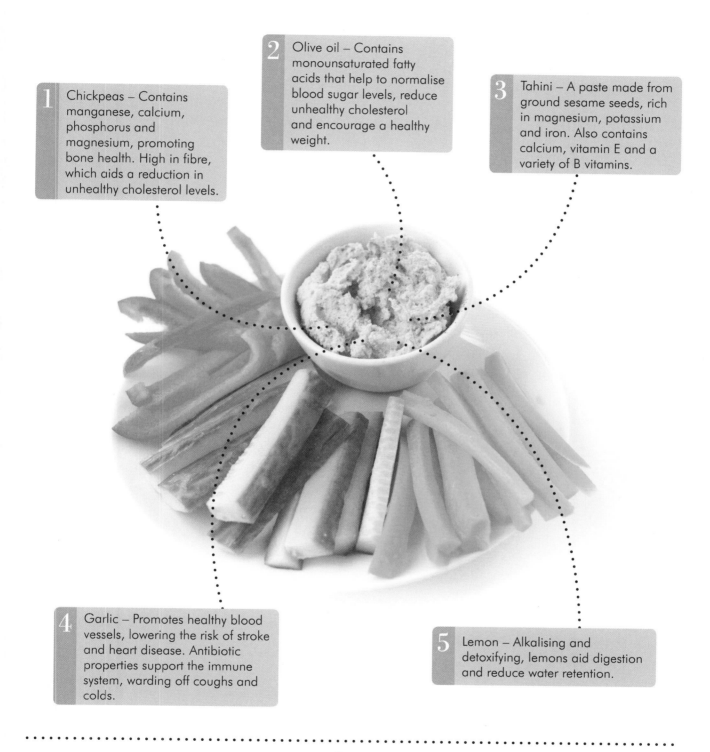

1 Chickpeas – Contains manganese, calcium, phosphorus and magnesium, promoting bone health. High in fibre, which aids a reduction in unhealthy cholesterol levels.

2 Olive oil – Contains monounsaturated fatty acids that help to normalise blood sugar levels, reduce unhealthy cholesterol and encourage a healthy weight.

3 Tahini – A paste made from ground sesame seeds, rich in magnesium, potassium and iron. Also contains calcium, vitamin E and a variety of B vitamins.

4 Garlic – Promotes healthy blood vessels, lowering the risk of stroke and heart disease. Antibiotic properties support the immune system, warding off coughs and colds.

5 Lemon – Alkalising and detoxifying, lemons aid digestion and reduce water retention.

Green Smoothie

A thirst-quenching smoothie that promotes a healthy immune system, soothes inflammation and boosts the metabolism. Rich in antioxidants and sweetened only by natural ingredients, this drink would be a suitable mid-morning or afternoon snack.

Total time: 00:05   Preparation time: 00:05   Cooking time: 00:00   Serves: 2

Ingredients

- 2 handfuls of spinach
- ½ glass of water/coconut water
- ½ banana
- ¼ pineapple (skin removed)
- ½ mango (skin removed)

Equipment

- Food processor

Instructions

1. Place all ingredients into a food processor and blend until smooth.
2. Serve immediately.

Hints and tips

- Fruit is rich in vitamins that promote health, but it is also naturally high in sugar, so should be eaten in moderation. On average, 1–2 portions of fruit per day would be a healthy recommendation. This smoothie would be considered as 1–2 portions.
- Experiment with a variety of different fruits and vegetables in smoothies, as preferred.

" Drinking this smoothie means that I've had my daily fruit portions but also had some green veg. It's also good to know that the banana and coconut water help to stabilise the water balance in my body, which is something I know is affected by purging. "

Lesley – recovering from bulimia

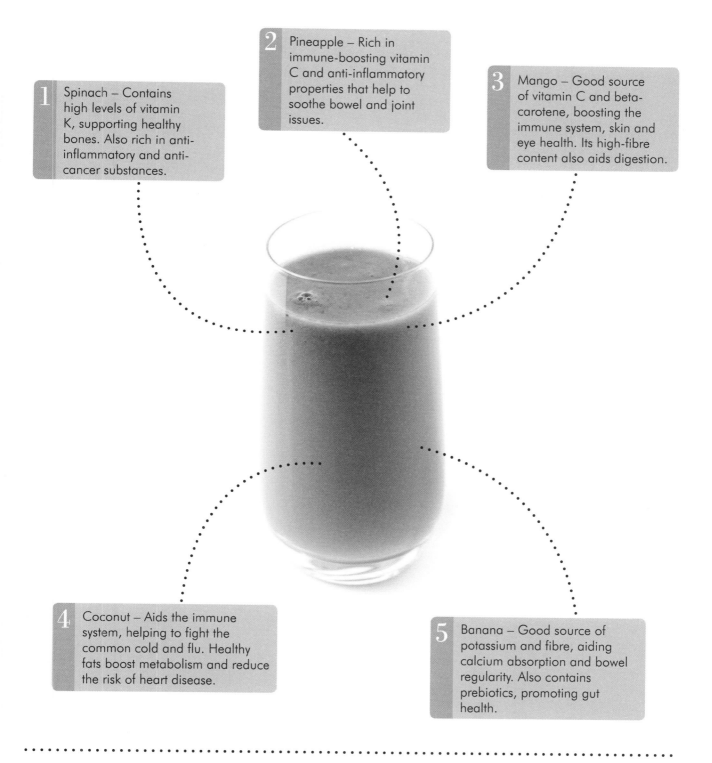

1 Spinach – Contains high levels of vitamin K, supporting healthy bones. Also rich in anti-inflammatory and anti-cancer substances.

2 Pineapple – Rich in immune-boosting vitamin C and anti-inflammatory properties that help to soothe bowel and joint issues.

3 Mango – Good source of vitamin C and beta-carotene, boosting the immune system, skin and eye health. Its high-fibre content also aids digestion.

4 Coconut – Aids the immune system, helping to fight the common cold and flu. Healthy fats boost metabolism and reduce the risk of heart disease.

5 Banana – Good source of potassium and fibre, aiding calcium absorption and bowel regularity. Also contains prebiotics, promoting gut health.

Artichoke and Cumin Dip

A nutritious dip made by placing all ingredients into a food processor – suitable for even the most novice chef! No cooking required. Just blend and eat.

Total time: 00:05   Preparation time: 00:05   Cooking time: 00:00   Serves: 2–4

Ingredients

- Juice and rind of ½ lemon
- Approx. 200g (scant cup) artichokes (canned or jarred)
- 4–5 tablespoons of cream cheese
- 1 tablespoon of Parmesan
- ¼ teaspoon of cumin
- Pinch of salt and pepper

Instructions

1. Grate the zest of the lemon into a food processor.
2. Add all other ingredients to the food processor and blend until combined.
3. Serve with wholemeal (wholewheat) crackers, crusty bread or crudités.

Equipment

- Food processor
- Kitchen scales
- Fine grater/zester
- Chopping board
- Sharp knife
- Tablespoon
- Teaspoon

Hints and tips

- Canned or jarred artichokes can often be found with antipasti food in the canned aisle of a supermarket.
- The cheese adds protein and flavour to the recipe.

> " I really love artichokes so was pleased to find this recipe. It's so easy to make and tastes great with crackers or crusty bread. I used to find dips a real challenge because I assumed them to be unhealthy, but making my own has helped to change my perception and enabled me to enjoy dips as a snack. "
>
> Lisa – overcoming body-image issues

1 Artichoke – Rich in antioxidants and fibre, aiding the digestive system and helping to maintain steady blood sugar levels. Helps to reduce cholesterol and ease indigestion.

2 Parmesan – A great source of protein, aiding cell growth and repair. Contains good levels of calcium, supporting healthy bones, teeth and nails.

3 Cream cheese – A great source of protein, aiding cell growth and repair. Contains good levels of calcium, supporting healthy bones, teeth and nails.

4 Lemon – Alkalising and detoxifying, lemons aid digestion and reduce water retention.

Ratatouille

A wonderful mix of vegetables in a tomato-rich sauce, served either hot or cold, as a main meal, side dish or snack. Prepared in just 10 minutes and then cooked on a low heat to reduce the sauce and intensify flavour. Delicious with rice or on top of a baked potato.

Total time: 00:60   Preparation time: 00:10   Cooking time: 00:50   Serves: 2–4

Ingredients

- 1 onion
- 1 yellow or red pepper
- 1 courgette (zucchini)
- ½ aubergine (eggplant)
- 2 cloves of garlic (skin removed)
- 1 tablespoon of oil
- ½ teaspoon of rosemary
- 1 can of chopped tomatoes (approx. 400g/1¾ cups)
- 1 can of water
- 1 handful of fresh basil leaves
- 1 tablespoon of balsamic vinegar

Equipment

- Oven hob (stovetop)
- Non-stick saucepan
- Chopping board
- Sharp knife
- Wooden spoon
- Tablespoon
- Teaspoon
- Can opener

Instructions

1. Cut the onion, pepper, courgette and aubergine into small pieces.
2. Peel and finely slice the garlic.
3. Heat the oil in a non-stick saucepan on a medium heat.
4. Add the aubergine and courgette to the oil and cook for 5 minutes, stirring regularly.
5. Add the onion, pepper, garlic and rosemary and cook for a further 5 minutes, stirring regularly.
6. Add the chopped tomatoes and water (using the empty can to measure the water).
7. Simmer for 40 minutes, without a lid, allowing the liquid to reduce.
8. Stir occasionally during cooking.
9. Tear the basil leaves into smaller pieces.
10. Finally, stir in the balsamic vinegar and basil leaves 5 minutes before serving.

Hints and tips

- Eating a variety of vegetables ensures consumption of all essential vitamins and minerals, especially when combined with meat, fish and dairy.
- This recipe can be batch cooked and stored in the fridge or freezer for later use.

"
As I eat my snacks, I tell myself that I need them to keep my metabolism working efficiently. Being aware of maintaining a stable blood sugar level has helped me to rationalise my thoughts and stabilise my weight.
"

Jacob – recovering from over-eating

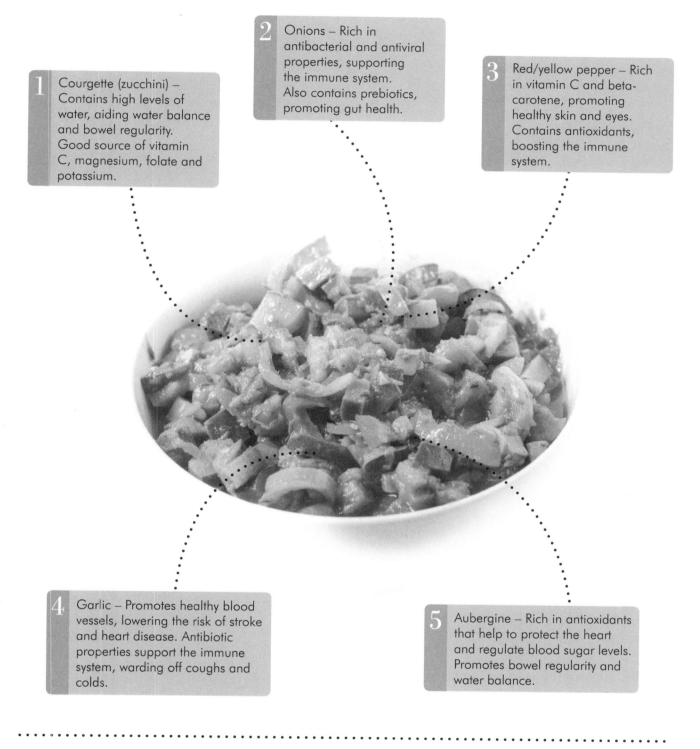

1 Courgette (zucchini) – Contains high levels of water, aiding water balance and bowel regularity. Good source of vitamin C, magnesium, folate and potassium.

2 Onions – Rich in antibacterial and antiviral properties, supporting the immune system. Also contains prebiotics, promoting gut health.

3 Red/yellow pepper – Rich in vitamin C and beta-carotene, promoting healthy skin and eyes. Contains antioxidants, boosting the immune system.

4 Garlic – Promotes healthy blood vessels, lowering the risk of stroke and heart disease. Antibiotic properties support the immune system, warding off coughs and colds.

5 Aubergine – Rich in antioxidants that help to protect the heart and regulate blood sugar levels. Promotes bowel regularity and water balance.

Pistachio Dukka

A delicious combination of nuts, seeds and spices. Perfect served with wholemeal (wholewheat) bread dipped in olive oil and then the dukka. Alternatively, sprinkle over salads to add extra flavour and crunch. Batch cook and store in an airtight container for later use.

Total time: 00:10   Preparation time: 00:05   Cooking time: 00:05   Serves: 2-4

Ingredients

- 4 tablespoons of shelled pistachio nuts
- 1 tablespoon of cumin seeds
- 1 tablespoon of coriander seeds
- 3 tablespoons of sesame seeds
- 1 fresh red chilli/teaspoon of dried chilli flakes
- Pinch of salt and pepper

Instructions

1. In a non-stick frying pan, heat the pistachios, cumin seeds and coriander seeds on a medium heat for 5 minutes.
2. Place all ingredients in a food processor and blend until desired consistency.
3. Serve with crusty bread and olive oil, or add to salads or sandwiches.

Equipment

- Oven hob (stovetop)
- Non-stick frying pan
- Food processor
- Tablespoon
- Teaspoon

Hints and tips

- Experiment with a variety of nuts, seeds and spices, according to your preference.
- If you don't have a food processor, you could use a pestle and mortar instead.
- Store in an airtight container.

> "
> This recipe offers a really interesting way of including nuts and seeds in my teenager's diet. We add the dukka to salads, providing a burst of flavour and a tasty crunch.
> "
>
> Kate – supportive parent

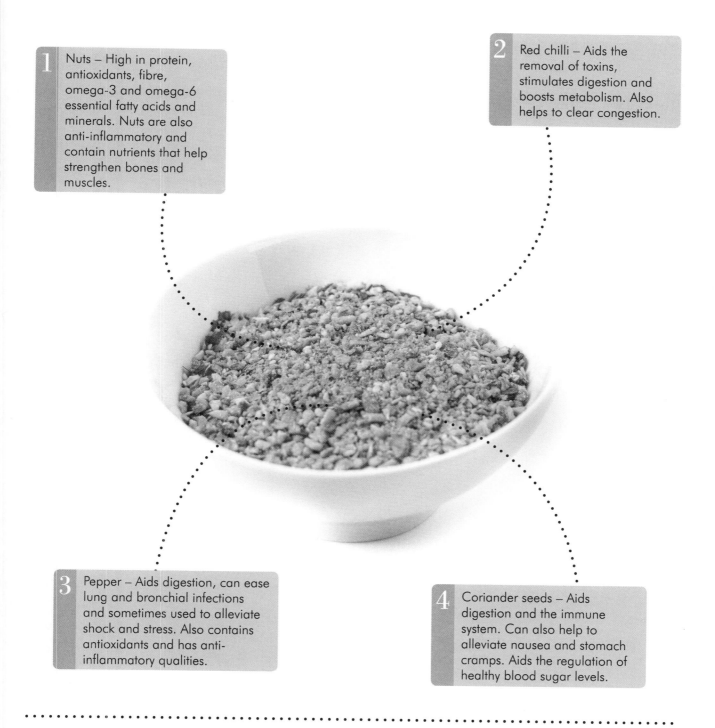

1 Nuts – High in protein, antioxidants, fibre, omega-3 and omega-6 essential fatty acids and minerals. Nuts are also anti-inflammatory and contain nutrients that help strengthen bones and muscles.

2 Red chilli – Aids the removal of toxins, stimulates digestion and boosts metabolism. Also helps to clear congestion.

3 Pepper – Aids digestion, can ease lung and bronchial infections and sometimes used to alleviate shock and stress. Also contains antioxidants and has anti-inflammatory qualities.

4 Coriander seeds – Aids digestion and the immune system. Can also help to alleviate nausea and stomach cramps. Aids the regulation of healthy blood sugar levels.

Smoked Salmon Stuffed Celery

A light snack high in protein and fibre, aiding cell repair and a healthy digestive system. This recipe is simple and refreshing to eat, at any time of day.

Total time: 00:05   Preparation time: 00:05   Cooking time: 00:00   Serves: 1

Ingredients

- 4 medium celery stalks
- 2 tablespoons of cream cheese or soured cream
- 2–3 slices of smoked salmon
- Pinch of salt and pepper
- Juice of ½ a lemon

Instructions

1. Wash and cut the celery as preferred.
2. Spread the cream cheese (or soured cream) over the celery.
3. Place the smoked salmon on top.
4. Add salt and pepper, as preferred.
5. Add lemon juice.

Equipment

- Chopping board
- Sharp knife
- Tablespoon

Hints and tips

- Pink Himalayan salt contains good levels of iodine and other minerals compared to table salt.
- See page 268 for salad dressings that could replace the cream cheese in this recipe.
- This recipe is also delicious served as a sandwich filler.

" My daughter loves this fresh recipe. Simple and healthy. Celery on its own is not enough of a snack, but the addition of cream cheese and salmon makes this dish a balanced snack. "

Teresa – mother of an anorexic

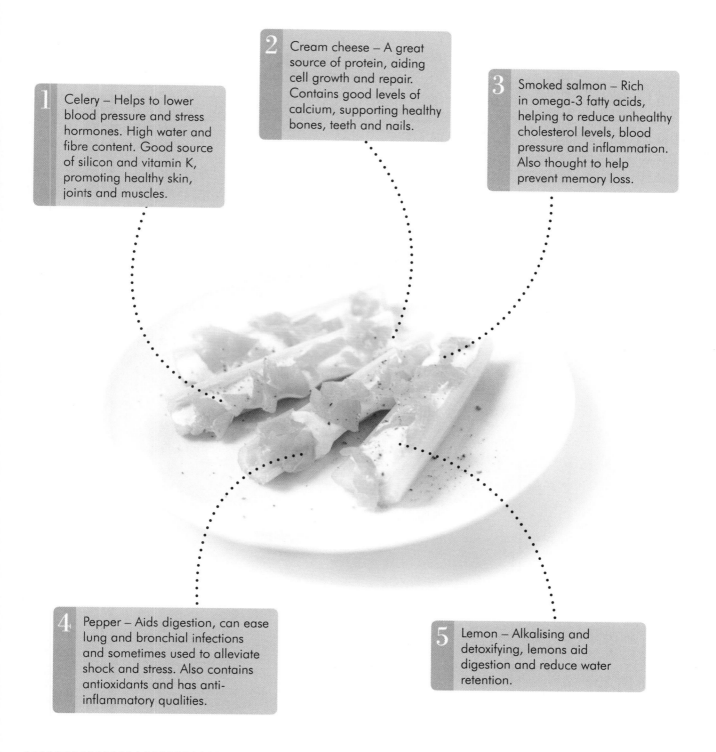

1 Celery – Helps to lower blood pressure and stress hormones. High water and fibre content. Good source of silicon and vitamin K, promoting healthy skin, joints and muscles.

2 Cream cheese – A great source of protein, aiding cell growth and repair. Contains good levels of calcium, supporting healthy bones, teeth and nails.

3 Smoked salmon – Rich in omega-3 fatty acids, helping to reduce unhealthy cholesterol levels, blood pressure and inflammation. Also thought to help prevent memory loss.

4 Pepper – Aids digestion, can ease lung and bronchial infections and sometimes used to alleviate shock and stress. Also contains antioxidants and has anti-inflammatory qualities.

5 Lemon – Alkalising and detoxifying, lemons aid digestion and reduce water retention.

Seeded Crackers

Wholesome crackers enriched with heart-healthy seeds, perfect served with hummus (see page 192), guacamole (see page 206) or beetroot dip (see page 190). Batch cook and store for later use, at any time of day.

Total time: 00:30   Preparation time: 00:10   Cooking time: 00:20   Serves: 6

Ingredients

- 100g (heaped cup) oats
- 2 tablespoons of flax seeds
- 2 tablespoons of chia seeds
- 100g (scant cup) wholemeal (wholewheat) flour
- Pinch of salt
- 100ml (½ cup) water
- 3 tablespoons of olive oil
- 2 tablespoons of organic honey

Equipment

- Oven
- Food processor
- Baking tray
- Kitchen scales
- Rolling pin
- Baking paper
- Sharp knife
- Tablespoon

Instructions

1. Preheat the oven to 170–180°C (325–350°F/Gas 3–4).
2. Place the oats, seeds, flour and salt in a food processor and blend for 30 seconds.
3. Add the water, olive oil and honey and blend until combined.
4. Roll out the mixture to 0.5cm thick, between two sheets of baking paper.
5. Remove the top layer of baking paper and sprinkle the mixture with a topping of your choice, for example black pepper, garlic powder, sesame seeds, poppy seeds, onion seeds or chilli flakes, rolling the topping into the dough.
6. Using a sharp knife, cut the mixture into 6 equal shapes.
7. Place these onto a sheet of baking paper on a baking tray.
8. Bake for 18–20 minutes.
9. Allow the crackers to cool before serving.
10. Store in an airtight container for future use.

Hints and tips

- Grinding flax seeds helps to release their nutrients and fibre; add to smoothies and soups for maximum benefits.
- Chia seeds are a great source of vegetarian protein.

"

One of the great things about this recipe is that I can make it in advance of eating. I can enjoy the process of cooking without the pressure of consuming.

"

Amy – recovering from an eating disorder

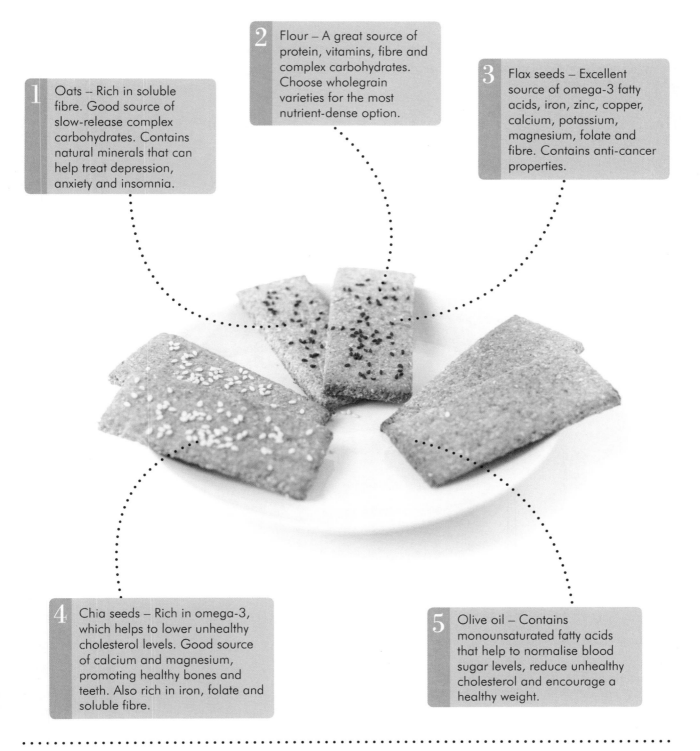

1 Oats – Rich in soluble fibre. Good source of slow-release complex carbohydrates. Contains natural minerals that can help treat depression, anxiety and insomnia.

2 Flour – A great source of protein, vitamins, fibre and complex carbohydrates. Choose wholegrain varieties for the most nutrient-dense option.

3 Flax seeds – Excellent source of omega-3 fatty acids, iron, zinc, copper, calcium, potassium, magnesium, folate and fibre. Contains anti-cancer properties.

4 Chia seeds – Rich in omega-3, which helps to lower unhealthy cholesterol levels. Good source of calcium and magnesium, promoting healthy bones and teeth. Also rich in iron, folate and soluble fibre.

5 Olive oil – Contains monounsaturated fatty acids that help to normalise blood sugar levels, reduce unhealthy cholesterol and encourage a healthy weight.

Guacamole

An immune-boosting dip made with just fruit, vegetables and a handful of green herbs. Serve with raw veg crudités, pitta bread or crackers. Also delicious served with chilli con carne and rice.

Total time: 00:05   Preparation time: 00:05   Cooking time: 00:00   Serves: 2

Ingredients

- 1 avocado
- 2 spring (green) onions
- 2–3 cherry tomatoes
- Juice of 1 lime
- Small handful of coriander (cilantro) leaves
- Pinch of salt and pepper

Optional: sliced fresh red chilli/dried chilli flakes

Equipment

- Food processor
- Measuring jug/cup
- Cling film (plastic wrap)
- Chopping board
- Sharp knife

Hints and tips

- Avocado is a fruit, which needs to be ripened before consumption. You can tell when it's ready to use by placing it in the palm of your hand and gently squeezing it. If it feels very firm, the avocado is not yet ready to eat, and should be allowed to ripen before use.
- Avocados are most nutrient-dense in the darkest area close to the skin.

Instructions

1. Prepare the avocado by slicing it in half lengthways, remove the central seed and peel the skin away from the half being used in the recipe.
2. Wrap the other half in cling film and place this in the fridge for future use.
3. Place the avocado, spring onions, tomatoes, lime juice, coriander, salt, pepper and chilli (if using) into a food processor.
4. Blend until smooth.
5. Alternatively, for a more textured, chunky guacamole (without the need for a food processor)...peel and then mash the avocado with a fork. Finely chop the spring onions, tomatoes and coriander. Combine all of the ingredients together.
6. Serve immediately, or refrigerate for later use.

"I used to avoid avocado because of misconceptions about it. Now, I understand its nutritional benefits and inlcude it in my food plan at least twice a week.

E – recovering from an eating disorder"

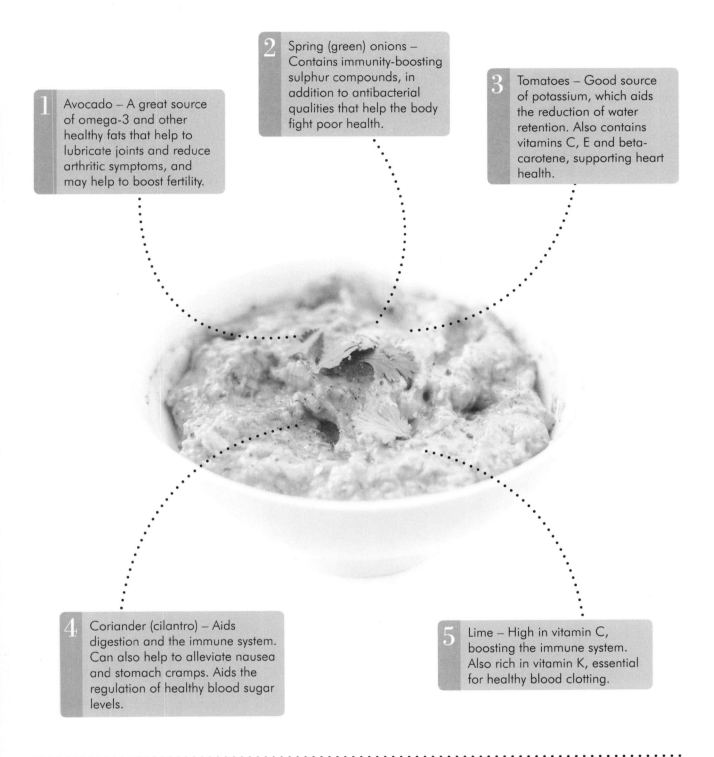

1 Avocado – A great source of omega-3 and other healthy fats that help to lubricate joints and reduce arthritic symptoms, and may help to boost fertility.

2 Spring (green) onions – Contains immunity-boosting sulphur compounds, in addition to antibacterial qualities that help the body fight poor health.

3 Tomatoes – Good source of potassium, which aids the reduction of water retention. Also contains vitamins C, E and beta-carotene, supporting heart health.

4 Coriander (cilantro) – Aids digestion and the immune system. Can also help to alleviate nausea and stomach cramps. Aids the regulation of healthy blood sugar levels.

5 Lime – High in vitamin C, boosting the immune system. Also rich in vitamin K, essential for healthy blood clotting.

Rainbow Coleslaw

A delicious combination of raw vegetables mixed with crème fraîche/sour cream (or Greek yoghurt), mustard and lemon juice. Often eaten alongside salad but also great with homemade burgers (see page 178 for a lamb burger recipe).

Total time: 00:10   Preparation time: 00:10   Cooking time: 00:00   Serves: 2-4

Ingredients

- 1 sweet potato
- 1 courgette (zucchini)
- 1 carrot
- ¼ white cabbage
- 3 spring (green) onions
- 2 tablespoons of crème fraîche/sour cream
- 1 teaspoon of Dijon mustard
- 1 teaspoon of olive oil
- Juice of ½ a lemon
- Pinch of salt and pepper

Optional: 1 apple or 1 stalk of celery

Instructions

1. Peel the sweet potato.
2. Grate the courgette, carrot, sweet potato and white cabbage (and apple/celery, if using) into a mixing bowl, using a grater or food processor with a grater accessory.
3. Finely slice the spring onions.
4. Add the crème fraîche/sour cream, Dijon mustard, olive oil, lemon juice, salt and pepper and mix together.
5. Serve immediately or store in the fridge for later use.

Equipment

- Grater (or food processor with grater accessory)
- Chopping board
- Sharp knife
- Tablespoon
- Teaspoon
- Mixing bowl
- Vegetable peeler

Hints and tips

- Including an array of colours in your diet ensures consumption of a variety of minerals and vitamins.
- Prepare a batch of grated vegetables to keep in the fridge, adding the condiments to a portion at a time as and when required. The vegetable mix could easily be added to other recipes as well.

> "
> I've avoided shop-bought coleslaw because I thought it unhealthy. But this recipe seems to include only healthy ingredients. So now I can enjoy coleslaw knowing that I'm feeding my body a great mix of vegetables!
> "
>
> Jenni – recovering from anorexia

1. Courgette (zucchini) – Contains high levels of water, aiding water balance and bowel regularity. Good source of vitamin C, magnesium, folate and potassium.

2. White cabbage – Contains vitamins B, C, K and other antioxidants that protect against free-radical damage. Also aids gut health, recovery from stomach ulcers and bone, teeth and nail strength.

3. Carrots – Good source of fibre, aiding digestion and the feeling of fullness. Contains anti-cancer substances. Also helps to maintain good eyesight.

4. Olive oil – Contains monounsaturated fatty acids that help to normalise blood sugar levels, reduce unhealthy cholesterol and encourage a healthy weight.

5. Sweet potato – Provides slow-release energy. Rich in vitamin C and beta-carotene, encouraging healthy skin and boosting the immune system.

Boiled Egg and Tomato

A simple snack providing all essential vitamins and minerals alongside the natural sweetness of tomato. Batch cook boiled eggs to be eaten as a snack or made into egg mayonnaise for salads or sandwiches. A perfect picnic snack!

Total time: 00:10   Preparation time: 00:02   Cooking time: 00:08   Serves: 1

Ingredients

- 1 free-range egg
- 1 large tomato
- Pinch of salt and pepper

Instructions

1. Half fill a saucepan with water and bring it to the boil.
2. Add the whole free-range egg to the water (shell on).
3. Cook for 6–8 minutes.
4. Drain the water from the saucepan and soak the egg in cold water to cool the shell enough to handle.
5. Slice the tomato, as preferred.
6. Remove the shell and slice the boiled egg.
7. Serve the egg and tomato together, with added salt and pepper, as preferred.

Equipment

- Oven hob (stovetop)
- Saucepan
- Chopping board
- Sharp knife

Hints and tips

- Sometimes the most simple idea is the best one!
- Place a wedge of lemon in the boiling water along with the eggs, when cooking, to help remove the egg shell once cooked.

"

Simple perfection! I boil a few eggs and keep them in the fridge, ready for use as a snack or with salads or egg mayonnaise.

"

Thomas – supportive parent

1 Eggs – Good source of protein, vitamin D and phosphorus, aiding strong bones and teeth. Excellent source of B vitamins and choline, boosting mental performance.

2 Tomatoes – Good source of potassium, which aids the reduction of water retention. Also contains vitamins C, E and beta-carotene, supporting heart health.

3 Pepper – Aids digestion, can ease lung and bronchial infections and sometimes used to alleviate shock and stress. Also contains antioxidants and has anti-inflammatory qualities.

Root Vegetable Crisps

Comforting vegetable crisps full of vitamins and minerals to boost general health. Baked rather than fried, these crisps can be enjoyed knowing that they are a healthy snack made from natural ingredients.

Total time: 00:40   Preparation time: 00:10   Cooking time: 00:30   Serves: 2–4

Ingredients

- 1 potato
- 1 sweet potato
- 1 parsnip
- 1 beetroot (beets)
- 2 tablespoons of oil
- 1 tablespoon of paprika
- Pinch of salt and pepper

Optional: sliced fresh red chilli or dried chilli flakes

Equipment

- Oven
- Non-stick baking tray
- Mixing bowl
- Vegetable peeler
- Tablespoon
- Optional: mandolin

Hints and tips

- A mandolin is a kitchen device designed to thinly slice vegetables safely and easily.
- Experiment with a variety of root vegetables and different oils – see page 13 for information about different oils.

Instructions

1. Preheat the oven to 150–170°C (300–325°F/Gas 2–3).
2. Wash, dry and peel the vegetables as necessary, leaving the skin on wherever possible.
3. Using a vegetable peeler (or mandolin), thinly slice the vegetables into a mixing bowl.
4. Coat the vegetables in the oil and paprika.
5. Add the chilli, if using.
6. Arrange the vegetables on a non-stick baking tray, in a single layer.
7. Bake for 25–30 minutes, or until the vegetable slices appear crisp but not burnt.
8. Allow the vegetable crisps to cool, before tossing them in salt and pepper, as preferred.

> I like to experiment in the kitchen so I tried these vegetable crisps. They were so easy to make and really tasty. A great way of getting some vegetables whilst also treating yourself to something that feels indulgent despite it being healthy.
>
> Emma

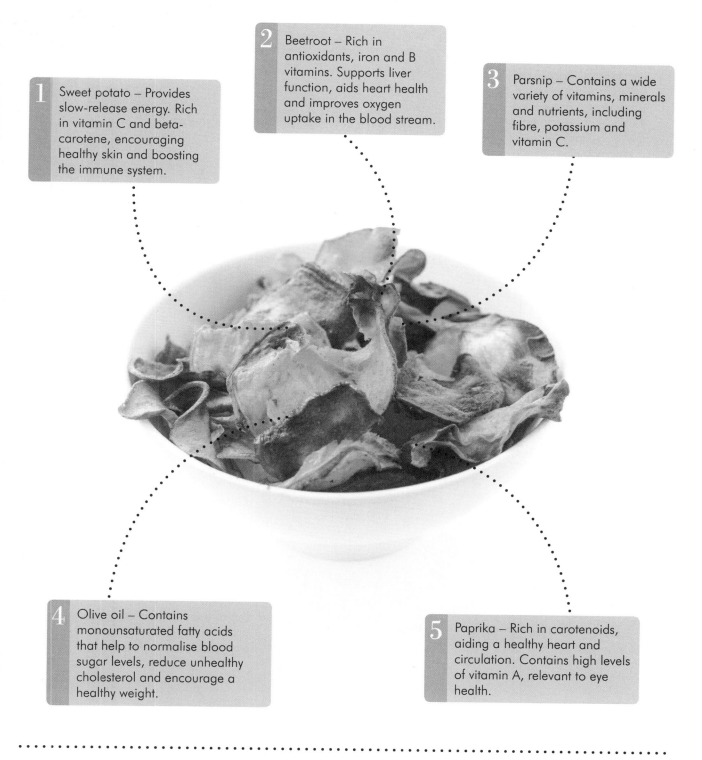

1 Sweet potato – Provides slow-release energy. Rich in vitamin C and beta-carotene, encouraging healthy skin and boosting the immune system.

2 Beetroot – Rich in antioxidants, iron and B vitamins. Supports liver function, aids heart health and improves oxygen uptake in the blood stream.

3 Parsnip – Contains a wide variety of vitamins, minerals and nutrients, including fibre, potassium and vitamin C.

4 Olive oil – Contains monounsaturated fatty acids that help to normalise blood sugar levels, reduce unhealthy cholesterol and encourage a healthy weight.

5 Paprika – Rich in carotenoids, aiding a healthy heart and circulation. Contains high levels of vitamin A, relevant to eye health.

Lime and Pepper Cashew Nuts

A simple natural snack rich in vitamins and minerals, aiding a healthy immune system and good bone and skin health. Experiment with alternative spices, according to your preference.

Total time: 00:10 Preparation time: 00:02 Cooking time: 00:08 Serves: 4

Ingredients

- 4 handfuls of cashew nuts
- 1–2 teaspoons of pepper
- Juice of 1 lime

Equipment

- Oven
- Baking tray
- Mixing bowl
- Chopping board
- Baking paper
- Sharp knife
- Teaspoon

Hints and tips

- Use different nuts, if preferred.
- Be careful not to burn the nuts – cook on a low heat and keep checking them regularly.

Instructions

1. Preheat the oven to 110°C (225°F/Gas ¼).
2. Line a baking tray with baking paper.
3. Combine the nuts, pepper and lime juice in a mixing bowl.
4. Arrange the nuts on the baking paper in a single layer.
5. Bake for 6–8 minutes, or until golden brown but not burnt.

> " I used to be terrified of nuts and thought my counsellor was crazy when she suggested that I have them as a mid-morning snack. But, throughout my recovery, I've learnt more about food as fuel and better understand the importance of healthy fats.
>
> Isabelle – recovering from anorexia "

1 Cashew nuts – Good source of monounsaturated fats, helping to protect against heart disease and cancer. Contains calcium, magnesium, iron, zinc and folate, contributing to good bone and skin health.

2 Lime – High in vitamin C, boosting the immune system. Also rich in vitamin K, essential for healthy blood clotting.

3 Pepper – Aids digestion, can ease lung and bronchial infections and sometimes used to alleviate shock and stress. Also contains antioxidants and has anti-inflammatory qualities.

Homemade Popcorn

A quick high-fibre snack that aids digestion and satisfies hunger. Flavour with a variety of nutritionally beneficial toppings for extra benefits. Batch cook and store in an airtight container for easy access to a healthy snack any time of day.

Total time: 00:05   Preparation time: 00:01   Cooking time: 00:04   Serves: 1

Ingredients

- 1 tablespoon of coconut oil
- 2 tablespoons of popcorn kernels

Topping examples:
- ½ teaspoon of salt and pepper
- ½ teaspoon of cinnamon
- 1 teaspoon of Marmite
- 1 teaspoon of organic honey
- 1 teaspoon of melted butter

Equipment

- Oven hob (stovetop)
- Non-stick frying pan (with a lid, or kitchen foil)
- Tablespoon
- Teaspoon

Instructions

1. Preheat the coconut oil in a non-stick saucepan or frying pan (with a lid).
2. Put 2–3 popcorn kernels into the pan.
3. Cover with the lid (or kitchen foil) and cook on a medium to high heat, until you've heard the kernels pop.
4. Remove the 2–3 pieces of popcorn.
5. Add the rest of the kernels in an even layer.
6. Cook, shaking the pan occasionally, until the sound of popping slows down (after approximately 2 minutes).
7. Remove from the heat and take the lid off the pan – this allows the steam to escape and keeps the popcorn crisp.
8. Add a topping, as preferred, and serve immediately.

Hints and tips

- Allow yourself a good portion to ensure that you stimulate the metabolism.
- Don't wait for all kernels to pop before removing from the heat otherwise the popcorn may burn.
- It's normal for a few kernels to remain un-popped.

> Making popcorn is actually a lot of fun. You can buy popcorn ready made nowadays but I prefer getting the pan on at home. A healthy, quick and simple snack that tastes even better when eaten during a movie with a friend!
>
> Becky – overcoming body-image issues

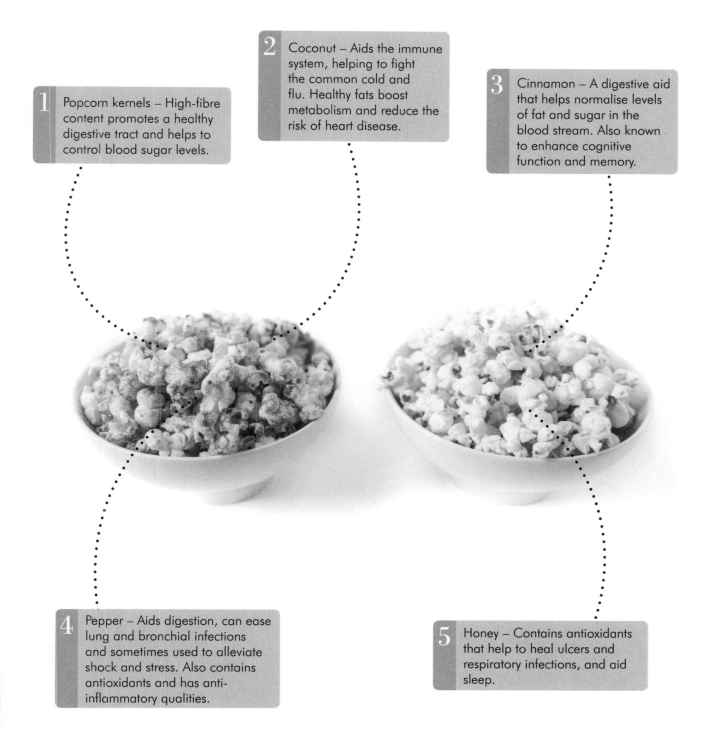

1 Popcorn kernels – High-fibre content promotes a healthy digestive tract and helps to control blood sugar levels.

2 Coconut – Aids the immune system, helping to fight the common cold and flu. Healthy fats boost metabolism and reduce the risk of heart disease.

3 Cinnamon – A digestive aid that helps normalise levels of fat and sugar in the blood stream. Also known to enhance cognitive function and memory.

4 Pepper – Aids digestion, can ease lung and bronchial infections and sometimes used to alleviate shock and stress. Also contains antioxidants and has anti-inflammatory qualities.

5 Honey – Contains antioxidants that help to heal ulcers and respiratory infections, and aid sleep.

NATURALLY SWEET

Bliss Balls... 220
Oatie Biscuits.. 222
Banana, Almond Butter and Chia Seeds........................... 224
Five-Minute Raw Brownies 226
Pecan Bis-Cakes.. 228
Choc and Nut Raw Tart.. 230
Melon, Yoghurt and Seeds 232
No-Bake Date Cakes.. 234
Soft-Serve Banana Ice Cream.. 236
Rejuvenating Chocolate Cake 238
Fruity Flapjacks.. 240

Bliss Balls

High-protein energy balls perfect for a mid-morning or afternoon snack. Especially good after exercise, aiding muscle repair and refuelling the body. Rich in antioxidants and only naturally occurring sugars, these little treats can be enjoyed knowing that they are good for you!

Total time: 00:10   Preparation time: 00:10   Cooking time: 00:00   Serves: 6

Ingredients

- 6 dates
- 3 figs
- 4 tablespoons of ground almonds
- 2 tablespoons of desiccated (dried) coconut
- 2 tablespoons of ground flax seeds
- 1 tablespoon of peanut/almond butter
- 1 tablespoon of coconut oil
- 1 tablespoon of water (plus water for soaking)
- ½ teaspoon of raw cacao powder
- ½ teaspoon of coffee granules (decaffeinated, if preferred)

Optional: desiccated (dried) coconut to cover

Instructions

1. Soak the dates and figs in a bowl of boiling water for 5 minutes.
2. Drain the fruit, which should now be softer to the touch.
3. Place all ingredients in the food processor.
4. Blend until fully combined and slightly sticky.
5. Shape the mixture into small balls (making approximately 12 balls in total).
6. Roll the balls in desiccated (dried) coconut, if desired.
7. Eat immediately if a soft texture is preferred. Otherwise, place the Bliss Balls in the fridge for at least 10 minutes for a firmer texture.
8. Store the Bliss Balls in an airtight container in the fridge for up to a week.

Equipment

- Food processor
- Kettle
- Bowl
- Tablespoon
- Teaspoon

Hints and tips

- Use whichever nuts you prefer.
- Bliss Balls can be frozen for up to 3 months, removing them from the freezer the day before you want them.
- Because Bliss Balls look a little like truffles, they make a great present for someone else… No need to worry about being offered one because they're full of goodness!

> " Initially I felt uncomfortable about eating Bliss Balls because they looked so delicious that my brain was convinced they must be unhealthy. I had to challenge my misconceptions about food – it really helped me to understand the nutritional benefits of the core ingredients…especially the fact that high-protein foods would help to repair my muscles after exercise. "
>
> S – recovering from anorexia

1 Dates – Great source of fibre, aiding digestion. Provides slow-release energy, helping to regulate blood glucose levels.

2 Figs – Rich in potassium, promoting healthy muscle contraction, nerve function and water balance. Contains calcium, relevant in bone health and growth.

3 Almonds/peanuts – High in protein and a variety of minerals that support brain, cardiovascular and respiratory health.

4 Flax seeds – Excellent source of omega-3 fatty acids, iron, zinc, copper, calcium, potassium, magnesium, folate and fibre. Contain powerful anti-cancer properties.

5 Coconut – Aids the immune system, helping to fight the common cold and flu. Healthy fats boost metabolism and reduce the risk of heart disease.

Oatie Biscuits

Homemade wholemeal (wholewheat) biscuits, providing slow-release energy, protein and a natural sweetness. Perfect served alongside a glass of milk or taken out and about for a portable snack.

Total time: 00:25   Preparation time: 00:10   Cooking time: 00:15   Serves: 6–8

Ingredients

- 100g (scant cup) wholemeal (wholewheat) or spelt flour
- 100g (heaped cup) porridge (oatmeal)
- 100g (½ cup) almond butter
- 100g (½ cup) butter
- 2–3 trablespoons organic honey
- 1 teaspoon of baking powder
- Pinch of salt

Instructions

1. Preheat the oven to 170–180°C (325–350°F/Gas 3–4).
2. Place all ingredients into a food processor and blend until combined.
3. Roll the dough to 0.5cm thick between two baking sheets.
4. Using a cookie cutter or sharp knife, cut the dough into cookie shapes of your preference.
5. Line a non-stick baking tray with baking paper.
6. Place the cookies onto the baking paper and bake for 12–15 minutes, or until golden brown.
7. Serve once cooled, or store in an airtight container for future use.

Equipment

- Oven
- Food processor
- Non-stick baking tray
- Kitchen scales
- Rolling pin
- Baking paper
- Cookie cutter or sharp knife
- Tablespoon
- Teaspoon

Hints and tips

- Wholemeal flour contains more nutrients and fibre than white flour.
- Spelt flour is thought to be more easily digested than most other flours.
- Almond butter can be purchased from most supermarkets. Choose no added salt/sugar varieties. Alternatively, consider making your own – see page 260 for recipe.

> " Even though I recognised that the ingredients are natural and healthy, I still found it hard to accept that biscuits should be included in my diet until I was reminded that restricting such things can result in cravings, especially when confronted with temptation. Everything in moderation, including moderation itself. "
>
> E – recovering from an eating disorder

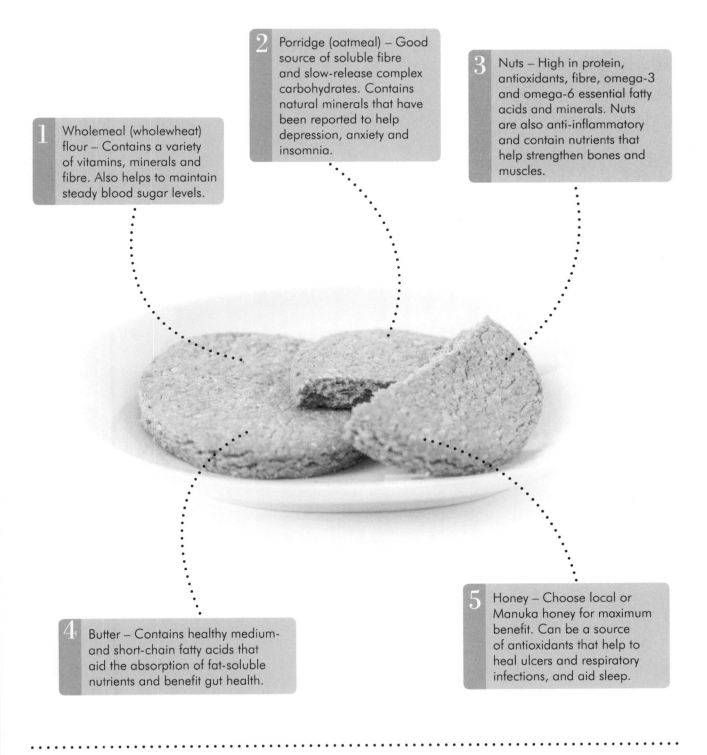

1 Wholemeal (wholewheat) flour – Contains a variety of vitamins, minerals and fibre. Also helps to maintain steady blood sugar levels.

2 Porridge (oatmeal) – Good source of soluble fibre and slow-release complex carbohydrates. Contains natural minerals that have been reported to help depression, anxiety and insomnia.

3 Nuts – High in protein, antioxidants, fibre, omega-3 and omega-6 essential fatty acids and minerals. Nuts are also anti-inflammatory and contain nutrients that help strengthen bones and muscles.

4 Butter – Contains healthy medium- and short-chain fatty acids that aid the absorption of fat-soluble nutrients and benefit gut health.

5 Honey – Choose local or Manuka honey for maximum benefit. Can be a source of antioxidants that help to heal ulcers and respiratory infections, and aid sleep.

Banana, Almond Butter & Chia Seeds

A simple snack providing a protein energy boost, eaten fresh or straight from the fridge or freezer. Easy and quick to prepare, with no fuss. Nutritious and delicious.

Total time: 00:05   Preparation time: 00:05   Cooking time: 00:00   Serves: 1

Ingredients

- 1 banana
- 1 tablespoon of almond, cashew or peanut butter
- 1 teaspoon of chia seeds

Equipment

- Chopping board
- Sharp knife
- Tablespoon
- Teaspoon

Instructions

1. Slice a banana into bite-size pieces.
2. Add almond, cashew or peanut butter to the top of each banana piece.
3. Sprinkle chia seeds over the top.
4. Serve immediately or freeze for later use (can be served frozen).

Hints and tips

- Chia seeds are a great source of vegetarian protein.
- Mix and match recipes – see page 236 for an alternative use for these banana bites.
- Experiment with different toppings, for example peanut butter, cashew butter, healthy chocolate spread – see pages 260 & 264 for recipes.

"The other day, I watched my nine-year-old son go into the kitchen and create this snack all by himself. He loves it! I felt so proud of him, and after reflection, proud of myself for inspiring him to make good food choices of his own. It's really important that I provide him with a good example of balance, without any extreme behaviour one way or another.

Emma

1 Banana – Good source of potassium and fibre, aiding calcium absorption and bowel regularity. Also contains prebiotics, promoting gut health.

2 Nut butter – High in protein, antioxidants, fibre, omega-3 and omega-6 essential fatty acids and minerals. Nuts are also anti-inflammatory and strengthen bones and muscles.

3 Chia seeds – Rich in omega-3, which helps to lower unhealthy cholesterol levels. Good source of protein, calcium and magnesium, promoting healthy bones and teeth. Also rich in iron, folate and soluble fibre.

Five-Minute Raw Brownies

A high-protein snack providing slow-release energy, anti-inflammatory and antioxidant properties. This naturally sweet treat can be eaten as a snack or dessert, on its own or combined with a glass of milk.

Total time: 00:05   Preparation time: 00:05   Cooking time: 00:00   Serves: 2

Ingredients

- Approx. 10 dates
- Approx. 20 pecans
- 1 tablespoon of organic honey
- 1 teaspoon of raw cacao powder

Instructions

1. Place all ingredients into a food processor and blend until smooth.
2. Shape the mixture into two equal squares.
3. Serve straight away or refrigerate for a more solid texture.

Equipment

- Food processor
- Tablespoon
- Teaspoon

Hints and tips

- Dried fruit is fairly high in natural sugar, so should be eaten in moderation. Combining dried fruit with nuts and seeds slows the subsequent release of energy, creating a balanced snack.
- Choose local honey whenever possible. Blended honey will have been purified. Manuka honey has the highest antibacterial/viral action.

> Sometimes I crave a sweet treat but know that if I make or buy a cake I will find it hard to resist eating too much. I can make this recipe knowing that the quantity is an appropriate amount for me and my partner, without having leftovers playing on my mind afterwards.
>
> Jacob – recovering from over-eating

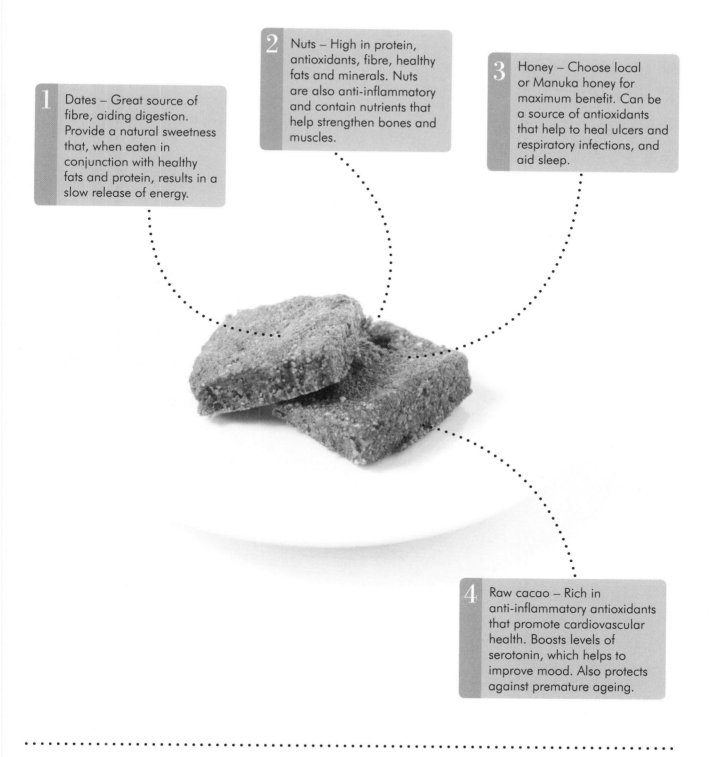

1 Dates – Great source of fibre, aiding digestion. Provide a natural sweetness that, when eaten in conjunction with healthy fats and protein, results in a slow release of energy.

2 Nuts – High in protein, antioxidants, fibre, healthy fats and minerals. Nuts are also anti-inflammatory and contain nutrients that help strengthen bones and muscles.

3 Honey – Choose local or Manuka honey for maximum benefit. Can be a source of antioxidants that help to heal ulcers and respiratory infections, and aid sleep.

4 Raw cacao – Rich in anti-inflammatory antioxidants that promote cardiovascular health. Boosts levels of serotonin, which helps to improve mood. Also protects against premature ageing.

Pecan Bis-Cakes

A protein-rich snack containing fibre, monosaturated fats and antioxidants, aiding metabolism and a healthy immune system. Nutritious and deliciously tasty – well received by guests or family members! Suitable for freezing.

Total time: 00:15   Preparation time: 00:05   Cooking time: 00:10   Serves: 8

Ingredients

- 150g (1¼ cups) ground almonds
- 75g (⅓ cup) pecans
- 50g (¼ cup) coconut butter
- 2 tablespoons of organic honey
- ¼ teaspoon of bicarbonate of soda (baking soda)
- Pinch of salt

Instructions

1. Preheat the oven to 170–180°C (325–350°F/Gas 3–4).
2. Place all ingredients in a food processor and blend until smooth.
3. Line a baking tray with baking paper.
4. Scoop heaped tablespoons of mix onto the baking paper, one inch apart, making 8 bis-cakes in total.
5. Bake for 8–10 minutes, or until golden brown.
6. Serve warm or cold, allowing the bis-cakes to cool before storing in an airtight container for future use.

Equipment

- Oven
- Food processor
- Baking tray
- Kitchen scales
- Baking paper
- Tablespoon
- Teaspoon

Hints and tips

- Almonds, hazelnuts, pecans and peanuts are actually fruit seeds (rather than 'nuts')!
- Choose local honey whenever possible. Blended honey will have been purified. Manuka honey has the highest antibacterial/viral action.
- Coconut butter is different to coconut oil. This recipe needs either coconut butter or creamed coconut.

> " Oh my goodness, these are amazing! It's hard to believe that they are just made of nuts, coconut and honey. I make a batch to share with family or freeze some for future use. "
>
> Emma

1 Almonds – High in protein and a variety of minerals that support brain, cardiovascular and respiratory health.

2 Pecans – Rich in fibre and monosaturated fats, aiding digestion and reducing the risk of heart disease, stroke and various cancers. Good source of phosphorus, relevant to bone health, and magnesium, offering anti-inflammatory benefits.

3 Coconut – Aids the immune system, helping to fight the common cold and flu. Healthy fats boost metabolism and reduce the risk of heart disease.

4 Honey – Choose local or Manuka honey for maximum benefit. Can be a source of antioxidants that help to heal ulcers and respiratory infections, and aid sleep.

Choc and Nut Raw Tart

An amazing snack so good for you that it could be eaten for breakfast or as a snack, or served as a nutritious dessert! Great served with yoghurt and berries, from the fridge, or soon after being removed from storage in the freezer.

Total time: 00:40   Preparation time: 00:40   Cooking time: 00:00   Serves: 8

Ingredients

Base:
- 125g (¾ cup) pitted dates
- 100g (¾ cup) ground almonds
- 2 tablespoons of flax seeds (preferably ground)
- 2 tablespoons of desiccated (dried) coconut
- 1 tablespoon of coconut oil
- Pinch of salt

Filling:
- 2 bananas
- 6 tablespoons of coconut oil
- 6 tablespoons of organic honey
- 6 tablespoons of raw cocoa powder
- 6 tablespoons of desiccated (dried) coconut

Equipment

- Food processor
- Kitchen scales
- Tart dish (approx. 23cm/9 inches)
- Tablespoon

Instructions

1. Place all base ingredients into a food processor and blend until combined.
2. Empty the mix into a tart dish.
3. Using a tablespoon, press the mixture into the base and sides of the tart dish evenly.
4. Place all filling ingredients into the food processor and blend until smooth.
5. Spoon the filling mix onto the tart base and refrigerate for at least 30 minutes.
6. Serve straight from the fridge or freeze for later use.

Hints and tips

- Grinding flax seeds helps to release their nutrients and fibre, so add to smoothies and soups for maximum benefits.
- Choc nut tart may be sliced and stored in the freezer. Remove the required portions from the freezer 5–10 minutes before serving (to allow them to soften a little).
- Raw cacao powder is unprocessed and contains antioxidants and flavanols.

" I really enjoyed this recipe, especially because you can make it in advance. I store the tart in the freezer so it lasts a long time. I therefore don't feel any pressure to eat it quickly. I can enjoy it once or twice a week, as part of a varied diet.

Sarah – recovering from bulimia "

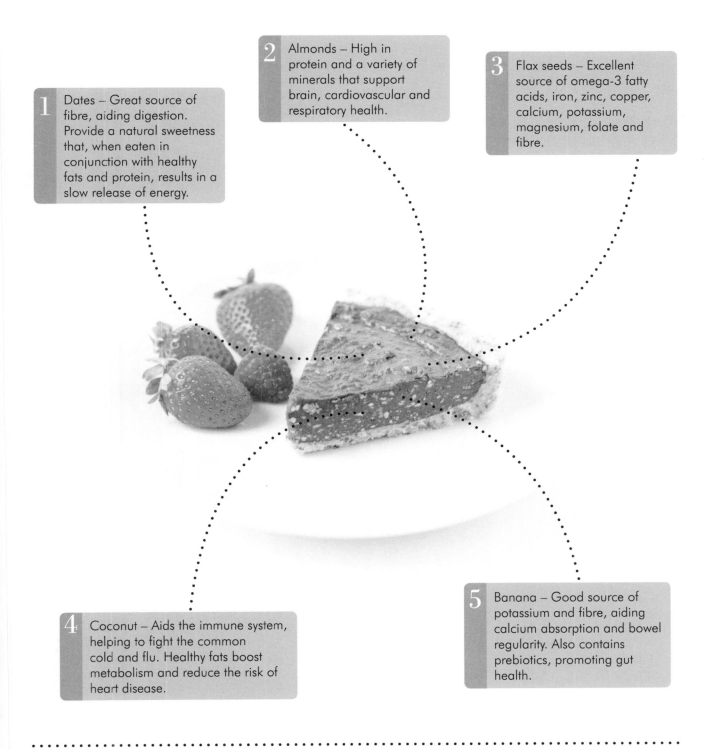

1 Dates – Great source of fibre, aiding digestion. Provide a natural sweetness that, when eaten in conjunction with healthy fats and protein, results in a slow release of energy.

2 Almonds – High in protein and a variety of minerals that support brain, cardiovascular and respiratory health.

3 Flax seeds – Excellent source of omega-3 fatty acids, iron, zinc, copper, calcium, potassium, magnesium, folate and fibre.

4 Coconut – Aids the immune system, helping to fight the common cold and flu. Healthy fats boost metabolism and reduce the risk of heart disease.

5 Banana – Good source of potassium and fibre, aiding calcium absorption and bowel regularity. Also contains prebiotics, promoting gut health.

Melon, Yoghurt and Seeds

A fresh natural snack, containing a variety of minerals that boost the immune system and support cardiovascular function. Feel free to experiment with different varieties of melon and seeds according to preference.

Total time: 00:05   Preparation time: 00:05   Cooking time: 00:00   Serves: 2

Ingredients

- ¼ cantaloupe melon
- 6 tablespoons of yoghurt
- 2 tablespoons of seeds (for example pumpkin seeds, sunflower seeds, flax seeds)

Optional: 2 teaspoons of organic honey

Instructions

1. Slice the melon to preferred size.
2. Spoon the yoghurt and seeds over the melon.
3. Drizzle with honey, if using.

Equipment

- Chopping board
- Sharp knife
- Teaspoon

Hints and tips

- Enjoy full-fat, natural and plain probiotic yoghurts for maximum benefit.
- Cantaloupe melon is the most nutritionally dense melon, containing around half the recommended daily amount of vitamin C and A in one portion.
- A ripe cantaloupe melon should smell fresh and give a little when gently squeezed (rather than feeling rock hard).

"Melon is really refreshing but doesn't tend to fill me up for very long, so adding the yoghurt and seeds makes this snack a more satisfying choice. It's good to find food that I really enjoy without feeling guilty.

Fleur – recovering from over-eating"

1 Melon – Rich in vitamin C and beta-carotene, supporting the immune system, and potassium, which helps to normalise blood pressure.

2 Pumpkin seeds – Great source of zinc, B vitamins, iron, magnesium and protein. Contains essential fatty acids that help to lower unhealthy cholesterol.

3 Yoghurt – Contains immune-boosting probiotics that support a healthy gut. Linked with maintenance of a healthy, stable weight.

4 Sunflower seeds – Excellent source of vitamin E, which promotes healthy hair and skin. Also contains B vitamins, supporting the immune system, protein and healthy fats that support the heart.

5 Flax seeds – Excellent source of omega-3 fatty acids, iron, zinc, copper, calcium, potassium, magnesium, folate and fibre.

No-Bake Date Cakes

A quick high-protein snack, rich in minerals that support brain, heart and respiratory health. A hands-on recipe that encourages tactile cooking – embrace the child in you!

Total time: 00:05   Preparation time: 00:05   Cooking time: 00:00   Serves: 4–6

Ingredients

- 10 dates
- 6 tablespoons of ground almonds
- 3 tablespoons of walnuts
- 2 tablespoons of organic honey

Equipment

- Food processor
- Tablespoon

Instructions

1. Place all ingredients into a food processor and blend until smooth.
2. Using your hands, shape the mixture into approximately 12 walnut-sized balls.
3. Store in an airtight container in the fridge.

Hints and tips

- Dried fruit is fairly high in natural sugar, so should be eaten in moderation. Combining dried fruit with nuts and seeds slows the subsequent release of energy, creating a balanced snack.
- Almonds are actually fruit seeds (rather than 'nuts')!
- Choose local honey whenever possible, as this will have the most nutritional value and the highest antibacterial/viral action.

"
I don't like coconut so this recipe offered me a great alternative to the Bliss Balls on page 220. I like having these to hand in the fridge because just one or two satisfy my craving for something sweet.

Rosie – overcoming low self-esteem
"

1 Dates – Great source of fibre, aiding digestion. Provide a natural sweetness that, when eaten in conjunction with healthy fats and protein, results in a slow release of energy.

2 Almonds – High in protein and a variety of minerals that support brain, cardiovascular and respiratory health.

3 Walnuts – Rich in omega-3, helping to lower unhealthy cholesterol levels. Good source of serotonin, a chemical that can help lift depression.

4 Honey – Choose local or Manuka honey for maximum benefit. Can be a source of antioxidants that help to heal ulcers and respiratory infections, and aid sleep.

Soft-Serve Banana Ice Cream

A naturally sweet dessert or snack rich in potassium. A topping of crushed nuts adds texture, healthy fats and protein, helping to strengthen bones and muscles. Conveniently kept in the freezer until ready to be eaten.

Total time: 00:05   Preparation time: 00:05   Cooking time: 00:00   Serves: 1

Ingredients

- 1 frozen banana
- 1–2 tablespoons of yoghurt
- 1 handful of crushed nuts (for example pecans, walnuts, cashews)

Instructions

1. Place the frozen banana and yoghurt into a food processor and blend until smooth.
2. Serve immediately, with the crushed nuts on top.

Equipment

- Freezer
- Food processor
- Tablespoon

Hints and tips

- Enjoy full-fat, natural and plain probiotic yoghurts for maximum benefit.
- Keep sliced banana in the freezer ready for this recipe at any time. See page 224 for an alternative use for the banana pieces.
- Experiment with flavours – consider adding 1 tablespoon of peanut butter, or a handful of berries, for example.

"
I could hardly believe my eyes when I saw this recipe. Healthy ice cream made from banana and yoghurt! Fantastic! I can now satisfy my cravings for a treat whilst eating something healthy.

Fleur – recovering from over-eating
"

1 Banana – Good source of potassium and fibre, aiding calcium absorption and bowel regularity. Also contains prebiotics, promoting gut health.

2 Yoghurt – Contains immune-boosting probiotics that support a healthy gut. Linked with maintenance of a healthy, stable weight.

3 Nuts – High in protein, antioxidants, fibre, omega-3 and omega-6 essential fatty acids and minerals. Nuts are also anti-inflammatory and contain nutrients that help strengthen bones and muscles.

Rejuvenating Chocolate Cake

A nutrient-dense tasty chocolate cake, boosting energy levels and supporting muscle strength and repair. Delicious served with Greek yoghurt and raspberries. Store in the fridge for a firmer texture, if preferred.

Total time: 00:30   Preparation time: 00:10   Cooking time: 00:20   Serves: 10

Ingredients

- 100g (scant ½ cup) coconut oil
- 3 free-range eggs
- 100g (⅓ cup) organic honey
- 100g (¾ cup) ground almonds
- 6 tablespooons of raw cacao
- 2 tablespoons of chia seeds
- Pinch of salt
- ½ teaspoon of bicarbonate of soda (baking soda)

Instructions

1. Preheat the oven to 170–180°C (325–350°F/Gas 3–4).
2. Grease a medium-sized cake tin with coconut oil.
3. Beat the eggs in a bowl.
4. Add all the other ingredients and fully combine.
5. Transfer the mix into the cake tin.
6. Bake for 20 minutes.
7. Serve warm or cold.

Equipment

- Oven
- Non-stick cake tin (approx. 23cm/9 inches)
- Kitchen scales
- Mixing bowl
- Whisk or fork
- Tablespoon
- Teaspoon

Hints and tips

- Serving a small portion of this cake alongside berries and yoghurt creates a wonderfully balanced snack or dessert.
- Enjoy full-fat, natural and plain probiotic yoghurts to maximise the benefits and avoid sweeteners.
- This recipe will be well received by guests!

"
An easy-to-make, high-protein cake adored by my whole family. I only need a small peice to satisfy my hunger. So delicious!

"
Emma

2 Almonds – High in protein and a variety of minerals that support brain, cardiovascular and respiratory health.

1 Eggs – Good source of protein, vitamin D and phosphorus, aiding strong [...]d teeth. Excellent [...] B vitamins and [...] boosting mental [...]nce.

3 Chia seeds – Rich in omega-3, which helps to lower unhealthy cholesterol levels. Good source of calcium and magnesium, promoting healthy bones and teeth. Also rich in iron, folate and soluble fibre.

4 Coconut – Aids the immune system, helping to fight the common cold and flu. Healthy fats boost metabolism and reduce the risk of heart disease.

5 Raw cacao – Rich in anti-inflammatory antioxidants that promote cardiovascular health. Boosts levels of serotonin, which helps to improve mood. Also protects against premature ageing.

Fruity Flapjacks

A heart-healthy snack combining porridge (oatmeal), nuts, seeds and the natural sweetness of dried fruit and local honey. Store in the fridge or freeze for later use. A satisfying mid-morning or afternoon snack.

Total time: 00:60   Preparation time: 00:10   Cooking time: 00:50   Serves: 10

Ingredients

- 2 bananas
- 1 apple
- 2 tablespoons of butter
- 2 tablespoons of almond butter
- 2 tablespoons of organic honey
- 100ml (scant ½ cup) of water
- 150g (¾ cup) dried fruit, for example cranberries or apricots
- 250g (2½ cups) porridge (oatmeal)
- 100g (¾ cup) mixed seeds, for example sunflower seeds or pumpkin seeds

Equipment

- Oven
- Oven hob (stovetop)
- Baking tray
- Non-stick saucepan
- Measuring jug/cup
- Kitchen scales
- Grater
- Baking paper
- Wooden spoon
- Tablespoon
- Sharp knife
- Chopping board

Hints and tips

- Dried fruit is fairly high in natural sugar, so should be eaten in moderation. Combining dried fruit with nuts and seeds slows the subsequent release of energy, creating a balanced snack.
- Use 100% natural porridge (without added sugar).

Instructions

1. Preheat the oven to 150–170°C (300–325°F/Gas 2–3).
2. Line a 20cm baking tray with baking paper.
3. Peel and mash 2 ripe bananas in a mixing bowl.
4. Grate the apple into the same bowl.
5. Add the butter, nut butter, honey and water.
6. Transfer the mixture to a non-stick saucepan and gently heat for 5 minutes, stirring occasionally.
7. Cut the dried fruit into small pieces, if necessary.
8. Remove the saucepan from the heat.
9. Add the oats, dried fruit and mixed seeds and fully combine.
10. Transfer the mixture to the lined baking tray.
11. Bake for 45 minutes, or until golden on top.
12. Cook in the tray before cutting into 12 equal slices.
13. Store in the fridge and consume within 5 days, or place in the freezer for later use (defrost before consuming).

> " These flapjacks are so tasty. They make a great snack before or after exercise so I make them for my daughter to eat between school and training. This book has helped her appreciate that she needs food to fuel her activities, keeping her strong and able to continue. "
>
> Kate – supportive parent

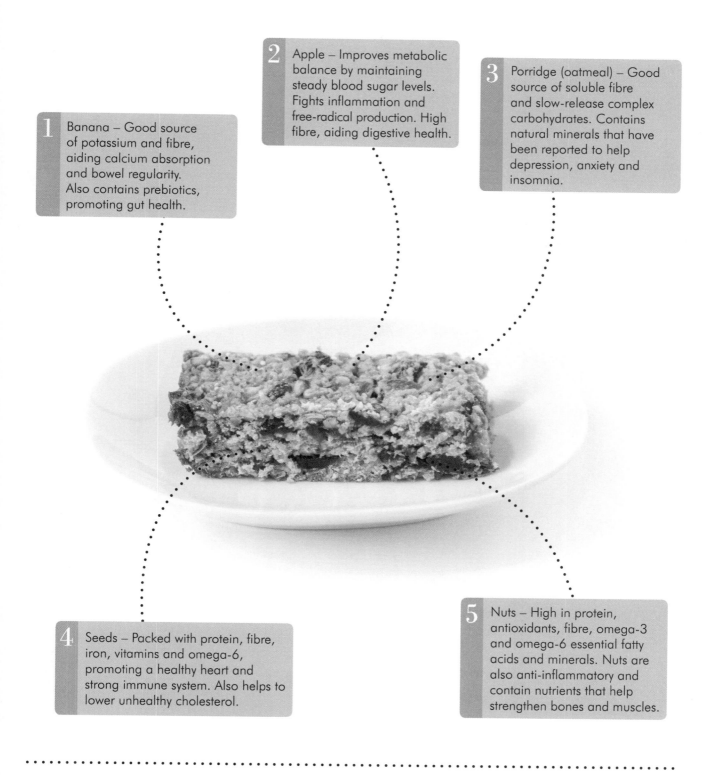

1 Banana – Good source of potassium and fibre, aiding calcium absorption and bowel regularity. Also contains prebiotics, promoting gut health.

2 Apple – Improves metabolic balance by maintaining steady blood sugar levels. Fights inflammation and free-radical production. High fibre, aiding digestive health.

3 Porridge (oatmeal) – Good source of soluble fibre and slow-release complex carbohydrates. Contains natural minerals that have been reported to help depression, anxiety and insomnia.

4 Seeds – Packed with protein, fibre, iron, vitamins and omega-6, promoting a healthy heart and strong immune system. Also helps to lower unhealthy cholesterol.

5 Nuts – High in protein, antioxidants, fibre, omega-3 and omega-6 essential fatty acids and minerals. Nuts are also anti-inflammatory and contain nutrients that help strengthen bones and muscles.

BREADS

No-Knead Seeded Spelt Loaf 244
Old-Fashioned Corn Bread 246
Wholemeal (Wholewheat) Soda Bread 248
Banana Bread 250
Simple Quick Bread 252

No-Knead Seeded Spelt Loaf

A simple wholemeal (wholewheat) loaf, made with spelt flour, which is more easily digested than traditional flours. No kneading or time for rising required – just mix, bake and serve! Delicious served with cream cheese and ham.

Total time: 00:55   Preparation time: 00:10   Cooking time: 00:45   1 loaf

Ingredients

- 500ml (18fl oz) warm water
- 2 tablespoons of fast-acting dried yeast (or 2 sachets)
- 2 tablespoons of organic honey
- 1 tablespoon of oil (e.g. olive oil)
- 500g (17.5oz) wholemeal (wholewheat) spelt flour
- 150g (5.5oz) sunflower seeds
- 1 teaspoon of baking powder
- 1 teaspoon of salt

Instructions

1. Preheat the oven to 170–180°C (325–350°F/Gas 3–4).
2. In a bowl, mix the warm water, yeast, honey and oil.
3. Leave to stand for 5 minutes (it may appear frothy).
4. In a separate mixing bowl, combine the flour, sunflower seeds (holding back a handful), baking powder and salt.
5. Pour the water mixture into the flour mixture and fully combine until it becomes a doughy consistency.
6. Place the dough into a loaf tin, sprinkling the reserved sunflower seeds on top.
7. Bake for 45 minutes.
8. Allow to cool before slicing, or store for later use.

Equipment

- Oven
- Loaf tin (medium-sized)
- Kitchen scales
- Measuring jug/cup
- 2 mixing bowls
- Tablespoon
- Teaspoon

Hints and tips

- This recipe can also be made with other types of flour.
- At its best the day of baking, but still delicious afterwards. Consider cutting the loaf into slices that can be frozen for later use (after being defrosted).

> " A dense, highly satisfying bread made from minimal ingredients. And so easy to make! This bread is really tasty – I know it might sound strange, but I like to have it with cream cheese, blackberries and honey! Try it – delicious! "
>
> E – recovering from an eating disorder

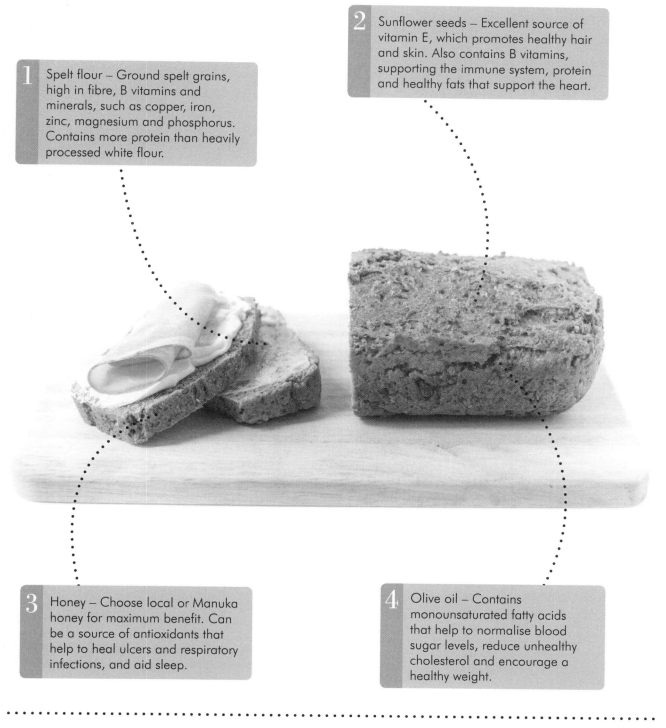

1 Spelt flour – Ground spelt grains, high in fibre, B vitamins and minerals, such as copper, iron, zinc, magnesium and phosphorus. Contains more protein than heavily processed white flour.

2 Sunflower seeds – Excellent source of vitamin E, which promotes healthy hair and skin. Also contains B vitamins, supporting the immune system, protein and healthy fats that support the heart.

3 Honey – Choose local or Manuka honey for maximum benefit. Can be a source of antioxidants that help to heal ulcers and respiratory infections, and aid sleep.

4 Olive oil – Contains monounsaturated fatty acids that help to normalise blood sugar levels, reduce unhealthy cholesterol and encourage a healthy weight.

Old-Fashioned Corn Bread

A delicious high-protein bread, providing one of your five a day! Perfect served with chilli con carne, meat or vegetarian stews and hearty soups. Corn bread could also be eaten as a healthy mid-morning or afternoon snack.

Total time: 00:40   Preparation time: 00:10   Cooking time: 00:30   Serves: 8

Ingredients

- 50g (¼ cup) butter
- 2 free-range eggs
- 250ml (1 cup) milk
- 125g (1 cup) strong white flour
- 150g (1¼ cup) polenta
- 1 can of sweetcorn (approx. 400g/1¾ cups)
- 1 tablespoon of baking powder
- 1 teaspoon of salt

Equipment

- Oven
- Microwave or non-stick saucepan
- Non-stick cake tin (23cm/9 inches)
- 2 mixing bowls
- Wooden spoon
- Sieve
- Can opener
- Tablespoon
- Teaspoon
- Kitchen scales

Instructions

1. Preheat the oven to 180–200°C (350–400°F/Gas 4–6).
2. Melt the butter in a microwave or non-stick saucepan (allowing it to cool but not solidify).
3. Carefully crack two eggs into a mixing bowl.
4. Add the milk and butter to the eggs.
5. Stir until fully combined.
6. Sieve the flour and polenta into a separate bowl.
7. Add the sweetcorn, baking powder and salt to the flour and polenta and mix together.
8. Add the egg mixture to the flour mixture and stir until just combined.
9. Spoon the mixture into a cake tin and bake for 25–30 minutes, or until the edges begin shrinking away from the side of the tin.
10. Cool before serving.

Hints and tips

- Polenta is made from ground corn. It looks like bright yellow flour and can be purchased from any supermarket.
- The sweetcorn could be placed into a food processor before it is added to the recipe, if you prefer a less chunky texture to the bread.

" Making this bread was actually fun! Knowing that the bread was mainly made from eggs and sweetcorn helped me to justify eating it. I've also made it in my food processor, meaning that the sweetcorn is broken down into smaller pieces, which was nice too. "

Lisa – overcoming body-image issues

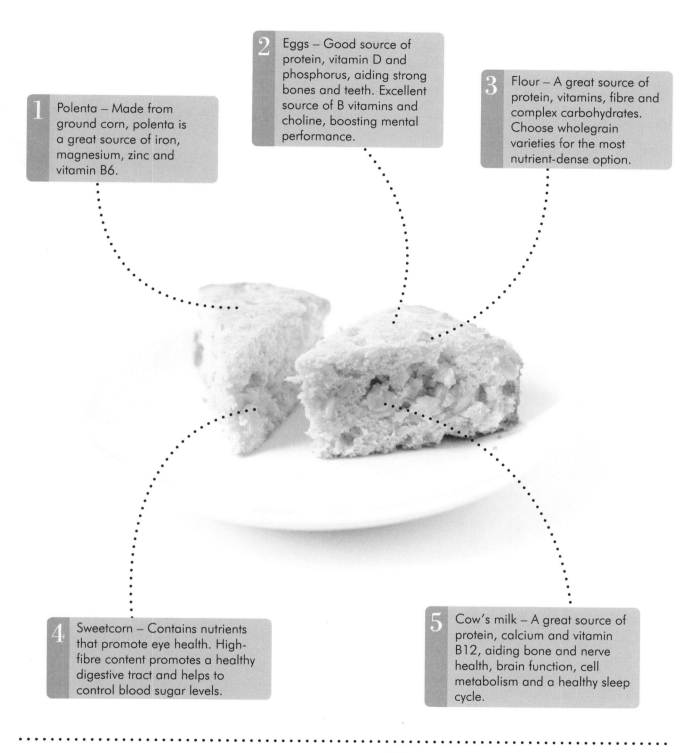

1 Polenta – Made from ground corn, polenta is a great source of iron, magnesium, zinc and vitamin B6.

2 Eggs – Good source of protein, vitamin D and phosphorus, aiding strong bones and teeth. Excellent source of B vitamins and choline, boosting mental performance.

3 Flour – A great source of protein, vitamins, fibre and complex carbohydrates. Choose wholegrain varieties for the most nutrient-dense option.

4 Sweetcorn – Contains nutrients that promote eye health. High-fibre content promotes a healthy digestive tract and helps to control blood sugar levels.

5 Cow's milk – A great source of protein, calcium and vitamin B12, aiding bone and nerve health, brain function, cell metabolism and a healthy sleep cycle.

Wholemeal (Wholewheat) Soda Bread

An amazing wholemeal (wholewheat) loaf that takes just minutes to prepare and needs no time to rise. Simple ingredients invite even the most novice cook to give this recipe a try. Experiment with different seeds and spices, according to preference.

Total time: 00:50   Preparation time: 00:10   Cooking time: 00:40   1 loaf

Ingredients

- 250g (2 cups) wholemeal (wholewheat) flour
- 250g (2 cups) plain flour
- 2 teaspoons of bicarbonate of soda (baking soda)
- 1 teaspoon of salt
- 2 tablespoons of chopped nuts or seeds, for example pine nuts, sunflower seeds, pumpkin seeds
- 400g (1½ cups) plain yoghurt

Optional: dash of milk

Equipment

- Oven
- Baking tray
- Mixing bowl
- Measuring jug/cup
- Sieve
- Baking paper
- Knife
- Tablespoon
- Teaspoon

Hints and tips

- You can use whichever nuts or seeds you prefer, whole or ground – they add protein, vitamins and minerals!
- Make sure that the bicarbonate of soda (baking soda) is well mixed in and not in clumps, to avoid a bitter taste.
- This bread requires no time to prove or rise.

Instructions

1. Preheat the oven to 180–200°C (350–400°F/Gas 4–6).
2. Line a baking tray with a baking sheet.
3. Sift both flours into a bowl. Add the bicarbonate of soda, salt, nuts and seeds.
4. Add the yoghurt to the bowl of flour and mix until all the ingredients have combined, adding a dash of milk to bring it all together if necessary.
5. Cover an area of your work surface with flour. Lightly knead the mixture with your hands, for just a couple of minutes.
6. Place the mixture onto the lined baking tray.
7. Cut a shallow line vertically across the centre of the loaf, approximately 2cm deep.
8. Bake for 20 minutes.
9. Reduce the oven temperature to 160–180°C (310–350°F/Gas 2½–4) and bake for a further 20 minutes.
10. Remove from the oven to cool.
11. Eat warm, or store for later use.

> "This is an amazing recipe, almost impossible to make badly. Much tastier than shop-bought bread, in my opinion. I love the crusty outside and soft inside.
>
> Nadia – overcoming low self-esteem

1 Nuts – High in protein, antioxidants, fibre, omega-3 and omega-6 fatty acids and minerals. Also anti-inflammatory and contain nutrients that help strengthen bones and muscles.

2 Wholemeal (wholewheat) flour – Contains a variety of vitamins, minerals and fibre. Also helps to maintain steady blood sugar levels.

3 Seeds – Packed with protein, fibre, iron, vitamins and omega-6, promoting a healthy heart and strong immune system. Also helps to lower unhealthy cholesterol.

4 Yoghurt – Contains immune-boosting probiotics that support a healthy gut. Linked with maintenance of a healthy, stable weight.

Banana Bread

A delicious snack, rich in protein, vitamins and minerals, enhancing heart and bone health. Serve as a snack, or use to make banana eggy bread for a healthy breakfast (see page 68 for recipe).

Total time: 00:50   Preparation time: 00:10   Cooking time: 00:40   1 loaf

Ingredients

- 75g (¼ cup) coconut oil
- 100g (scant cup) wholemeal (wholewheat) flour
- 75g (½ cup) ground almonds
- 1 handful of crushed walnuts
- 1 teaspoon of cinnamon
- 1 teaspoon of baking powder
- 1 teaspoon of bicarbonate of soda (baking soda)
- ¼ teaspoon of salt
- 3 ripe bananas
- 3 free-range eggs
- 125g (½ cup) almond or cashew butter

Equipment

- Oven
- Non-stick baking loaf tray
- Kitchen scales
- Measuring jug/cup
- Baking paper
- Teaspoon
- 2 mixing bowls
- Wooden spoon
- Fork

Instructions

1. Preheat the oven to 170–180°C (325–350°F/Gas 3–4).
2. Melt the coconut oil in a microwave or non-stick saucepan (allowing it to cool but not solidify).
3. Line the base of a baking loaf tray with baking paper.
4. In a bowl, mix the wholemeal (wholewheat) flour, almonds, walnuts, cinnamon, baking powder, bicarbonate of soda and salt.
5. In a separate mixing bowl, mash 3 ripe bananas with a fork.
6. Add the eggs, nut butter and coconut oil to the bananas and mix until fully combined.
7. Place the egg mixture into the flour mixture and stir together, creating a lumpy consistency.
8. Pour the mix into the loaf tray.
9. Bake for 35–40 minutes, or until lightly browned and starting to shrink away from the side of the tray.
10. Cool in the tray for 5 minutes.
11. Remove from the tray and serve immediately, or store for later use.

Hints and tips

- Oven temperatures may vary, so the cooking time might alter a little from person to person. When the banana bread is cooked, it should be springy to the touch.
- If the banana bread appears to be burning on the top but doesn't seem cooked through, place a piece of foil over the top whilst you finish baking.

> Eating little and often throughout the day and planning my meals and snacks has helped me to stop binging. It took my mind off food for a little while, meaning that I was able to concentrate and focus on other areas of my life.
>
> James – recovering from anorexia

1 Eggs – Good source of vitamin D and phosphorus, aiding strong bones and teeth. Excellent source of B vitamins and choline, boosting mental performance.

2 Nuts – High in protein, antioxidants, fibre, omega-3 and omega-6 essential fatty acids and minerals. Nuts are also anti-inflammatory and contain nutrients that help strengthen bones and muscles.

3 Banana – Good source of potassium and fibre, aiding calcium absorption and bowel regularity. Also contains prebiotics, promoting gut health.

4 Coconut – Aids the immune system, helping to fight the common cold and flu. Healthy fats boost metabolism and reduce the risk of heart disease.

5 Almonds – High in protein and a variety of minerals that support brain, cardiovascular and respiratory health.

Simple Quick Bread

An easy bread recipe using very simple ingredients. Shape the bread dough into rolls, flatbreads or pizza bases, as preferred. Double the recipe if batch cooking to freeze portions for later use. Delicious served with soup, hummus or healthy stews.

Total time: 00:40   Preparation time: 00:20   Cooking time: 00:20   Serves: 2-3

Ingredients

- 125ml (½ cup) warm water
- 1 tablespoon of fast-acting dried yeast
- 1 tablespoon of organic honey
- 1 tablespoon of oil
- 225g (2 cups) flour of choice
- ½ teaspoon of salt
- ½ teaspoon of baking powder
- ½ tablespoon of milk of choice

Equipment

- Oven
- Baking tray
- 2 mixing bowls
- Measuring jug/cup
- Sieve
- Baking paper
- Knife
- Tablespoon
- Teaspoon
- Optional: pastry brush

Hints and tips

- Absolutely delicious, but best eaten on the day of baking.
- Make this recipe in any shape you prefer, varying cooking times according to the thickness of the dough. Have a little fun experimenting!

Instructions

1. Preheat the oven to 170–180°C (325–350°F/Gas 3–4).
2. Line a baking tray with a baking sheet.
3. In a mixing bowl, combine the warm water, yeast, honey and oil.
4. Leave to stand for 5 minutes (it may appear frothy).
5. In a separate bowl, mix the flour, salt and baking powder.
6. Combine the wet and dry ingredients in one bowl and mix to form a doughy consistency.
7. Empty the dough onto a floured service and knead with your hands for 5–10 minutes.
8. Cut and mould into preferred shapes, for example 3 rolls, 3 flatbreads or 1 pizza base.
9. Place the pieces of dough onto the lined baking tray.
10. Apply a small amount of milk to the surface of each piece of dough using fingers or a pastry brush.
11. Bake in the oven until cooked through and lightly browned (approximately 18 minutes for rolls, 15 minutes for flatbreads, 10 minutes for pizza bases).
12. Serve immediately or cool and store in an airtight container for later use.

> " This was the first bread recipe that I have tried to make. I was attracted by the minimal ingredients list. I've previously been afraid of eating bread, but making it myself has helped me to feel more comfortable with it. Kneading the dough was surprisingly therapeutic. "
>
> Rosie – overcoming low self-esteem

1 Wholemeal (wholewheat) flour – Contains a variety of vitamins, minerals and fibre. Also helps to maintain steady blood sugar levels.

2 Honey – Choose local or Manuka honey for maximum benefit. Can be a source of antioxidants that help to heal ulcers and respiratory infections, and aid sleep.

3 Cow's milk – A great source of protein, calcium and vitamin B12, aiding bone and nerve health, brain function, cell metabolism and a healthy sleep cycle.

HEALTHY SPREADS AND SAUCES

Homemade Mayonnaise 256
Pizza/Pasta Sauce 258
Cashew Butter 260
Pesto Sauce 262
Healthy Chocolate Spread 264
Fresh Berry and Lime Compote 266
Salad Dressings 268

Homemade Mayonnaise

A versatile condiment that can be easily made and stored in the fridge for two weeks. Made from natural ingredients offering various nutritional benefits, homemade mayonnaise can be enjoyed in moderation, without guilt.

Total time: 00:10   Preparation time: 00:10   Cooking time: 00:00   Serves: 12–16

Ingredients

- 2 free-range eggs
- 1 tablespoon of apple cider vinegar
- ½ teaspoon of salt
- 2 teaspoons of Dijon mustard
- 475ml (16fl oz) sunflower oil or rapeseed oil

Instructions

1. Break the eggs into a food processor and blend for 30 seconds.
2. Add the apple cider vinegar, salt and mustard and blend again until combined.
3. Continually mix whilst adding the oil very, very slowly, taking approximately 8–10 minutes to pour the oil. Do not rush this process otherwise the mixture will split. If this happens, add another egg yolk and further oil, very slowly.
4. Use 1–2 tablespoons per serving.
5. Store in the fridge for up to 2 weeks.

Equipment

- Food processor
- Measuring jug/cup
- Tablespoon
- Teaspoon

Hints and tips

- This recipe provides the information needed to make your own mayonnaise, but it is equally fine for you to buy it pre-made. It would be emotionally unhealthy if you felt unable to eat food made by others so you should challenge yourself to have a variety of foods, from a variety of sources and venues. Everything in moderation, including moderation itself.

" I really like mayonnaise but would never allow myself to have it. I didn't feel worthy of food that I liked or wanted, especially when I thought of it as an indulgence. However, learning how to make my own mayonnaise has changed this. I am starting to appreciate the benefits of different ingredients and am more able to challenge my eating disorder thoughts. Slowly but surely. "

Isabelle – recovering from anorexia

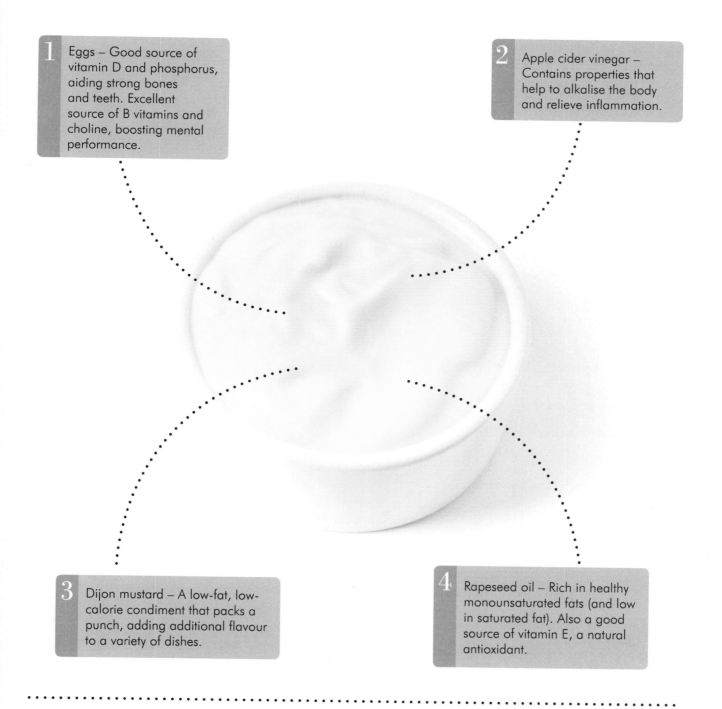

1 Eggs – Good source of vitamin D and phosphorus, aiding strong bones and teeth. Excellent source of B vitamins and choline, boosting mental performance.

2 Apple cider vinegar – Contains properties that help to alkalise the body and relieve inflammation.

3 Dijon mustard – A low-fat, low-calorie condiment that packs a punch, adding additional flavour to a variety of dishes.

4 Rapeseed oil – Rich in healthy monounsaturated fats (and low in saturated fat). Also a good source of vitamin E, a natural antioxidant.

Pizza/Pasta Sauce

A simple but nutritious tomato sauce, made with a variety of vegetables and immune-boosting garlic. Batch cook and store this recipe in the fridge for up to a week. Add to pastas and stews, spread on top of pitta bread or even eat it as a soup!

Total time: 00:15   Preparation time: 00:05   Cooking time: 00:10   Serves: 4

Ingredients

- 1 red or white onion
- 1 red pepper
- 1 courgette (zucchini)
- 1–3 cloves of garlic (skin removed)
- 1 tablespoon of oil
- 1 can of mixed beans (approx. 400g/1¾ cups)
- 1 can of chopped tomatoes (approx. 400g/1¾ cups)
- 1–2 tablespoons of dried herbs (or a small handful of fresh herbs), for example basil or oregano

Optional: sliced fresh red chilli or dried chilli flakes

Equipment

- Oven hob (stovetop)
- Non-stick saucepan
- Colander
- Chopping board
- Can opener
- Sharp knife
- Wooden spoon
- Tablespoon
- Teaspoon

Instructions

1. Finely chop the onion, red pepper, courgette and garlic.
2. Gently heat the oil in a non-stick saucepan.
3. Add the chopped vegetables and garlic and sauté over a medium heat for 3–5 minutes, or until the vegetables are soft but not browned.
4. Drain and rinse the can of beans.
5. Add the tinned tomatoes, beans and herbs to the saucepan and simmer for a further 5 minutes. Add the chilli now too, if using.
6. If you prefer a smoother texture, pour the mixture into a food processor and blend for 1 minute.
7. Use straight away or cool and store in the fridge for later use.

Hints and tips

- Add fresh herbs on top to maximise nutritional benefits.
- Spread on top of pitta bread to make a brilliant pitta pizza (see page 162).
- Batch cook and freeze for convenience.

> " Wow. This recipe is a great thing to make and eat. I'm not used to cooking so was nervous the first time I tried it, but was really surprised by how easy it was. My version even looked like the photograph! Hopefully, I can build my confidence in cooking to enable me to try other new things as well. "
>
> S – overcoming low self-esteem

1 Onions – Rich in antibacterial and antiviral properties, supporting the immune system. Also contains prebiotics, promoting gut health.

2 Courgette (zucchini) – Contains high levels of water, aiding water balance and bowel regularity. Good source of vitamin C, magnesium, folate and potassium.

3 Tomatoes – Good source of potassium, which aids the reduction of water retention. Also contains vitamins C, E and beta-carotene, supporting heart health.

4 Mixed beans – High protein, supporting cell repair and growth. Good source of complex carbohydrates and fibre, stabilising blood sugar levels and cholesterol.

5 Basil – Can ease digestion and be a good remedy for headaches and insomnia. Oregano – Rich in vitamin K, promoting bone growth and maintenance of bone density.

Cashew Butter

A smooth natural spread, providing the body with a great source of protein, healthy fats and an array of minerals that promote a healthy heart and strengthen bones. Experiment with a variety of different nuts, according to preference.

Total time: 00:10   Preparation time: 00:10   Cooking time: 00:00   Serves: 6

Ingredients

- Approx. 200g (heaped ¾ cup) unsalted cashews (or Brazils, almonds, pecans, peanuts or hazelnuts)
- Pinch of salt

Equipment

- Oven hob (stovetop)
- Non-stick frying pan
- Food processor

Hints and tips

- Eat hazelnuts with skin on to benefit from an increased level of antioxidants.
- Almonds eaten with the skin on offer double the antioxidant power!
- The food processor gets hot when it is working for a long time, so you may need to allow it to cool a little halfway through.

Instructions

1. Heat the cashews in a dry non-stick frying pan on a low-medium heat for 1–2 minutes.
2. Add the nuts and salt to a food processor and blend for 5–8 minutes, or until smooth.
3. Store in an airtight container in the cupboard for up to 2 weeks.

> " I eat cashews, so I thought it worth trying cashew butter. It took quite a long time to blend, but was worth the wait. Really tasty on wholemeal toast, but also good added to baking recipes. "
>
> Lucus – recovering from anorexia

1 Cashew nuts – Good source of monounsaturated fats, helping to protect against heart disease and cancer. Contains calcium, magnesium, iron, zinc and folate, contributing to good bone and skin health.

2 Brazil nuts – Good source of protein. Also contains monounsaturated fats and selenium, associated with lower cholesterol levels and a healthy heart.

3 Almonds – High in protein and a variety of minerals that support brain, cardiovascular and respiratory health.

4 Pecans – Rich in fibre and monounsaturated fats, aiding digestion and reducing the risk of health issues. Good source of phosphorus, relevant to bone health, and magnesium, offering anti-inflammatory benefits.

5 Hazelnuts – Great source of protein, vitamin K and E. Contains monounsaturated fat, associated with healthy cholesterol levels. Also contains folate, B vitamins and copper.

Pesto Sauce

A delicious high-protein pasta sauce bursting with flavour and nutritional benefits. Add to pasta (see page 142), pizza (see page 162) or even spread on sandwiches, if desired. This recipe can be made and stored in the fridge for later use.

Total time: 00:05   Preparation time: 00:03   Cooking time: 00:02   Serves: 2

Ingredients

- Approx. 50g (¼ cup) pine nuts or cashew nuts
- 1 clove of garlic
- Approx. 50g (1.75oz) Parmesan
- 1 handful of fresh basil leaves
- Juice of 1 lemon
- 2 tablespoons of water
- 1 tablespoon of olive oil
- Pinch of salt and pepper

Instructions

1. Heat the pine nuts/cashew nuts in a dry non-stick frying pan on a low-medium heat for 1–2 minutes.
2. Peel the garlic clove.
3. Add the garlic, nuts and all other ingredients to a food processor.
4. Blend until fully combined.
5. Serve with pasta, in sandwiches, on burgers or with vegetables. Can be stored in the fridge for up to a week.

Equipment

- Oven hob (stovetop)
- Non-stick frying pan/saucepan
- Food processor
- Kitchen scales
- Tablespoon

Hints and tips

- Most people use olive oil to make pesto sauce, however, you could use alternative oils if preferred.
- Pine nuts are expensive because of the process involved in farming them. You can use cashew nuts instead, if preferred.

> "Making this sauce was really fun! A friend had suggested that I try making some recipes without having to even think about eating them. This enabled me to enjoy the making process, without any stress. The rest of my family ate pesto pasta that night, and I've since managed to join them. Cooking my own food really has helped me to feel more comfortable about eating."
>
> F – recovering from an eating disorder

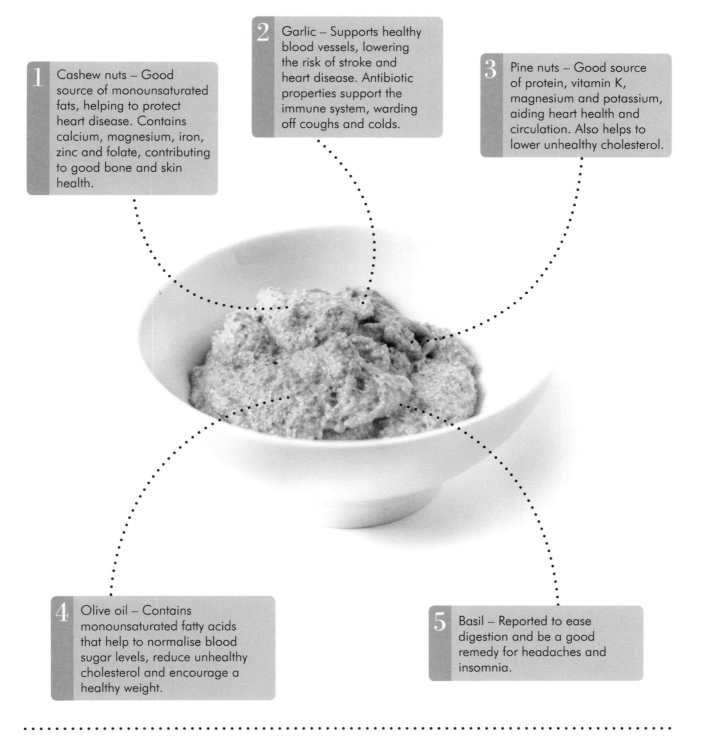

1 Cashew nuts – Good source of monounsaturated fats, helping to protect heart disease. Contains calcium, magnesium, iron, zinc and folate, contributing to good bone and skin health.

2 Garlic – Supports healthy blood vessels, lowering the risk of stroke and heart disease. Antibiotic properties support the immune system, warding off coughs and colds.

3 Pine nuts – Good source of protein, vitamin K, magnesium and potassium, aiding heart health and circulation. Also helps to lower unhealthy cholesterol.

4 Olive oil – Contains monounsaturated fatty acids that help to normalise blood sugar levels, reduce unhealthy cholesterol and encourage a healthy weight.

5 Basil – Reported to ease digestion and be a good remedy for headaches and insomnia.

Healthy Chocolate Spread

A healthy alternative to shop-brought chocolate spreads, bursting with antioxidants that promote good health and vitality. Made from only nuts, seeds, honey and raw cacao powder, this spread can be enjoyed on toast or crumpets as a healthy breakfast option.

Total time: 00:05   Preparation time: 00:05   Cooking time: 00:00   Serves: 4–6

Ingredients

- 6 tablespoons of ground almonds
- 2 tablespoons of mixed seeds
- 2 tablespoons of coconut oil
- 1 tablespoon of raw cacao powder
- 1 tablespoon of organic honey
- 1 tablespoon of water

Equipment

- Food processor
- Tablespoon

Instructions

1. Add all ingredients to a food processor and blend until fully combined and smooth.
2. Store in an airtight container for up to 2 weeks.

Hints and tips

- Store in an airtight container in the cupboard or fridge, depending on how firm you would rather have the spread.
- Nuts are rich in protein and healthy fats.
- Unlike cocoa powder, raw cacao powder is unprocessed and therefore retains an impressive amount of antioxidants and flavanols. You can buy cacao powder from health food shops or online.

> " Healthy chocolate spread! Healthy chocolate spread! My prayers have been answered! No, seriously, I know that I shouldn't eat the whole jar in one go. In fact, I don't want to... Having this spread on a couple of crumpets or pieces of toast feels more than enough. I'm so pleased that I can have this knowing that it's all healthy. Thank you!
>
> M – recovering from an eating disorder "

1 Coconut – Aids the immune system, helping to fight the common cold and flu. Healthy fats boost metabolism and reduce the risk of heart disease.

2 Almonds – High in protein and a variety of minerals that support brain, cardiovascular and respiratory health.

3 Seeds – Packed with protein, fibre, iron, vitamins and omega-3, promoting a healthy heart and strong immune system. Also helps to lower unhealthy cholesterol.

4 Cacao – Rich in anti-inflammatory antioxidants that promote cardiovascular health. Boosts levels of serotonin, which helps to improve mood. Also protects against premature ageing.

5 Honey – Contains antioxidants that help to heal ulcers and respiratory infections, and aid sleep.

Fresh Berry and Lime Compote

An amazing berry sauce with a zing, delicious served with homemade pancakes and yoghurt (see page 60 for recipe). Made from just fruit and honey, this naturally sweet sauce is also great on eggy bread (see page 26) or served with Greek yoghurt, nuts and seeds (see page 30).

Total time: 00:10   Preparation time: 00:01   Cooking time: 00:09   Serves: 1

Ingredients

- 1 handful of blackberries
- 1 handful of blueberries
- Zest and juice of ½ lime
- 1 tablespoon of water
- 1–2 teaspoons of organic honey

Equipment

- Oven hob (stovetop)
- Non-stick saucepan
- Wooden spoon
- Tablespoon
- Teaspoon
- Grater

Instructions

1. Add all ingredients to a non-stick saucepan and bring to the boil.
2. Reduce to a simmer and cook for a further 8 minutes, stirring occasionally.
3. Serve warm, or refrigerate for later use.

Hints and tips

- Choose local honey whenever possible, as this will contain the most nutritional value and have the highest antibacterial action.
- Consider picking your own seasonal fruit, as and when appropriate. Some farmers advertise 'pick your own' opportunities, but you may also be able to forage – blackberries can often be found in countryside hedges during the autumn.

> "I like to experiment with food, creating delicious foods from healthy ingredients. I want to enjoy eating without feeling guilty or greedy. Recovering from an eating disorder has taught me that it's important to appreciate food as fuel for the mind and body. Everything in moderation, including moderation itself."
>
> Emma

1 Blackberries – Shown to improve cognitive function and memory. High in vitamin C and antioxidants, in addition to other anti-cancer substances.

2 Blueberries – Rich in antioxidants. Thought to improve cognitive function and memory, improve eye health and slow the growth of cancer cells.

3 Lime – High in vitamin C, boosting the immune system. Also rich in vitamin K, essential for healthy blood clotting, and vitamin A, aiding liver function.

4 Honey – Contains antioxidants that help to heal ulcers and respiratory infections, and aid sleep.

Salad Dressings

An array of vitamin- and mineral-rich dressings created to add flavour and nutritional value to any salad. Experiment with the below ingredients according to your personal preferences. Make and store these dressings in the fridge for convenient later use.

Total time: 00:05   Preparation time: 00:05   Cooking time: 00:00   Serves: 2

Ingredients

- See individual dressings in the instructions.

Equipment

- Mixing bowl
- Tablespoon
- Teaspoon

Instructions

- **Balsamic dressing** – 2 tablespoons of olive oil, 1 tablespoon of balsamic vinegar, ½ teaspoon of Dijon mustard, juice of ½ a lemon, pinch of salt and pepper.
- **Simple salad dressing** – 2 tablespoons of olive oil, 1 tablespoon of apple cider vinegar, juice of ½ a lemon, pinch of salt and pepper.
- **Italian herb dressing** – 2 tablespoons of olive oil, ½ teaspoon of honey, ¼ teaspoon of garlic powder, pinch of dried thyme, pinch of dried oregano, pinch of dried basil, pinch of salt and pepper.
- **Cucumber dressing** – 2 tablespoons of Greek yoghurt, 2 inches of finely chopped cucumber, 1 teaspoon of olive oil, 1 teaspoon of balsamic vinegar, ½ teaspoon of dill, pinch of salt and pepper.
- **Citrus vinaigrette** – 1 tablespoon of orange juice, 1 tablespoon of lemon juice, 1 teaspoon of olive oil, 1 teaspoon of soy sauce, ½ teaspoon of Dijon mustard, ½ teaspoon of honey.
- **Honey and mustard dressing** – 2 tablespoons of Greek yoghurt, ½ teaspoon of Dijon mustard, 1 teaspoon of honey, juice of ½ a lemon.

Hints and tips

- All of these salad dressings have nutritional value to add to other recipes.
- Rather than focusing on food fears, calories and rigid rules, focus attention on the nutritional benefits of wholesome foods.
- These salad dressings can be prepared and stored in the fridge for later use.
- Experiment with different combinations of the ingredients, according to your preferences.

"
I assumed that salad dressing were unhealthy and unnecessary. I was wrong! I've enjoyed trying each of these dressings, knowing that they're adding nutritional value to our meals.
"

Kate – supportive parent

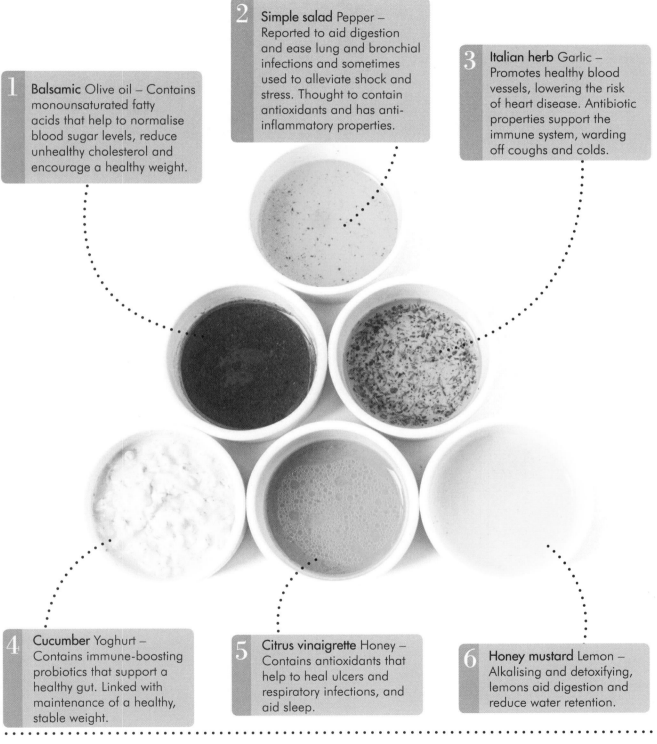

1 **Balsamic** Olive oil – Contains monounsaturated fatty acids that help to normalise blood sugar levels, reduce unhealthy cholesterol and encourage a healthy weight.

2 **Simple salad** Pepper – Reported to aid digestion and ease lung and bronchial infections and sometimes used to alleviate shock and stress. Thought to contain antioxidants and has anti-inflammatory properties.

3 **Italian herb** Garlic – Promotes healthy blood vessels, lowering the risk of heart disease. Antibiotic properties support the immune system, warding off coughs and colds.

4 **Cucumber** Yoghurt – Contains immune-boosting probiotics that support a healthy gut. Linked with maintenance of a healthy, stable weight.

5 **Citrus vinaigrette** Honey – Contains antioxidants that help to heal ulcers and respiratory infections, and aid sleep.

6 **Honey mustard** Lemon – Alkalising and detoxifying, lemons aid digestion and reduce water retention.

SELF-HELP TOOLS

Self-reflection 272
Personal Bliss List 273
Wellness Self-assessment 274
Doodle Page 280

Self-reflection

One of the most important things to remember and accept is that nobody is perfect, and nor should they try to be. Everyone makes mistakes. Sometimes, mistakes teach you the greatest lessons, helping to make you a better person. Being real and honest is beautiful.

> 'Today I will do my best. If I have a good day, I will be proud of myself. If I have a bad day, I will not dwell on it, I will forgive myself and learn from my experiences. I will continue to move forward, day by day, evolving as a person.'

No matter how many mistakes you make or how slow your progress, you are still way ahead of anyone who isn't trying. Live life day by day, appreciating the positives and learning from any negatives, allowing your personality to evolve and develop continuously. And remember – the happiest people don't have the best of everything, they just make the best of everything.

My personal responsibility checklist

This checklist may help you learn how to be accountable to yourself. Ask yourself:

- Am I being kind and considerate to myself?

- Am I surrounding myself with supportive influences?

- Do I listen to positive advice?

- Am I seeking the things I need?

- Do I express my feelings openly?

- Am I trying my best to be well?

- Am I being honest with myself and others?

- Do I seek additional support when needed?

- Considering my answers to the above, what could I do to improve my situation?

Personal Bliss List

Use the space below to note activities that make you emotionally happy. These must not be related to food, weight or body image. Some examples have been provided for you, with space for you to personalise the list according to your individual preferences. Refer to your bliss list regularly, including the activities in your daily life whenever possible.

- Enjoy a hot bubble bath
- Take the dog for a walk
- Read a book
- Chat with a friend

- Go horse riding
- Practise yoga
- Watch a film
- Paint a picture

Wellness Self-assessment

Use the checklists below to evaluate your thoughts and behaviours. Your answers may indicate areas that would benefit from more consideration. You might like to revisit the checklists in the future, enabling you to see your personal progress over time. Use the blank lines to personalise the table according to your individual needs.

1=Untrue   2=Mostly untrue   3=Somewhat true   4=Mostly true   5=Absolutely true

My eating habits

		1	2	3	4	5
1	I practise healthy eating habits	1	2	3	4	5
2	I eat three meals a day (plus snacks, when appropriate)	1	2	3	4	5
3	I eat a sufficient amount of calories for my lifestyle needs	1	2	3	4	5
4	I am able to enjoy eating	1	2	3	4	5
5	I eat a variety of foods on a regular basis	1	2	3	4	5
6	I am able to eat in company	1	2	3	4	5
7	I can decide what to eat without too much procrastination	1	2	3	4	5
8	I am comfortable talking about food	1	2	3	4	5
9	I am comfortable food shopping	1	2	3	4	5
10	I eat at least 5 portions of fruit and veg a day	1	2	3	4	5
11	I eat from every food group, including carbohydrates, proteins, fats and dairy	1	2	3	4	5
12	I am able to buy and eat food out and about	1	2	3	4	5
13	I can make spontaneous choices about food	1	2	3	4	5
14	I do not feel the need to maintain a rigid/restricted food plan	1	2	3	4	5
15	I do not punish myself for eating	1	2	3	4	5
16	I do not criticise myself in relation to my weight or food intake	1	2	3	4	5
17	I do not binge	1	2	3	4	5
18	I do not make myself sick after eating	1	2	3	4	5
19	I do not use laxatives	1	2	3	4	5
20	I do not use diuretics	1	2	3	4	5
21	I do not take slimming pills	1	2	3	4	5
22	I do not abuse alcohol	1	2	3	4	5
23		1	2	3	4	5
24		1	2	3	4	5

1=Untrue   2=Mostly untrue   3=Somewhat true   4=Mostly true   5=Absolutely true

My body image

		1	2	3	4	5
1	I treat my body well	1	2	3	4	5
2	I have a positive attitude towards my body	1	2	3	4	5
3	I am accepting of my body shape	1	2	3	4	5
4	I give my body care and consideration	1	2	3	4	5
5	I feel psychologically connected to my body	1	2	3	4	5
6	I exercise to be fit and healthy rather than to change my body	1	2	3	4	5
7	I am comfortable with being in a photo or video	1	2	3	4	5
8	I have realistic thoughts and expectations of my body	1	2	3	4	5
9	I am comfortable with other people seeing my body	1	2	3	4	5
10	I am happy to participate in physical activities	1	2	3	4	5
11	I am comfortable looking in a mirror	1	2	3	4	5
12	I am comfortable shopping for clothes	1	2	3	4	5
13	I am able to be physically close to someone else	1	2	3	4	5
14	My body image is not affected by other people's thoughts and opinions	1	2	3	4	5
15	My body image is not affected by what other people look like	1	2	3	4	5
16	I do not feel too big/small	1	2	3	4	5
17	I am not obsessed with checking my body	1	2	3	4	5
18	I am not preoccupied with controlling my weight	1	2	3	4	5
19	I do not take any illegal or harmful substances to alter my body	1	2	3	4	5
20	I do not change my posture just to avoid seeing myself in certain positions	1	2	3	4	5
21	I do not need lots of make-up or fake tan to feel comfortable with myself	1	2	3	4	5
22	I do not feel the need to seek constant reassurance about my body	1	2	3	4	5
23	I do not abuse sunbeds	1	2	3	4	5
24	I do not criticise myself in relation to my weight	1	2	3	4	5
25	I do not feel it necessary to have cosmetic surgery	1	2	3	4	5
26		1	2	3	4	5
27		1	2	3	4	5

Body confidence does not come from trying to achieve the perfect body, it comes from embracing the one you've already got.

1=Untrue   2=Mostly untrue   3=Somewhat true   4=Mostly true   5=Absolutely true

My physical health

		1	2	3	4	5
1	My weight is within a normal range for my age and height	1	2	3	4	5
2	My weight has been stable for three months or more	1	2	3	4	5
3	I have regular periods (women only)	1	2	3	4	5
4	I have plenty of energy	1	2	3	4	5
5	My bones and joints are healthy and strong for my age	1	2	3	4	5
6	My body temperature is within a normal range	1	2	3	4	5
7	My blood pressure is within a normal range	1	2	3	4	5
8	My heart rate is within a normal range	1	2	3	4	5
9	I feel comfortable visiting a health professional	1	2	3	4	5
10	My hair and nails are strong	1	2	3	4	5
11	My skin looks and feels healthy	1	2	3	4	5
12	I have healthy teeth and gums	1	2	3	4	5
13	I have a normal sleeping pattern	1	2	3	4	5
14	I do not have problems with my digestive system	1	2	3	4	5
15	I do not have issues with constipation	1	2	3	4	5
16	I do not feel overly tired	1	2	3	4	5
17	I do not have to visit my GP for regular tests	1	2	3	4	5
18	I am not unwell very often	1	2	3	4	5
19	When I am unwell, I recover quickly	1	2	3	4	5
20		1	2	3	4	5
21		1	2	3	4	5

'When I began to look physically well, people around me assumed that I was no longer struggling with my eating disorder. It was important for me to help them understand that challenging my eating disorder thoughts was emotionally draining and that I actually needed their support more than ever. Otherwise, I think people might have unknowingly triggered a relapse by expecting me to cope with more than I could handle. I needed time to come to terms with my new body and some space to reflect upon who I wanted to be and what I wanted from my future.'

Emma

1=Untrue   2=Mostly untrue   3=Somewhat true   4=Mostly true   5=Absolutely true

My psychological health

		1	2	3	4	5
1	I have plenty of self-esteem	1	2	3	4	5
2	I am able to relax	1	2	3	4	5
3	Most of the time, my thoughts are rational and fair	1	2	3	4	5
4	My self-esteem is not affected by my weight	1	2	3	4	5
5	I am able to accept compliments graciously	1	2	3	4	5
6	I am not a perfectionist to the detriment of enjoying life	1	2	3	4	5
7	My self-worth is not related to strict exercise or diet plans	1	2	3	4	5
8	My self-worth is not dependent on other people's approval	1	2	3	4	5
9	I am able to concentrate on things	1	2	3	4	5
10	People around me would say I have a realistic view of myself	1	2	3	4	5
11	I welcome new experiences	1	2	3	4	5
12	I am able to take responsibility for myself	1	2	3	4	5
13	I feel happy most of the time	1	2	3	4	5
14	I feel positive about the future	1	2	3	4	5
15	I feel like a worthy person	1	2	3	4	5
16	I am aware of my personal preferences	1	2	3	4	5
17	I do not struggle with an inner critical voice	1	2	3	4	5
18	I do not have obsessive/compulsive thoughts and behaviours	1	2	3	4	5
19	I do not have suicidal thoughts	1	2	3	4	5
20	I do not suffer with anxiety/panic attacks	1	2	3	4	5
21	I do not fear failure to the extent that I will avoid its possibility	1	2	3	4	5
22	I am not restricted by constant negative thoughts	1	2	3	4	5
23		1	2	3	4	5
24		1	2	3	4	5

'Although I sometimes have negative thoughts about myself, I am now able to recognise them as nervous self-doubt. I don't have to react or punish myself anymore. I am able to accept that I may not be perfect, but I am perfectly me, and that's more than good enough! Overcoming my challenges has made me a stronger person.'

Emma

1=Untrue   2=Mostly untrue   3=Somewhat true   4=Mostly true   5=Absolutely true

My coping skills

1	I am able to recognise and be considerate towards my needs and emotions	1	2	3	4	5
2	I feel able to express positive thoughts and feelings	1	2	3	4	5
3	I feel able to express negative thoughts and feelings	1	2	3	4	5
4	I am able to be calm and rational with myself and others	1	2	3	4	5
5	I have a range of positive tools that I use to help me cope with life	1	2	3	4	5
6	I can enjoy being spontaneous	1	2	3	4	5
7	I can cope well with change	1	2	3	4	5
8	I am not afraid of having a different opinion to someone else	1	2	3	4	5
9	I can cope with stress in a healthy way	1	2	3	4	5
10	I have a healthy relationship with exercise	1	2	3	4	5
11	I feel comfortable resting my body when I am tired, injured or unwell	1	2	3	4	5
12	I am able to ask for help when I need it	1	2	3	4	5
13	I am aware of triggers that may cause me anxiety	1	2	3	4	5
14	I do not struggle with frequent low moods	1	2	3	4	5
15	I do not weigh myself in a ritualistic way	1	2	3	4	5
16	I do not abuse recreational drugs or alcohol	1	2	3	4	5
17	I do not abuse food or exercise to manage my emotions	1	2	3	4	5
18	I am not challenged by obsessive compulsive disorder (OCD)	1	2	3	4	5
19	I do not cause myself physical pain as a way of coping with emotions	1	2	3	4	5
20	My needs do not depend on someone else's approval	1	2	3	4	5
21	I do not do things just to please others, to the detriment of myself	1	2	3	4	5
22		1	2	3	4	5
23		1	2	3	4	5

Being positive does not mean ignoring the negative, it means overcoming the challenges you face, with determination and hope. Remember – you can only do your best, with what you have, and what you know, in that very moment. Be honest and brave and you'll always have reason to feel proud of yourself.

1=Untrue   2=Mostly untrue   3=Somewhat true   4=Mostly true   5=Absolutely true

My relationships

		1	2	3	4	5
1	I have a network of people I can turn to	1	2	3	4	5
2	I enjoy personal hobbies that are good for my physical and/or emotional health	1	2	3	4	5
3	I am able to initiate conversations with other people	1	2	3	4	5
4	I feel comfortable talking about personal thoughts and experiences	1	2	3	4	5
5	I choose to participate in social events and activities on a regular basis	1	2	3	4	5
6	I am comfortable with the relationship that I have with my parents	1	2	3	4	5
7	I am comfortable with the relationship that I have with my other family members	1	2	3	4	5
8	I am able to study/work, if required	1	2	3	4	5
9	I am in a position to consider volunterring, if desired	1	2	3	4	5
10	I am able to consider travelling without it causing significant anxiety	1	2	3	4	5
11	I have some good friends who I can trust	1	2	3	4	5
12	I am able to be myself with other people	1	2	3	4	5
13	I am comfortable with the idea of being in a personal relationship	1	2	3	4	5
14	I am comfortable spending time with myself	1	2	3	4	5
15	I am able to ask others for help	1	2	3	4	5
16	I do not feel isolated or lonely	1	2	3	4	5
17		1	2	3	4	5
18		1	2	3	4	5

When you have completed the above checklists you will better understand how you feel about your body, eating habits and relationships. Circling the number 1 or 2 indicates that you have negative thoughts and behaviours that should be addressed with care and support. Circling the number 3 suggests that your thoughts on a subject could be improved. Circling the number 4 or 5 represents a positive, healthy mindset that allows you to experience a happy, fulfilled life.

Be proud of any acheivements and pro-active about the self-care still needed to meet your full potential. Give yourself permission to strive for happiness.

Doodle Page

Use this page to doodle positive affirmations that inspire long-term recovery.

Everything in moderation, including moderation itself.

You can only do your best, with what you have and what you know in that very moment.

If you always do what you've always done, you'll always get what you've always got.

I want to be strong, fit and healthy.

If I eat a balance of healthy, nutritious food and exercise smart, my body will be what it should be

Eating regularly will aid my metabolism and stabilise my weight.

Spending money on good-quality food is an investment in my health and wellbeing...my future.

Breathe. Pause. Breathe. Move forward.

I need to show my body that I can be trusted to fuel it responsibly and consistently.

Once you've run out of space here, buy yourself a special notebook for more doodling.

INDEX

Example Food Plan..284
My Food Plan...285
Measurement Index 286
Photographic Index of Ingredients 288
Photographic Index of Recipes 290

Example Food Plan

The table below provides an example of a healthy, balanced food plan. However, a person's specific nutritional requirements are dependent on many factors, including height, weight, daily activity levels and general health.

This book includes a variety of food choices, allowing you to personalise an eating plan according to your individual needs and preferences. Please note pages 8–13 for general nutritional advice that will help you to create a balanced way of eating. Should you still feel overwhelmed and wish for additional support, seek help from a qualified professional who is sensitive to your issues.

	BREAKFAST	SNACK	LUNCH	SNACK	DINNER
MONDAY	Mug muffin with yoghurt and raspberries	Popcorn	Tuna pasta salad	Beetroot dip with crackers	Chicken and roast vegetable tray bake
TUESDAY	Cinnamon eggy bread with berries	Bliss Balls	Chicken, sweetcorn and avocado wrap	Melon and yoghurt	Asian style salmon with veg rice
WEDNESDAY	Porridge (oatmeal) with apple and walnuts	Smoked salmon stuffed celery	Mango and feta salad	Beetroot dip with crackers	Chilli con carne with rice (batch cook and store)
THURSDAY	Banana smoothie	Hummus with crudités	Mackerel pâté with salad	Popcorn	Quinoa, sundried tomato and feta
FRIDAY	Ham, spinach and Parmesan eggs	Bliss Balls	Chilli con carne in a wholemeal (wholewheat) wrap	Banana, almond butter and chia seeds	Lentil cottage pie with broccoli
SATURDAY	Pancakes with fruit compote	Lime and pepper cashew nuts	Quinoa Greek salad	Hummus with crudités	Fish pie with peas
SUNDAY	Poached egg and avocado on toast	Green smoothie	Mixed bean salad	Bliss Balls	Pesto pasta with chicken

My Food Plan

If you find it helpful to plan your meals ahead, feel free to photocopy the below table as a template food plan.

	BREAKFAST	SNACK	LUNCH	SNACK	DINNER
MONDAY					
TUESDAY					
WEDNESDAY					
THURSDAY					
FRIDAY					
SATURDAY					
SUNDAY					

The space below may be used to note your shopping items.

Measurement Index

Weights

METRIC	IMPERIAL
15g	½oz
20g	¾ oz
30g	1oz
60g	2oz
85g	3oz
115g	4oz (¼lb)
140g	5oz
170g	6oz
200g	7oz
230g	8oz (½lb)
255g	9oz
285g	10oz
310g	11oz
340g	12oz (¾lb)
370g	13oz
400g	14oz
425g	15oz
450g	16oz (1lb)
680g	24oz
0.9kg	32oz (2lb)
1.4kg	48oz (3lb)
1.8kg	64oz (4lb)
1g=0.035oz 1oz=28.35g	
1kg = 35oz/2.2lbs	

Liquids

METRIC	CUPS	FLUID OZ	UK PINTS
100ml		3½	
125ml	½	4½	
150ml		5	¼
200ml		7	
250ml	1	9	
275ml		10	½
300ml		11	
400ml		14	
500ml	2	18	
570ml		20	1
750ml	3	26	
1.0L	4	35	1¾
1.1L		40	2
1.3L	5	46	
1.7L		60	3
2.0L	8	70	

Cups

ONE CUP	METRIC	IMPERIAL
Flour	140g	5oz
Caster sugar	225g	8oz
Butter	225g	8oz
Uncooked rice	200g	7oz
Grated cheese	110g	4oz
Oats	90g	3oz
Honey	350g	12oz
Ground nuts	120g	4oz
Couscous	180g	6oz

Food terms

BRITISH	AMERICAN
Aubergine	Eggplant
Beetroot	Beets
Bicarbonate of soda	Baking soda
Cling film	Plastic wrap
Coriander	Cilantro
Cornflour	Cornstarch
Courgette	Zucchini
Eggy bread	French toast
Desiccated (coconut)	Dried
Green/red peppers	Bell peppers
Grill	Broil
Hob	Stovetop
Kipper	Smoked herring
Kitchen paper	Paper towel
Mangetout	Snow peas
Mince	Ground
Plain flour	All-purpose flour
Porridge oats	Oatmeal
Prawn	Small shrimp
Rocket	Arugula
Slow cooker	Crockpot
Spring onions	Green onions
Sweetcorn	Corn
Tomato purée	Tomato paste

In an attempt to make this book easier to use we have included various UK/US food terms. For a more complete list please visit: the-shoppers-market.com/misc/f/foodterms.html

Oven temps

°C	°F	GAS	DESCRIPTION
120	250	½	VERY SLOW
140	275	1	
150	300	2	SLOW
170	325	3	
180	350	4	MODERATE
190	375	5	
200	400	6	MOD. HOT
220	425	7	
230	450	8	HOT
240	475	9	VERY HOT

$$°C \times 1.8 + 32 = °F$$
$$°F - 32 \div 1.8 = °C$$

Note that fan oven temperatures should be reduced by around 20°C

WATER

Boils at:	100°C	212°F
Freezes at:	0°C	32°F

1 litre	=	1.76 pints
1 pint (UK)	=	568 ml
1 pint (US)	=	16 fl oz

1 fl oz	=	28.41 ml
1 ml	=	0.035 fl oz
1 cup (US)	=	250 ml

Photographic Index of Ingredients

Use this page to identify ingredients used in the recipes throughout the cookbook.
*For American terminology, please see page 287.

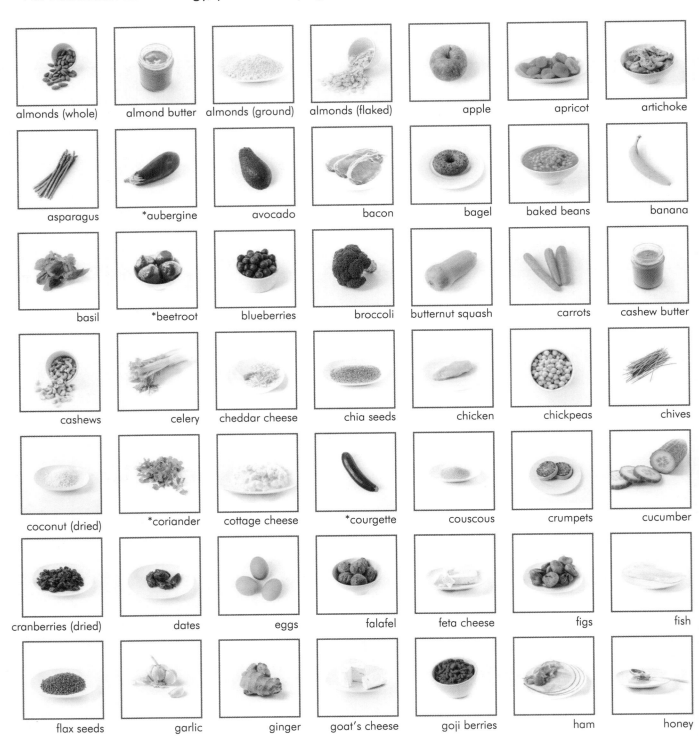

almonds (whole)	almond butter	almonds (ground)	almonds (flaked)	apple	apricot	artichoke
asparagus	*aubergine	avocado	bacon	bagel	baked beans	banana
basil	*beetroot	blueberries	broccoli	butternut squash	carrots	cashew butter
cashews	celery	cheddar cheese	chia seeds	chicken	chickpeas	chives
coconut (dried)	*coriander	cottage cheese	*courgette	couscous	crumpets	cucumber
cranberries (dried)	dates	eggs	falafel	feta cheese	figs	fish
flax seeds	garlic	ginger	goat's cheese	goji berries	ham	honey

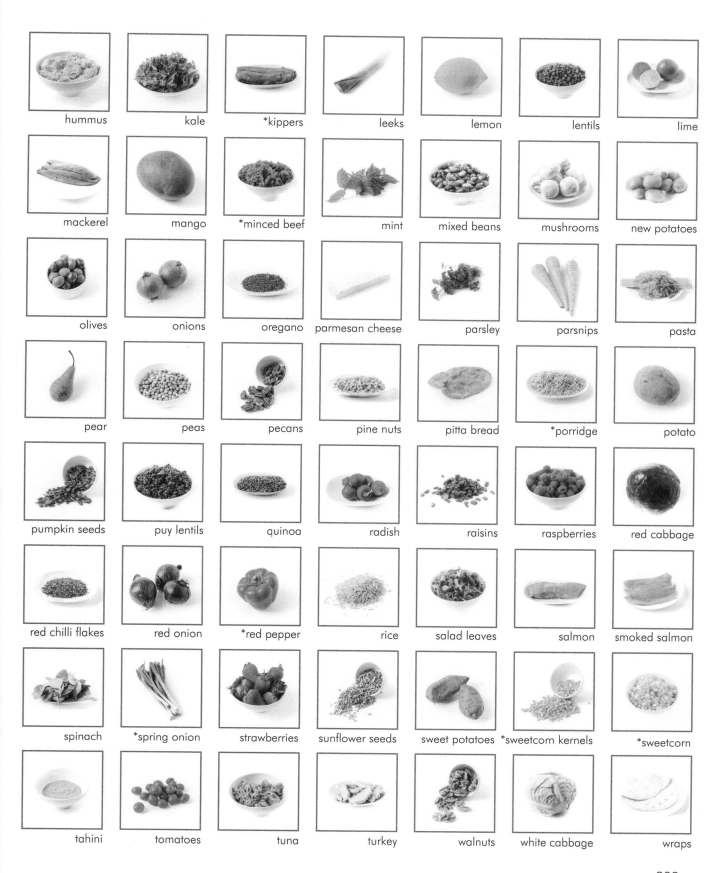

hummus	kale	*kippers	leeks	lemon	lentils	lime
mackerel	mango	*minced beef	mint	mixed beans	mushrooms	new potatoes
olives	onions	oregano	parmesan cheese	parsley	parsnips	pasta
pear	peas	pecans	pine nuts	pitta bread	*porridge	potato
pumpkin seeds	puy lentils	quinoa	radish	raisins	raspberries	red cabbage
red chilli flakes	red onion	*red pepper	rice	salad leaves	salmon	smoked salmon
spinach	*spring onion	strawberries	sunflower seeds	sweet potatoes	*sweetcorn kernels	*sweetcorn
tahini	tomatoes	tuna	turkey	walnuts	white cabbage	wraps

Photographic Index of Recipes

page 20   page 22   page 24   page 26   page 28

page 30   page 32   page 34   page 36   page 38

page 40   page 42   page 44   page 46   page 48

page 50   page 52   page 54   page 58   page 60

page 62   page 64   page 66   page 68   page 70

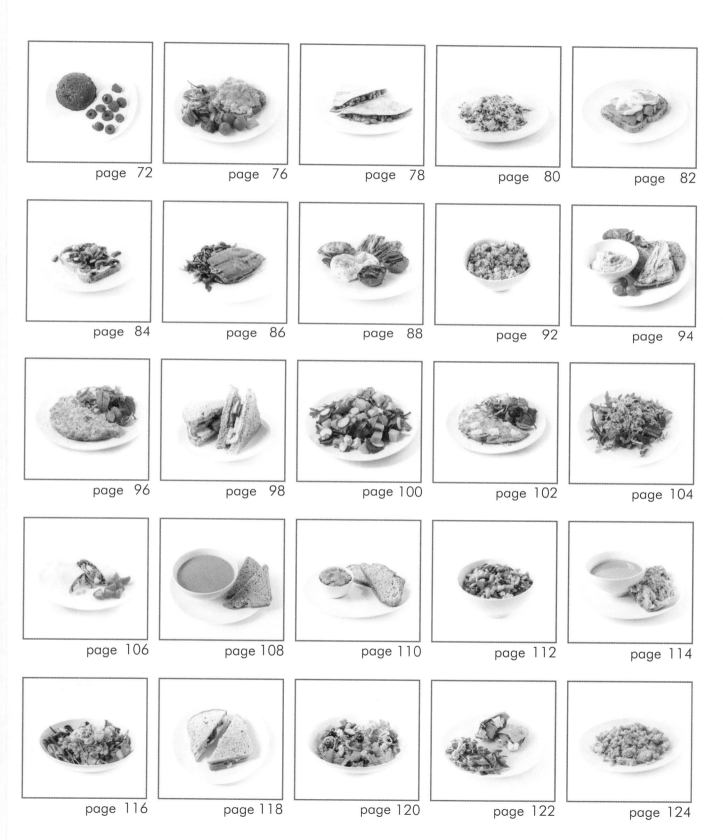

page 72

page 76

page 78

page 80

page 82

page 84

page 86

page 88

page 92

page 94

page 96

page 98

page 100

page 102

page 104

page 106

page 108

page 110

page 112

page 114

page 116

page 118

page 120

page 122

page 124

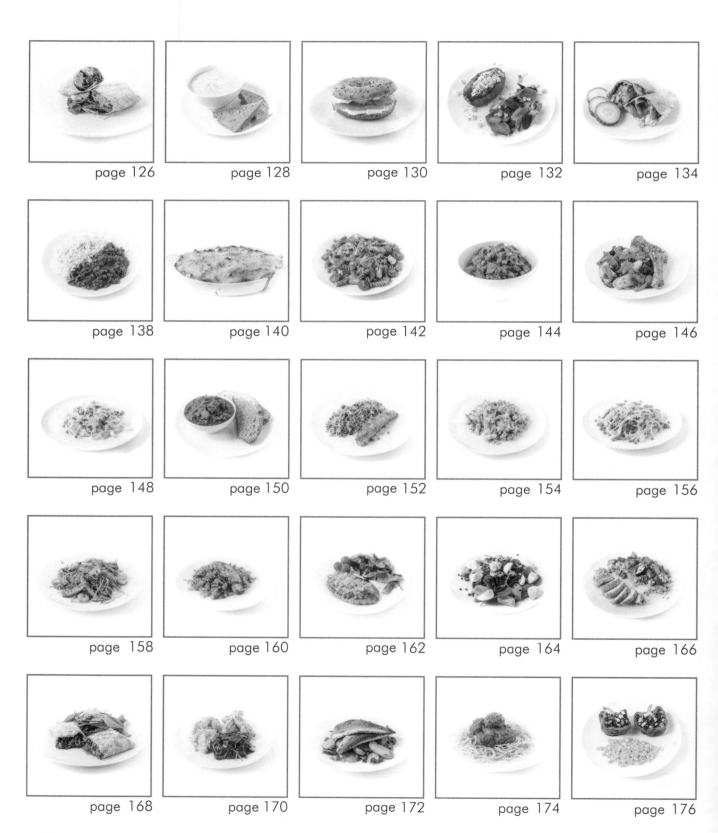

page 126

page 128

page 130

page 132

page 134

page 138

page 140

page 142

page 144

page 146

page 148

page 150

page 152

page 154

page 156

page 158

page 160

page 162

page 164

page 166

page 168

page 170

page 172

page 174

page 176

page 178

page 180

page 182

page 184

page 186

page 190

page 192

page 194

page 196

page 198

page 200

page 202

page 204

page 206

page 208

page 210

page 212

page 214

page 216

page 220

page 222

page 224

page 226

page 228

page 230

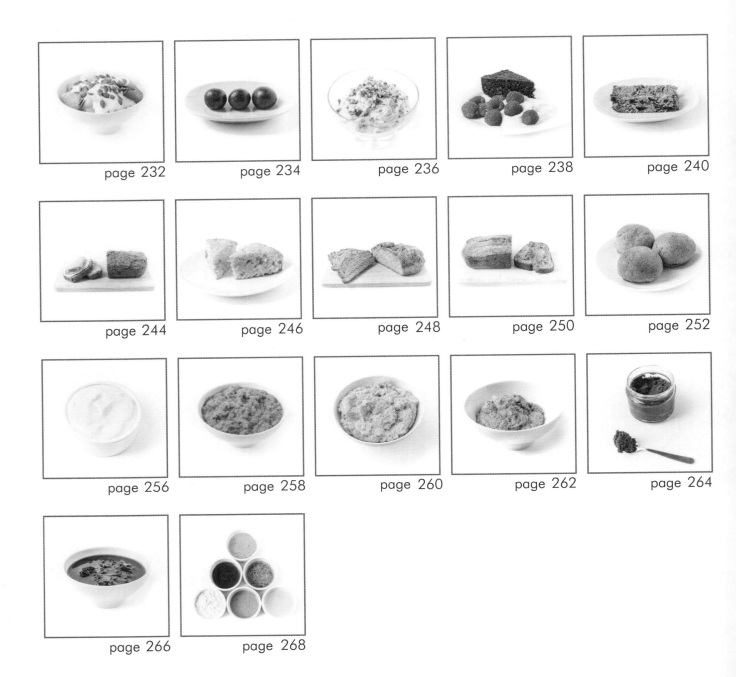

page 232

page 234

page 236

page 238

page 240

page 244

page 246

page 248

page 250

page 252

page 256

page 258

page 260

page 262

page 264

page 266

page 268

Contributors Information

Emma Bacon – author

Emma Bacon is the founder and project manager of an eating disorder support service called BalancED MK (www.balancedmk.co.uk), set up in response to her recovery from anorexia nervosa. She mentors long-term sufferers and facilitates a recovery-focused self-support group for sufferers and carers, spreading awareness and understanding about eating disorders whenever possible. Her pursuit to encourage and inspire a healthy lifestyle has led her to qualify as a personal trainer and martial arts instructor, enabling her to guide clients searching for the combination of emotional and physical wellbeing. Website: www.rebalancing-me.com. Instagram: rebalancing-me

Laura Osborne – photographer

Laura started her photography journey in 2010, and through self-teaching, has had much joy in photographing all walks of life from newborn babies to weddings and everything in between, including her three young children. With a first-class honours degree in biomedical science, Laura understands how important nutrients in food are, and how crucial it is to have the correct balance to promote a healthy body and mind. See www.lauraophotography.com

LezLee Williams – graphic designer

LezLee is a former Graphic Design, Multimedia and Web Design teacher from Texas. Her passion has always been helping others, creativity and design. Whilst living as an expat in the UK, she decided to ulitlise her skills by helping Emma to create a calm and aesthetically pleasing book. Lezlee is thrilled to have been part of something that will positively impact the lives of so many.

Dr Elisabeth Phillipps – nutritional therapist

Dr Elisabeth Phillipps, DPhil, BSc (Hons), BSc Nutr Med FNTP, is a renowned nutrition and wellbeing consultant. For over six years she has run her private practice, Hartwell Nutrition (www.hartwellnutrition.co.uk), working with clients to achieve better health through nutrition. Elisabeth was happy to evaluate the balance of recipes created by Emma, knowing this would give reassurance to the reader at home.